# Pension Scheme Deficits

Practical Solutions

Consulting Editor **Steven Hull**

**Consulting editor**
Steven Hull

**Publisher**
Sian O'Neill

**Editor**
Carolyn Boyle

**Marketing manager**
Alan Mowat

**Production**
John Meikle, Russell Anderson

**Publishing directors**
Guy Davis, Tony Harriss, Mark Lamb

***Pension Scheme Deficits: Practical Solutions***
**is published by**
Globe Law and Business
Globe Business Publishing Ltd
New Hibernia House
Winchester Walk
London Bridge
London SE1 9AG
United Kingdom
Tel +44 20 7234 0606
Fax +44 20 7234 0808
Web www.gbplawbooks.com

Printed by Antony Rowe Ltd

ISBN 1-905783-08-6 / 978-1-905783-08-3

# Table of contents

# Preface

**Steven Hull**
Ashurst

Pension deficits are rarely out of the press and frequently generate headlines in the mainstream media, as well as in the educated and informed pensions press. The preponderance of deficits has produced the most substantial piece of pensions legislation since the Maxwell disaster, centring on the discovery of pension fund deficits and the subsequent recovery of assets.

This book is not intended as an all-embracing intellectual treatise. It is designed to appeal to a wide audience, from pension managers to finance directors; from prospective pension fund members to pensioners; from those who benefit from schemes which are exceptionally well funded and backed by a substantial employer to those whose schemes are on the brink of falling into the Pension Protection Fund (PPF) or may have already done so. We also hope that professionals operating in the pensions world will find the book of interest. The contributors are pension lawyers and actuaries, and therefore one would suspect that the issues covered by the book will be most familiar to others within these professions. However, the aim of the book is to introduce the lay pensions reader to the key issues and provide a basic grounding in the complexities encountered when finding money to plug a hole. As readers will appreciate, and as this book demonstrates, even with the benefit of tax relief this is easier said than done.

The book takes the reader through a historical development of the most recent issues that have driven the growing expertise in reducing pension fund deficits and their substantially wider impact today. The Pensions Act 2004, creating the Pensions Regulator and the PPF, has had the most dramatic impact on the UK pensions world since the Maxwell disaster – itself probably the most significant single event in the history of defined benefit pension schemes. Trustees, in particular, have been thrust into the limelight and are now seized with such obligations that doing anything other than seeking the best professional advice in relation to most steps they take is just not an option.

Likewise, the effects of a pension fund deficit are now felt far more widely within corporate structures – both nationally and internationally – than merely by the employers that participate in the scheme. Deficits now have the potential to impact on everyday corporate activity and have spawned a degree of creativity within the pensions world that has been matched only by Alan Pickering's Simplification Review and the Goode Committee report following the Maxwell disaster.

We are very fortunate to have had so many high-calibre contributors willing to dedicate their time and expertise in contributing to this book, and special thanks go to them for their efforts. I would also like to give special thanks to my professional development lawyer, Chris Holmes, who has assisted me throughout in numerous research requests and without whom I would have been unable to complete my task.

I hope that readers find the end result a helpful and informative introduction to a highly topical and complex area.

*Steven Hull is a partner at the international law firm Ashurst and leads the London pensions team. He has over 18 years' legal experience of a wide range of pension-related matters in acting for employers and trustees. He has particular expertise in pension scheme reorganisations and mergers, deficit reduction and surplus resolution strategies, changing benefit structures, the pension aspects of corporate transactions and dealing with the new legislative regime following the Pensions Act 2004 and Finance Act 2004.*

*Prior to joining Ashurst in 2005, Mr Hull established and led the pensions team for over five years in the London office of a large US law firm. Prior to that, he spent over 12 years training, qualifying (in 1989) and working in the pensions team at a well-known London law firm that for many years was widely acknowledged as having the most highly regarded pensions team of any law firm in the United Kingdom. His time there included a two-year secondment to the employee benefits department of a well-known New York law firm.*

# Why are schemes in deficit?

**Jonathan Seres**
Sacker & Partners LLP

---

**1. The exam answer: "liabilities, prudence, tax"**

The three parts of the answer – liabilities, prudence and tax – are outlined in this paragraph and expanded in the rest of this chapter.

Liabilities of UK pension schemes have soared in the last 20 years. Key drivers have been:

- legislation protecting early leavers;
- legislation conferring inflation protection, sex equality and part-timer access;
- corporate restructures conferring early retirement;
- seriously increased life expectancy; and
- escalating buy-out costs.

Prudence has brought a double whammy:

- lower expected returns if investments in equities are switched to bonds; and
- bonds' discount rate for liability measurement, under the new accounting standard that has been applicable from 2005 (at latest), even if investments stay in equities. Effectively, the expected returns from equities can be booked only when earned, while accrued liabilities (for future payment) are discounted to a present capital cost on a bonds' rate.

Prudence now questions the traditional mismatch of assets and liabilities in 'defined benefit' schemes. If prudence dictates a move from volatile equities to government stocks and derivatives, to match expected pension outgo, this could, in broad terms, double the regular cost of accrual and have a similar (or greater) result on an existing deficit. Further influences on prudence have been:

- accounting standards using corporate bond discount rates to measure liabilities; as the years 2006/07 have shown, this can drive investments into bonds to minimise unmatched volatility;
- the effect of contribution 'holidays' in the 1990s, with hindsight regarded as imprudent in many cases; and
- the replacement of the potentially misleading 'minimum funding requirement', applicable from 1997 to 2005, with the prudence obligations of the new regime.

Tax changes in 1991 and 1997 have materially damaged asset returns; after decades of fiscal encouragement for qualifying schemes, the dividend tax credit of 25% was reduced to 20% in 1991. Recovery of the credit was abolished in 1997. The 1997 change alone was generally estimated to cost the pensions industry £5 billion per year at then asset levels. The major 2006 tax changes have not reversed this tax cost. Only interest and capital gains continue to have advantaged tax treatment in pension schemes. The dividend change led to an immediate reduction in measured solvency levels, as the discount method generally used at the time was based on expected returns, and the dividend change had the obvious actual effect of reducing returns.

Deficits generally apply just to 'defined benefit' schemes, but can also apply to the risk benefits that some 'defined contribution' schemes provide at the employer's expense, such as life insurance or enhanced early retirement. Further, legislation has extended eligibility for all schemes. However, most of this chapter applies to defined benefit schemes, as is clear from the context.

## 2. Liabilities – cost of legislation

Legislation has turned pension schemes from long-service awards for clerical staff (typically) to deferred pay for all the sponsor's employees. Socially this has been of great importance in the United Kingdom, but it has also been akin to a creeping set of stealth taxes. By contrast, when the state's earnings-related pension, introduced in 1978, was reassessed just a decade later in the light of improved mortality and falling birth rates, its benefits were progressively reduced over a 20-year period. Legislation prevents the private sector from adopting a similar remedy.

The United Kingdom has kept a very low state pension while obliging the occupational sector to extend its coverage. The increasing cost of that coverage is therefore not surprising when compared to social security contributions in Belgium in 2007/8 exceeding 37% of pay (plus state subsidies), and in the recent past exceeding 50%. The corresponding figure in the United Kingdom is below 24% (on the main band of contracted-in earnings).

The 1978 changes affected both the state and the occupational sector. National insurance contributions were changed from flat rate to earnings related. For the occupational sector:

- existing schemes could be improved to qualify for a partial 'rebate' of the new national insurance contributions. Since the early 1990s, the rebate is generally regarded as having fallen behind the cost of the required benefits; and
- new schemes, typically for non-clerical staff, could also qualify (from 1978) for the new rebate and this encouraged extended coverage to non-pensioned staff; from 1988, for a five-year period, new schemes received an incentive payment in addition to the rebate.

From 1985, legislation increased the cost of all occupational coverage where an employer had an existing scheme or chose to establish a new one. The key headings of the imposed cost areas are:

- wider preserved accrual for early leavers (with a cash transfer option to a registered personal pension scheme). Previously, preservation had applied only to leavers over age 26 with at least five years' accrual. Progressive changes, starting with removal of the age threshold, give the present leaver a right to a transfer option after only three months;

- inflation proofing of the preserved pensions between leaving service and start of pension (up to 5% per year compounded over the period); partially introduced in 1985, it was extended in 1991;
- inflation proofing of pensions in payment. While this applies only to pension accrued since 1997, there were powerful commercial reasons why some schemes had adopted a similar rule in the 1980s;
- equalisation of male and female retirement ages, often to the costly earlier age, under a 1990 European Court of Justice interpretation of the EU Treaty;
- extension to part-timers from 1986 under EU sex legislation if this group was mainly female, and under a later EU directive regardless of sex;
- a raft of UK regulations implementing EU directives by extending eligibility of existing schemes to fixed-term workers and other categories that previously might have been excluded from a scheme;
- compliance with burgeoning administration requirements, some examples being:
  - information disclosure – introduced in 1986 and steadily expanded, with only a brief simplification *en route* before further expansion;
  - accounting and fund management regulations from 1997;
  - data protection from 2000, both for general security and at the individual's level for sensitive data; and
  - trustee knowledge and understanding requirements from 2006; and
- potentially outweighing all the above, for a sponsor seeking to wind up a scheme, the imposed debt to fund any shortfall of assets required to meet the annuity cost, announced in 2003 and fully effective the following year. A subsequent regulation impacts on the withdrawal of a participating employer from an ongoing scheme and, therefore, impacts on mergers and acquisitions.

The last bullet leads to mention of the powers, introduced from 2005, for the Pensions Regulator to issue contribution notices and financial support directions, with a clearance procedure for mergers, acquisitions, dividends and other relevant circumstances. The existence of the clearance procedure and the withdrawal cost under the above regulation gives scheme trustees a lever to demand a share in financial receipts from corporate transactions.

Over the past 30 years this increasing cost of occupational coverage has fallen on sponsors that had chosen voluntarily to establish their pension schemes. While taxes (primarily national insurance) to pay current state benefits have risen for all employers, to meet the increasing proportion of dependants to those in work, the whole burden of increased occupational coverage required by legislation has fallen on existing sponsored schemes. Effectively, many small employers, and some in new industries, have escaped this burden completely, as they have never established their own pension schemes. New proposals from the government, which would add a mere 3% to the latter's payroll costs, offer no help to sponsors facing legal difficulties in closing existing schemes.

**3. Corporate restructuring**

Defined benefit schemes have been useful management tools to ease out staff at times of restructuring. Typically, scheme members aged 50 (the earliest permitted age under tax rules – but to rise to 55 from 2010, except for protected rights) have received immediate pensions. While voluntary leavers who choose an age 50 commencement would ordinarily suffer a reduction to offset the cost of the 10 or 15-year longer period of payment, some schemes automatically disapply this reduction on redundancy and almost all can disapply it at the request of the employer. The effect is generally to double the pension cost. Often this cost is not noticed by the employer because no apparent credit is given to the individual for the 10 or 15 lost potential years of service. The cost, however, to the pension scheme of paying the accrued pension during those years is new and is capitalised as a further liability at the next valuation.

Few employers paid to their schemes lump sums to meet this aspect of restructuring cost during the 1990s when schemes were in surplus. Some, however, made advance provision in the assessed liabilities. Either way, the extra liability is there and adds cost in the supplementary areas of longevity and compliance.

**4. Increased life expectancy**

Increased life expectancy has been a triple whammy for pension schemes:

- Traditionally, valuations have been slow to adopt new demographic assumptions, so the creep of improved mortality from 1970 onwards may not have been recognised until nearer 2000, with a sudden valuation deficit.
- Research published by insurance companies and the government actuary in the period 2000 to 2003 showed that earlier projections of mortality improvement were too low. The research alerted insurers to consider a range of future projections, rather than a single curve, labelled short, medium and long 'cohort'. A number of well-publicised pension schemes have adopted the medium cohort, with a significant increase in liabilities. Some mature schemes are analysing the effect of a long cohort out-turn. Either way, the cost of insurance annuity purchase has increased just when schemes are obliged, for the first time, to inform members annually of the discontinuance solvency level – meaning insurance buy-out (unless the scheme is too large) plus expenses.
- The above introduction of future mortality projections on alternative bases creates a difficulty for both the sponsor and scheme trustees. Both face the potential expense of modelling the alternative outcomes. Sponsors will generally prefer not to reserve for an uncertain outcome, while trustees with an eye to the sponsor's covenant may feel the need for just such a reserve. The different interests may lead to cost, uncertainty and a difficult negotiation on the scheme funding valuation under the new Pensions Act (effective for any valuation date after September 2005, the latest effective date being in 2008).

Company analysts are beginning to note the mortality assumptions used for the purpose of sponsor accounts. In section 7, the new accounting standards are mentioned. While they may be criticised for measuring liabilities on a single day's market level of interest rates, they contain a latitude for mortality assumptions that is surprising in such prescriptive standards. Industry surveys of published accounts are now commenting on the reported bases.

Many sponsors are therefore commissioning their own advice as to the range of life expectancy that can properly be used, with a particular focus on their own retired 'population'. For the sponsor, the double purpose is to avoid surprises and reduce the opportunity for analysts to mark down forecast profits.

In a typical scheme that may have last updated its mortality tables in the early 1990s, the adoption of the medium cohort projection might increase the value placed on liabilities by 5%. A 'what if' consideration of the long cohort might have increased the figures by a further 10%.

## 5. Increased insurance buy-out cost

While pension scheme liabilities are rarely assessed by direct reference to annuity buy-out costs, the solvency level on a potential discontinuance and the potential employer's debt are measured that way.

In section 6, reference is made to the 'buffer' of potential liabilities that, until changes in legislation (and in some cases to rules too), would fall away on scheme discontinuance and might have enabled scheme assets to be sufficient for annuity purchase. That buffer is no longer available. Further, section 2 refers to the legislation of 2003 and 2004 that imposes a debt on the participating employers if they withdraw, or a scheme winds up, with insufficient assets to meet the annuity cost.

The two key drivers of annuity cost are:

- long-term interest rates on the stocks of which regulated insurers must hold an appropriate proportion to back their liabilities; and
- mortality tables – and increasingly, the projected changes to these.

Long-term interest rates began a decline as retail price inflation fell in the early 1990s, with a consequential increase in the price of corresponding new investment stocks. While 2007 has seen an increase in interest rates, this has been less marked at the long end of the market. At the same time, mortality experience tables began to show a significant increase in longevity. Annuity costs have therefore more than doubled over a 20-year period.

The effect has been to increase the potential cost of winding up a pension scheme and the probable debt on the sponsor if that were to happen.

## 6. Prudence – including 'liability-driven investment'

From 1970 through to the mid-1990s, defined benefit schemes in the United Kingdom were overwhelmingly invested in equities, typically as much as 80% of the portfolio. Taking the period as a whole, this kept down the cost of maintaining the scheme. However, if the trustees could not rely on the employer's financial strength, this investment policy might have been imprudent for at least the following three reasons – but for the 'buffer' mentioned below that was, however, progressively removed during that period, mainly by legislation (but also, in some cases, by rule changes):

- Equities have no guaranteed maturity value – their market price is inherently volatile, as illustrated by the 1974 market crash and the steady fall from 2000 to 2003. In both cases the market had recovered within four years, but there was no certainty that this would happen.
- It is pure chance whether the assumed returns, for the assessment of the contribution rate at a valuation, will comprise the eventual outcome. The resulting deficit or surplus at the next valuation is met by adjusting the sponsor's contribution rate, usually with a view to a 10-year (or longer) convergence towards precise equality of assets and discounted liabilities. In practice, an adjustment is usually needed at each successive valuation.
- Even where the valuation shows exactly equal assets and liabilities, if the employer became insolvent the trustees could not usually risk a continuance of the equities' investment policy as there would be no backer if a fall in value were not followed by a sufficient rise to compensate and replace the income reduction too. A switch to bonds at that point in time would reduce the expected returns, with a solvency reduction. A purchase of insurance annuities would be likely to show an even greater solvency reduction. Most scheme rules would require an annuity purchase (on the employer's insolvency) unless the trustees had reason to defer it.

While these bullets seem to rely on the employer as backer, during the 1970s and early 1980s most large defined benefit schemes had a 'buffer' to the liabilities which resulted in a discontinuance level sufficient to buy annuities (if there had been sufficient capacity in the insurance market). The buffer comprised potential liabilities, taken into account when assessing the contribution rate, which would fall away on discontinuance.

The three main elements of the buffer were as follows:

- Reserve for potential pension for members in service – until legislation effective from 1975, typically on discontinuance there was a 10-year qualifying period. For those with under 10 years, the reserve was available for the scheme's general buy-out cost. Progressive legislation did reduce the qualifying period, but not to a negligible amount until 1988.
- Salary reserve for those above the 10-year threshold – typically, the scheme assumed salaries to increase at a rate of 1% to 2% below equities' returns and accumulated a reserve for the effect of future salary rises on accrued service. This too would be available on discontinuance. It remained relevant when the 10-year threshold was reduced, but became less significant when legislation introduced partial indexation to deferred pensions in 1985 and extended it in 1991 at a time when salary inflation was converging (downwards) on price inflation.
- Pension increases' reserve – from the early 1970s onwards, most large pension schemes awarded, at discretion, annual increases to pensions in payments, to compensate for retail price inflation. This exercise of discretion, typically under a rule needing both sponsor and trustee to agree, was widespread during the high increases in retail price inflation of the 1970s (26% in 1975) and the still

> high inflation, by today's standards, of the 1980s (5.5% in 1982). Valuations then, as today, included an allowance for these pension increases, but until 1997 there was no legislation to require their award (apart from a very small element for schemes contracted out of the state's upper tier) – so there was a capital reserve available on discontinuance. For some schemes, this element of the buffer is still available as the rule relating to pre-1997 accrual remains discretionary. However, many schemes introduced an entitlement in the 1980s after merger and acquisition activity revealed that purchasers of corporates could otherwise wind up the pension scheme and claim the buffer as 'surplus'.

With these elements of the buffer no longer available, and the experience of large assessed deficits due to the fall in equities from 2000 to 2003 (not recovering until late 2006), many trustees have questioned the prudence of an equity-reliant investment policy. They have also been obliged to consider 'prudence' and the appropriateness of the assets to the liabilities, by the Pensions Act 2004 and its scheme funding regulations, effective (for practical purposes) from 2006.

The importance to trustees of the sponsor's financial strength to meet unexpected contribution requirements has therefore become much more significant. The importance of this has also been stressed by guidance issued by the Pensions Regulator from 2005 onwards. Trustees might take the view that the insolvency of the employer is remote, but that is a hard call over the long-term perspective of a pension scheme. More likely, the trustees will assess the employer's ability to meet the discontinuance annuity cost. For many sponsors, this would be covered many times over by their net asset value, but not in the case of mature schemes with legacy liabilities from old industries.

Some trustees may discuss with the sponsor a move away from equities. This would bring a higher contribution cost. A strong employer might be willing to build up an asset 'buffer' within the scheme to increase the prudence of maintaining an equities investment policy.

In complete contrast, some sponsors may be willing (or eager) to move (fully or partially) to a liability-driven investment policy. The key features of liability-driven investment are:

- assessment of monthly cash outgo over the future life of the scheme;
- purchase of bonds to deliver a predictable income; and
- swap of that income (through the derivatives market) to match the predicted outgo, including swaps of nominal income for retail price inflation indexed income.

Liability-driven investment does not remove all risk. Mortality improvements are a key uncertainty – as is the possibility that obesity could reverse the trend.

The reinvestment basis of bonds at maturity cannot be predicted, although swaps may be able to reduce the importance of this unknown.

Liability-driven investment as a policy will generally be costly. In the years 2005 and 2006 this was particularly the case, as the demand for inflation-linked long-dated bonds pushed real returns below 1% per annum.

An alternative, or a complement to a partial liability-driven investment, is to seek to offset the volatility of equities by spreading the return-seeking investments across a variety of asset classes. This is a particularly important development for trustees. Traditionally, property has been the main alternative to equities for return-seeking investments, either directly or through unitised funds.

Recent studies suggest that commodities have a low correlation with equity markets and can therefore spread risk, even though in themselves a volatile asset class. The studies have also included high performance bonds and entirely skill-based funds such as global tactical asset allocation. Market capacity in some of these classes (and in other 'alternative' investments), at a given time, may limit investment opportunities and result in the need to add new classes to a portfolio. The governance of the classes and assessment of new opportunities can impose a considerable burden and cost on trustees. Even allowing for this, there is apparent scope to reduce risk and therefore, with prudence, maintain some exposure to return-seeking assets, even where the sponsor's covenant is regarded as not the strongest. This, however, is a new area where conclusions have to be scheme-specific.

Some schemes are in deficit because they moved out of equities at a sub-optimal time during the fluctuations of recent years; others because their trustees have decided that the volatility renders the asset class imprudent at the high percentage previously held. They may have done so before the use of alternative return-seeking asset classes became more generally recognised.

## 7. Recent accounting standards – FRS17 and IAS19

Financial Reporting Standard (FRS) 17 was required to be implemented in full by scheme sponsors (in their own accounts) for accounting periods starting on or after January 1 2005, although for listed companies this was overridden by the requirement to adopt International Accounting Standard (IAS) 19, the international standard.

For defined benefit schemes, the most radical changes in FRS17, compared to the previous standard, were:

- market value accounting for assets (the previous standard was profit and loss orientated rather than balance-sheet driven);
- market value accounting for liabilities, on a bonds' discount rate applicable on the single relevant date – see below regarding volatility;
- no smoothing for actuarial gains or losses; and
- balance-sheet recognition of pension scheme surplus or deficit.

IAS19 contains an option. Either it can be very similar to FRS17 or the third bullet can be replaced by a smoothing mechanism. However, the latter involves initially the reworking of earlier years and has not been widely adopted in the United Kingdom.

The lack of smoothing will tend to increase the volatility of the sponsor's balance sheet – unless the pension scheme assets are in corporate bonds or hedged against interest rate changes. The typical bonds discount rate might have been of the order of 5.1% in January 2007 and 5.8% in July 2007. As indicated in section 6, a move of assets to bonds (or to liability-driven investment) tends to increase cost. Similarly, an interest rate hedge will incur a cost – at its simplest, the premium cost of an option.

The assessment of liabilities on a bonds' discount rate, fixed on a given date, seems normal to corporate treasurers but inappropriate to some trustees who assess returns and liabilities on the basis of projections and chosen asset classes. However, the accounting standards are unlikely to change, and while long-term bond rates are low, they are likely to result in reported deficits for many schemes that trustees and sponsors regard, on an agreed funding basis, as in surplus. Pressure on trustees to adopt the accounting standard, despite its disadvantages, may arise from two sources:

- the employer's dislike of confusion arising from different bases; and
- the Pensions Regulator's use of the accounting standard for screening purposes and initially for other purposes – although published guidance indicates that scheme-specific funding data, if different, will be used when valuations are available under the Pensions Act 2004.

Both FRS17 and IAS19 provide that the actuarial assumptions are ultimately the responsibility of the sponsor's directors, although actuarial advice is expected to be obtained (as explicitly stated in FRS17). The key latitude for sponsors has been the mortality table, as mentioned in section 4. This latitude can be defended on the grounds that, while mortality tables (or particular scheme experience) are matters of fact, projected improvements are matters of speculation. However, unless the adopted tables are rebased regularly, there is the possibility of unexpectedly high adjustment to balance-sheet liabilities at a future date.

## 8. Contribution 'holidays'

The bull market of the 1980s and resultant scheme valuation surpluses were followed for many schemes by a pause in sponsor contributions – colloquially known as a 'holiday'. With hindsight, a more prudent response would have been to spread the surplus over a longer period, but there was also a tax driver for a holiday, in that surplus above 5% (on a specified basis) had to result in benefit improvements or a contribution holiday if tax on part of scheme returns was to be avoided.

The inevitable delay in completing scheme valuations meant that in some cases a market downturn, or other factors, had in the meanwhile turned the surplus into a deficit.

## 9. Minimum funding requirement

The minimum funding requirement (MFR) was an unsuccessful attempt to ensure reasonable funding of defined benefit pension schemes. Its original purpose, proposed in 1993, was weakened before its introduction in April 1997 and further weakened following the tax changes of July that year.

Following misuse of pension funds by the late Robert Maxwell in 1991, a report on pension schemes as a whole was commissioned by the government and received in 1993. Its recommendations included a 'minimum solvency requirement', but industry responses pointed out that:

- schemes were not funded to an insurance buy-out level and, if this were to be required, many would be promptly closed; and
- if a lower requirement were to be introduced, as government had indicated, it would be better named 'minimum funding requirement' – as was then done by the Pensions Act 1995, effective from April 1997.

The government's intention was that the MFR should set a minimum standard but that it should have little practical effect for most large schemes which were generally funded to a higher level. Such schemes, on their first three-yearly valuation after 1997, typically reported funding levels around 100% on their established basis and much higher levels on the MFR basis. While some schemes continued to target the established basis, companies looking to trim contributions or re-start after a 'holiday' funded to the lower MFR basis. The stock market fall from 2000 to 2003 accentuated the difference between the two approaches, as the MFR in many cases remained over 100% or else comfortingly near it.

The MFR was a scheme funding target, not a reporting standard for sponsors' accounts. However, the old corporate reporting standard (SSAP24) was, in many cases, comforting during the early stages of the bear market, as it was profit and loss account driven, rather than a balance-sheet measure, and took into account sustained dividend levels. As a result, both pension schemes and sponsors were, in many cases, reporting optimistic funding figures that required heavy downgrading when the MFR and SSAP24 were both replaced with a strong emphasis on prudence.

The Pensions Act 2004 replaced the MFR with an objective of 100% funding with assets "appropriate" to liabilities, and provision for a recovery plan where there was a shortfall. The driver for this part of the act was an EU directive of 2003 born out of concern that the Maxwell scandal revealed that pension funds were outside the regulatory net of banking and insurance directives. The directive also contained a requirement that investments should be "prudent". For the United Kingdom, the prudence requirement is now in both the funding and the investment regulations issued under the Pensions Act, applicable in full to a scheme's first valuation date after September 22 2005. Trustees are obliged to:

- reach agreement with the sponsor on a contribution schedule; or
- report to the Pensions Regulator the failure to agree. The Pensions Regulator can then impose a schedule.

The potential uncertainty of an imposed contribution schedule has been one of the factors that have driven many sponsors to accept a significantly more prudent funding basis than they might otherwise have agreed to. The other main factor has been the corporate reporting of their liabilities under the new accounting standards, generally being a more conservative basis. In the background has been the new disclosure requirement – also EU driven – to inform members, annually since September 2005, of the pension scheme's solvency level.

Another background factor, both to the acceptance by sponsors and trustees of the greater need for prudence and to the discrediting of the MFR, has been the series of well-publicised scheme funding failures since 1997. In many cases, despite the

MFR being met, on the insolvency of the sponsor the obligation on the trustees to purchase annuities brought home the materially higher annuity buy-out cost. As the MFR was accompanied by a statutory priority sequence for the application of available assets, those who were not in receipt of pensions met the whole shortfall before pensions were cut back. This was exacerbated by transitional regulations that gave priority to future inflation-linked increases to those pensions, in the early years, and increased their purchase cost, to the further detriment of those not in receipt of pensions. The assets available for the future pensions of this latter group have in some cases been little more than 10% of the required sums, and (in the publicised examples) rarely reached 50%.

Sponsors are therefore now well aware of the statutory changes and the irrelevance of the MFR to the new prudence requirements. They may be less aware that equities can still be an available asset class to generate an expectation of higher returns than bonds, because the headline corporate accounting measure of liabilities is at a bonds discount rate, but either way the corporate results have in almost all cases been adversely affected by the combination of legislation and events of recent years.

One of the features of the MFR was to increase the demand for gilt-edged stocks, which its replacement was intended to alleviate, but the effect of the new accounting standards and the greater understanding of the inherent mismatch of defined benefit scheme liabilities and the supporting assets has been to increase that demand and thus drive up the price. The UK corporate bonds market is relatively small, so gilts have been an expensive proxy (with just a small additional return for sophisticated schemes creating synthetic bonds by, for example, selling credit default swaps related to a basket of bonds equivalent in amount to the gilts held). The MFR demand driver for gilts applied to mature schemes with significant pensions in payment, as the measure of liabilities for the pensions was based on a gilts discount rate. Although large schemes, with liabilities for pensions in payment exceeding £100 million, could use an equities measure for part of the liabilities, by 2000 a shortage of gilts had been identified by government, with a dual response:

- a published intention to skew new gilts issues towards longer terms; and
- a reference to scheme-specific investment policies as one of the objectives of the Pensions Act 2004.

The second of these objectives has not reduced demand, as the combination of prudential matters has outweighed the removal of the MFR driver. The equities bear market of 2000 to 2003 was therefore accompanied by a rising cost in the gilts market, creating a double whammy for solvency levels if a switch from equities began in, say, 2003.

## 10. Tax

For the sponsor, the key difference between defined benefit and defined contribution schemes is that for defined benefit the balance of cost is payable by the sponsor. Any increase in tax on a defined benefit scheme reduces surplus or increases deficit, and thus flows through to the sponsor's accounts.

In section 1, the highly material tax change of 1997 has been mentioned. The risk of further tax changes should be borne in mind. While change to the capital gains tax exemption is unlikely, as it would inhibit trustees' investment policy (and thus distort capital markets, contrary to the government's apparent policy to avoid distortions), tax on interest remains a less remote possibility. There is also a risk of some pension fund activities being regarded as trading rather than investment, resulting in a tax charge, as happened with respect to some underwriting activities in the 1980s.

In the less visible area of value added tax, there have been numerous tax changes affecting pension schemes. Some have been just a change in Revenue practice (but difficult to challenge). When investment managers are also administrative custodians, the practice regarding partial recovery by a non-grouped employer (if it has sufficient value added tax (VAT) output) of VAT on its administration fees has been changed at least twice in the past 20 years. The treatment of brokerage fees relating to overseas investment has also been changed materially (by regulations). Apart from the change in tax cost, considerable advisory fees may be incurred.

For defined benefit schemes currently in deficit, the likelihood is that the 1997 abolition of dividend tax credits contributed to the deficit. For all defined benefit schemes, the risk to the sponsor remains that future tax changes may adversely affect it.

# Traditional methods of assessing and dealing with a deficit

**Stephen Yeo**
Watson Wyatt

## 1. What is a deficit?

### 1.1 Types of actuarial valuation

There are a number of reasons why it is necessary to determine the value of a defined benefit pension scheme's liabilities. The value of the liabilities differs depending on the reason for the valuation. All methods now tend to value assets at market value, although this was not always the case. The three most important measures of a scheme's liabilities are summarised below.

*(a)* ***Valuation for determining employer contributions***

A funding valuation is carried out at least every three years. The main purpose of this actuarial valuation is to determine the level of future employer contributions required so that after a suitable period, there will be sufficient assets to pay all benefits earned to that date. It is assumed that the scheme will continue indefinitely, with employed members' benefits continuing to increase in line with members' earnings until they leave service or retire. The assumed rates of future investment returns, price inflation, how long members live and other assumptions are in most cases agreed between the trustee, employer and actuary, and are designed to be prudent. Occasionally, when the rules of the scheme permit, the trustees and the actuary are the only parties involved in such decision making.

In future, this valuation will be known as the 'scheme-specific funding valuation' as described in section 1.7.

The actuary's report to the trustees must contain information such as membership data, the contributions paid since the last valuation, the funding objective and key assumptions made.

*(b)* ***Valuation for the employer's accounts***

Companies are required to disclose various details relating to their pension arrangements in their annual accounts. The relevant accounting standard is known as Financial Reporting Standard (FRS) 17 (which, for quoted companies, has been replaced by the broadly similar International Accounting Standard IAS19 from 2005). The FRS17 accounting standard prescribes both the method and the assumptions which should be used to value the liabilities. In particular, the liabilities are valued using the yield on AA-rated corporate bonds. For most schemes, this valuation currently places a higher value on the liabilities than the funding valuation would.

*(c)* ***Valuation to show what happens if the employer fails***

A discontinuance valuation shows the financial position of a scheme in the hypothetical situation of the employer failing (ie, the employer can no longer pay any future contributions). In that instance, all employed members would be granted deferred pensions based on earnings and pensionable service at the valuation date, and trustees would have to choose between:

- winding up the scheme and buying out the benefits with an insurance company (although for some large schemes and others with unusual benefits, this may not be possible); and
- continuing the scheme and investing in low-risk assets with the aim of paying all benefits to members as they fall due.

The discontinuance liabilities are very much higher than the liabilities measured using the funding or accounting valuations. If, on winding-up, an employer's assets are not sufficient to make up the shortfall, it will not be possible to pay all members' benefits in full. In that situation the Pension Protection Fund (PPF) provides a safety net designed to ensure that members receive the level of benefits specified in Schedule 7 to the Pensions Act 2004.

If there is a deficit, the actuary must quantify approximately the impact of the applicable priority order on different categories of benefit had the scheme been wound up on the valuation date. The actuary must also state what the overall solvency level of the scheme would have been had the statutory funding objective been exactly met on the valuation date.

Trustees should also be aware of the separate valuation for PPF levy calculation purposes, often called a Section 179 valuation. This indicates the ability of the scheme to provide the PPF compensation level of benefits in the event of employer insolvency.

## 1.2 Assumptions

The assumptions made by the actuary in carrying out a valuation can be split between demographic (sometimes termed statistical) and economic.

*(a)* ***Demographic assumptions***

These assumptions are usually based on past experience, with adjustment if there is an expectation that the future will differ from the past. Larger schemes may have enough data for their own experience to be used. In smaller schemes, the experience of larger populations of other similar schemes will be used. Assumptions are likely to be needed for:

- post-retirement mortality;
- family statistics (eg, proportion of married members and age of spouse);
- options (eg, frequency of commutation or transfer);
- additional liabilities (eg, additional voluntary contributions);
- ill-health retirement;
- pre-retirement mortality;

- voluntary withdrawal – this can be service related; and
- promotional pay increases.

**(b) Economic assumptions**

History has shown that while the absolute level of various economic variables has fluctuated widely, their level relative to price inflation has been much more stable. It is therefore common to express the economic assumptions in terms of their real (ie, relative to price inflation) level. The main economic assumptions are as follows.

*(i) Investment return (or discount rate)*

The expected rate of return on fixed interest securities can be estimated from the redemption yield of good-quality corporate bonds of appropriate duration to maturity, depending on the term of the liabilities. It may be appropriate to allow for the risk that money will have to be reinvested at lower returns than are currently available. Where the actuary's method requires an assumption about the expected rate of return on shares, this can be derived from the current dividend yield, with an upward adjustment to allow for the expectation that dividends will increase faster than inflation. The excess return of shares over bonds, known as the equity risk premium, varies with time, but has averaged around 3% a year over the last century. Essentially, this is the return demanded by the market as compensation for the risk that equity returns will be less than those on bonds.

*(ii) Price inflation*

A view on future price inflation can be formed from the target set by the government for the Bank of England (BoE), recent levels of price inflation and inflation forecasts implied by bond market data. The current BoE target is expressed as inflation of 2% a year measured by the Consumer Prices Index (CPI). The Retail Price Index (RPI) includes housing costs, notably mortgage interest payments, and for mathematical reasons to do with the construction of the index, the 2% CPI target is considered to be equivalent to an RPI target of about 2.75%.

*(iii) Pension and deferred pension increases*

These are usually related to price inflation, possibly with a cap (eg, limited price indexation, which requires indexation in line with the RPI subject to an annual limit of 5%) or a collar in the form of a minimum increase. Detailed modelling can be carried out to determine the appropriate allowance.

*(iv) Pay escalation*

Statistical analysis of past pay escalation figures indicates that the rate of pay escalation over time has been relatively stable in real terms (ie, net of price inflation), and a rolling 10-year average of general annual pay increases varies between 1% and 2.5% a year in real terms. However, pay figures (as used in the calculation of pension benefits) can be influenced by the definition of 'pay' (eg, total pay, basic salary, pay less an offset or pay subject to a cap) and the employer's remuneration policy.

Prudent assumptions can allow for some degree of out-performance of scheme assets relative to bonds, depending on the specific circumstances of the scheme. In particular, the trustees should consider the scheme's investment policy and the ability of the employer to cope with the financial consequences of assumptions not being borne out by experience.

## 1.3 Deterministic and stochastic techniques

One problem inherent in the conventional actuarial valuation is that only a single answer emerges – that is, the fund is required to pay all benefits if all assumptions are precisely borne out by experience. Most assumptions can be regarded as one point in a range of possibilities.

To illustrate this, stochastic modelling techniques have been developed, often seen in the form of 'asset-liability' models, which might assist trustees when assessing the prudence of either individual assumptions or the overall calculation of technical provisions. The main characteristics of these techniques are that they:

- attempt to model the course of events as they might emerge based on randomly generated simulations of the future in line with an economic model; and
- result in a range of outcomes with probabilities attached. They are not meant as a predictive tool; rather, they are illustrative of possible outcomes.

The use of stochastic modelling techniques may not be appropriate for all schemes and trustees normally discuss with their actuary possible approaches to illustrating variability. A simpler and less costly analysis could take the form of carrying out the valuation on a few different sets of assumptions simply to illustrate the width of the potential outcome range and the sensitivity of results to particular assumptions.

The actuary's report must draw attention to those assumptions to which the valuation results are particularly sensitive. The actuary must describe or illustrate how the results will differ if these assumptions are not borne out so that the reader may understand the sensitivity of the results to the assumptions chosen. In particular, this analysis must include the susceptibility of the results to variations in future mortality experience compared with that assumed.

## 1.4 Single discount rate v dual discount rate

The appropriate overall investment portfolio, or that for individual groups such as pensioners or employed members, can be considered using asset-liability modelling techniques. In practice, many schemes currently have an investment strategy that is consistent with a portfolio for pensioners that is predominantly (but not exclusively) bond based, while that for employed members and deferred pensioners includes a substantial amount of equity (ie, traded shares) and real property. The discount rates derived for each liability class based on these implied portfolios is therefore likely to differ.

Possible approaches that could be used to derive a discount rate for these liabilities include:

- a single discount rate, derived as a combination of the discount rates for each

asset class, reflecting the weighted average of the trustees' current strategy;
- different discount rates in perpetuity for each liability class; or
- the discount rate derived for employed members and deferred pensioners for the period before retirement, and the pensioner discount rate for the period after retirement of employed members, deferred pensioners and pensioners.

The first two approaches would be expected to produce very similar results. Both effectively assume that the current mix of assets produced in aggregate by combining the portfolios for each of the liabilities implied by the current investment strategy will continue in perpetuity. The third approach reflects an expectation that the total asset allocation will move over time to a higher bond content that is considered more appropriate for pensioners.

For mature closed schemes, the third approach, which assumes a changing asset allocation over time, is the most robust.

### 1.5 Valuation methods

There are a number of ways to derive the cost of the future accrual of benefits arising from employed members' service after the valuation date. Typically, the 'projected unit' method is used. Under this approach, the capital cost of the projected future benefits arising from the single year of service following the valuation date is calculated and expressed as a percentage of current pensionable salary. This method is expected to produce a stable contribution rate if the age and salary profile of the membership remains stable. However, in schemes that are closed to new entrants, the average age of the membership will increase over time. The contribution rate calculated on this methodology would increase at successive valuations. Alternative methodologies can be used which produce a more stable rate as the membership grows older.

### 1.6 Analysis of deficit

Where the funding objectives include a target funding level, the report must state the position of the scheme relative to that target funding level and include a reconciliation of the actuarial deficit, or funding level, on the basis being used for the current valuation with the position disclosed by the previous valuation. The description must be sufficient to identify the relative significance of the items of actuarial gain or loss which the actuary considers to be material, including changes in the valuation method and the valuation assumptions. The report should normally include some quantification of these items.

### 1.7 Balance of power between employer and trustees and role of actuary

For many years the balance of power between the employer and the trustees over determining the contribution rate and the role of the actuary in this process were determined only by the rules of the scheme.

Under the new, scheme-specific funding regime introduced by Sections 221 to 233 of the Pensions Act 2004, this balance may have changed. The 'standard' position is that the decisions in connection with scheme funding must be agreed between the trustees and the employer. The trustees will have to agree with the employer the appropriate funding target (technical provisions) and recovery plan, after considering advice from the actuary. However, there are two special cases:

- where the trustees have the power under the trust deed and rules to set contributions; and
- where the actuary previously had the power to set contributions.

These are described in paragraph 23 of the Pensions Regulator's Code of Practice on Funding Defined Benefits. The code is available at www.thepensionsregulator.gov.uk/trustees/guidance/schemeFunding/index.aspx.

Where the trustees have sole power under the rules to set the employer's contribution rate, the trustees retain this power and merely have to consult the employer on funding matters. However, there is a complication, in that these special provisions apply only if no one other than the trustees can reduce the contribution rate or suspend contributions altogether. Where this is the case, the 'standard' procedures will apply.

Where the actuary is given the power to set the employer's contribution rate, the legislation is modified to require the trustees (and the Pensions Regulator, if the trustees and employer cannot agree) to "take into account the recommendations of the actuary", rather than simply consider advice. In addition, the actuary must certify that the contributions specified in the schedule of contributions are not less than those he would have set had the decision still been his. These modifications apply only if it is the scheme actuary (appointed under Section 47(1)(b) of the Pensions Act 1995) who had the power to set the employer's contribution rate. If the trust deed does not specify this, the 'standard' procedure will likely apply.

The modification to the standard arrangements described above is subject to any constraints or conditions on the original powers set out in the trust deed. So if, for example, the trustees could set the contribution rate subject to such rate not exceeding 12% per annum, the 12% limit would still apply under the new requirements.

In many cases, understanding the correct interaction of the specific wording of the scheme's own documentation with the general requirements of the scheme-specific funding regime as laid down in the Pensions Act 2004 and in the scheme-specific funding regulations is far from straightforward and legal advice should be taken.

## 1.8 Employer covenant and asset allocation

In order to inform decisions on both the technical provisions and any recovery plan needed, the trustees need to form an objective assessment of the employer's financial position and prospects, as well as its willingness to continue to fund the scheme's benefits known as the employer's covenant.

As well as using information from the employer, the trustees will consider using commercially available services or other sources of information such as:

- rating agencies or credit scoring institutions;
- credit specialist advisers;
- reports of industry regulators (in the case of certain regulated industries);
- information which may become available in connection with the risk-based element of the PPF's levy; and

- any new developments in the credit advisory services market aimed at assisting the trustees to evaluate the employer's financial standing.

**1.9 Financial economics**

In recent decades, first in the United States and more recently in the United Kingdom, actuaries have increasingly applied the principles of financial economics to the funding of defined benefit pension schemes. In simple terms, these assert that a market value can be placed on a series of future cash flows; this market value is independent of ownership and risk can be properly allowed for only if explicit allowances are made, relative to a risk-free value. Those who have adopted this approach have argued that the asset class most closely matching fixed future liabilities is risk-free bonds and that to anticipate returns in excess of this is imprudent.

Other actuaries have argued that the supply of bond investments of suitable duration to maturity is limited; not all pension liabilities are fixed and it is reasonable to anticipate the higher investment returns that might be expected to be earned from return-seeking assets such as equities or bonds, not least because the risk/return balance applying to a pension scheme is not the same as that of other investors. These arguments have been given added focus by recent fluctuations in the real yield on long-term gilts, with the 50-year index-linked issue reaching a low of 0.38% in January 2006 but since recovering to close to 1%.

**1.10 Accounting rules for pensions costs in company accounts**

Defined benefit pension schemes often constitute a significant corporate liability and accounting conventions have therefore been developed to govern the manner in which company accounts disclose pension liabilities.

***(a) 1988: Statement of Standard Accounting Practice 24***

Statement of Standard Accounting Practice (SSAP) 24 was developed by the Accounting Standards Board to provide a framework for companies to recognise the cost of providing pension benefits in their published accounts. In addition, SSAP24 set out information about pension arrangements that had to be disclosed in the company's accounts. The standard applied to accounting periods beginning on or after July 1 1988. It applied to:

- explicit, implicit and *ex-gratia* pension arrangements;
- funded and unfunded schemes;
- insured and self-administered schemes; and
- both UK and overseas schemes of UK companies.

SSAP24 covered defined benefit and defined contribution schemes and other post-retirement benefits (eg, medical expenses cover).

***(b) 2001: FRS17***

FRS17 was developed by the Accounting Standards Board and was initially introduced alongside SSAP24. It required figures to be shown in the notes to the accounts for financial years ending on or after June 22 2001 (balance sheet) and for the next accounting year (profit and loss). FRS17 was initially introduced on a voluntary basis but replaced SSAP24 as the mandatory standard for accounting periods beginning on or after January 1 2005.

The overall objective of the standard is to ensure that the financial statements of companies reflect the 'fair value' of the assets and liabilities arising from the employers' retirement benefit obligations and any related funding. In addition, it requires that the operating costs of providing retirement benefits are recognised in the accounting period in which the benefit is earned, and that changes in the values of assets and liabilities are recognised in the accounting period in which those changes arise. It also aims to ensure that financial statements contain adequate disclosure of the cost of retirement benefits and the related gains, losses, assets and liabilities.

The significant elements in the valuation of assets and liabilities are that assets are measured at market value and liabilities are calculated using a discount rate equal to the yield on AA corporate bonds of duration appropriate for the liabilities. This yield is lower than the rate of return most actuaries use for a funding valuation, with the consequence that the value placed on the liabilities is higher. Most schemes have the bulk of their assets in asset classes whose value shows little correlation with that of AA bonds. As a result, FRS17 deficits can change rapidly in a short period.

#### *(c) 2005: IAS19*

All companies listed on an EU stock exchange had to comply with International Accounting Standards (IAS) with effect from the accounting year beginning on or after January 1 2005. The international standard relating to pensions is IAS19, which is broadly similar to FRS17, with minor differences relating to asset valuations, risk benefits and the treatment of expenses. The more significant difference arises because IAS19 does not incorporate a statement of recognised gains and losses, which, under FRS17, had been used to allow for experience gains and losses.

### 1.11 Law affecting funding

Although there has always been a body of professional guidance underpinning the approach which actuaries must take when conducting scheme valuations, there have been few regulatory constraints until recent decades. These began with the contracting-out arrangements that accompanied the introduction of the State Earnings-Related Pension Scheme (SERPS) in 1978.

#### *(a) April 1978: contracting out*

From 1978, the government allowed employers operating more generous pension schemes the option of guaranteeing to provide a specified level of benefit in place of the SERPS benefit, known as the 'guaranteed minimum pension', in return for a reduction in the rate of National Insurance contributions paid by the employer and the member.

The government of the day wanted to make sure that those contracted-out benefits that were being offered in lieu of SERPS had the backing of adequate assets.

In order to remain contracted out, schemes were required to produce a certificate from an actuary certifying that, in the normal course of events over the next three years and assuming the continuation of a specified rate of contributions, the scheme would be expected to have sufficient resources to meet certain priority liabilities if it were to wind up. Broadly speaking, the priority liabilities were pensions in payment and guaranteed minimum pensions for non-pensioners. As most schemes were providing significantly higher benefits, such a certificate could normally be provided without difficulty.

*(b)* ***April 1987: restriction on surpluses***

In the late 1980s many defined benefit schemes found themselves with assets surplus to those required to meet expected liabilities. In some cases such surpluses were large and there was little prospect of the employer making use of the surplus beyond suspending contributions. Some employers sought to extract surpluses from schemes by payment of all or part to the employer, necessitating negotiations with the schemes' trustees and the Inland Revenue.

At the same time, the Treasury became concerned at the cost to the Exchequer of allowing schemes with large surpluses to continue to receive tax relief.

To satisfy these twin needs, new legislation (Schedule 22 of the Income and Corporation Taxes Act 1988) stipulated an upper funding limit which, if exceeded, would result in a partial loss of tax relief, in that investment returns from the assets in excess of the limit would be subject to tax, unless the excess could be extinguished by means of a contribution holiday, benefit improvement or surplus payment to the employer. Any surplus paid to the employer was subject to a free-standing corporation tax charge of 40%. In this way the surplus legislation both permitted and encouraged payments of surplus to the employer.

The legislation permitted assets to be held in the scheme equal to 105% of the liabilities before the tax disbenefits began to apply. The actuarial basis underlying the calculation of liabilities was very cautious and, looking back, some commentators have suggested that today's funding difficulties could have been ameliorated if surplus payments or other uses of surplus to the benefit of the employer had not been permitted, or if a limit higher than 105% had been specified. This is true, but the effect is often overstated because emphasis is put on the seemingly low margin of 5% and little attention is paid to the strength of the actuarial basis specified to determine liabilities.

*(c)* ***April 1997: minimum funding requirement***

In the wake of the Maxwell debacle, the 1995 Pensions Act introduced the minimum funding requirement (MFR) which provided a common yardstick against which to measure scheme solvency. However, the MFR did not signify adequacy; it simply provided a standard measure which was intended to protect fully pensions already in payment and provide younger members with a transfer value that would give them an even chance of replicating scheme benefits if they transferred to an occupational scheme or a personal pension scheme. Unfortunately, the combination of the increasing cost of annuities, the collapse in the value of shares between 2000 and 2003 and legislation which required that pensioners took priority over all other beneficiaries when schemes wound up meant that tens of thousands of employees and former employees of bankrupt employers have lost part or all of their pension, due to the underfunded position of their schemes. Some commentators have argued that the MFR, rather than improving security, actually reduced security in some pension schemes because it became a benchmark which employers could use to restrict the contributions they needed to pay.

***(d) September 2005: statutory funding objective***

The Pensions Act 2004 replaced the MFR with a statutory funding objective, which is intended to be scheme specific and more robust than the MFR. The Pensions Regulator has issued a Code of Practice on Funding Defined Benefits, which covers valuations with effective dates on or after September 22 2005 referred to in section 1.7.

Under the statutory funding objective, where there is a shortfall at the effective date of the actuarial valuation, the trustees must aim to eliminate it by means of a recovery plan over a specified period. Some new terms were defined:

- 'Statutory funding objective' – every scheme is subject to the statutory funding objective which is to have sufficient and appropriate assets to cover its 'technical provisions'.
- 'Technical provisions' – these are an estimate, made on actuarial principles, of the assets needed at any particular time to make provision for benefits already accrued under the scheme.

Full actuarial valuations must be carried out at least once every three years. In intervening years, trustees of schemes with at least 100 members must commission an actuarial report giving an actuary's estimate of changes to the funding position of the scheme since the last full actuarial valuation. Unlike the actuarial valuation, it will not usually be based on such detailed member-by-member calculations.

The Pensions Regulator has issued a statement explaining how it will approach the regulation of defined benefit scheme funding. This sets out some triggers which, if exceeded, will result in schemes having to submit information in excess of the basic information submitted by all schemes. The Pension Regulator has been keen to stress that the triggers are merely resource allocation tools, not targets that should influence trustees.

Trustees of schemes with at least 100 members must issue a summary funding statement containing prescribed information to all members and beneficiaries each year.

## 1.12 Impact of increased longevity

Over the last 50 years, mortality rate declines in the United Kingdom for older age groups have tended to run in the 1% to 2% per annum range, but in the 1990s decline rates of 2% to 3% were observed for 60 to 90-year-old men and for 60 to 80-year-old women. In 1983 it was estimated that life expectancy for a man who reached 65 in 2005 would be about 15 years. By 2005 the unanticipated improvements had increased this to 19.5 years. When interest rates were high and few pension increases were guaranteed, such an increase in life expectancy might have added only about 10% to the cost of pensions. However, with lower interest rates and near index-linked pensions, the cost increase is more than 20%.

Because of its growing significance and the sustained trend in one direction – that of longer life expectancy – actuaries are required to pay particular attention to assumptions about future mortality. In their application to a particular scheme, it is normal to adjust standard mortality tables to reflect scheme, employer or geographic factors where evidence exists to support this. Consideration must also be given as to the likely persistence of these differences in the future and to the likely rate of improvement in longevity.

### 1.13 Special issues for maturing schemes

Some issues may require a different emphasis in mature schemes or those that can be expected to mature relatively quickly. They are of particular relevance to closed schemes, as such schemes will mature, possibly rapidly, over time.

It is likely that the funding objectives for a closed scheme are significantly different from those for an open scheme. With the latter, it is likely that the sponsoring employer's perception of risks inherent in defined benefit schemes is different.

For both closed and open schemes, the sponsor will often consider its funding strategy together with the scheme's investment strategy – enhanced investment returns from equity-based investment strategies are likely to be considered necessary and appropriate in order for it to provide benefits at an acceptable cost. The funding objectives will often assume, implicitly or explicitly, continuation of equity-based investment strategies.

For a mature or maturing scheme, it will often not be appropriate to assume that an aggressive investment strategy can continue *ad infinitum*. More generally, the assumption that the scheme will continue indefinitely will no longer apply. As a result, the effect on the discontinuance position of any actions taken in the ongoing operation of the scheme will need to be considered.

As a scheme matures, there will be an increasing convergence in the ongoing and discontinuance funding objectives. This is primarily for two reasons:

- The chances of the scheme winding up in the foreseeable future, for reasons beyond the control of the trustees, are likely to be greater (eg, if wind-up is triggered once the last active member leaves pensionable service).
- The trustees may need to consider more actively their duties to protect members' benefits in a winding-up situation and this may mean that they exercise their powers of investment, setting contributions or winding-up differently. Equally, employers will need to understand the implications of any change in emphasis (albeit over time) in the way in which trustees exercise their powers.

This change in emphasis will be of importance to many employers that have recently closed their defined benefit schemes. In many cases, employers will have taken this decision as one part of a strategy of managing and minimising defined benefit risks, so funding objectives may be very different from what they were in the past.

A particular funding strategy that may appeal to employers and trustees in these circumstances is one that aims for a fully funded status on a 'least risk' basis, with a view to removing as much risk as possible once this fully funded status has been achieved. However, one employer's or trustee's perception of a 'least risk' basis may be different from another's.

For example, consider a closed scheme where the intention is to wind it up and buy out benefits when the last active member leaves service. A sensible funding strategy in these circumstances would aim for a fully funded status on a buy-out basis by the time of winding-up. The funding strategy would need to be coupled with a consistent investment strategy, which might be one that is aligned with premium bases used by insurers.

Alternatively, consider a large closed scheme which the employer/trustees intend to continue running as a closed scheme after the last active member leaves service. A 'least risk' investment strategy for such a scheme in the long run may be one consisting predominantly of corporate bonds or government bonds, perhaps with some equity exposures. The funding objectives would need to be consistent with this and it may be necessary to aim in the long run for a target funding level somewhat higher than 100% measured on a bonds basis. Targeting a funding level of more than 100% would be desirable because the trustees would seek to build a cushion to protect members' benefits from risks, such as increasing longevity, and for reinvestment.

An important consideration is the timescale over which the target funding level is to be achieved. The aim may be to get there gradually, over the lifetime of the active membership or over shorter periods. An understanding of how quickly the scheme will mature will be important.

## 2. Methods of addressing a deficit

Various strategies can be used to address a pension deficit.

### 2.1 Paying additional cash contributions

The most common is to make additional cash contributions. From the perspective of the trustees and the Pensions Regulator, this is likely to be the preferred method of providing employer collateral to meet the pension promise.

From the employer's perspective, there are likely to be various issues with providing more cash, such as affordability, impact on operating cash flow, opportunity cost of the contribution and the difficulty in recovering any subsequent surplus that would potentially emerge. While contributions will attract corporation tax relief, this may need to be spread if the contributions in any year are greater than 210% of the contributions in the previous year. Conversely, the PPF risk-based levy should be reduced if additional contributions are paid, which may be considered as an additional return on taking this approach.

## 2.2 Financing cash contribution with debt

How the additional contributions are financed is also an important consideration. Some well-known employers have issued bonds and paid the proceeds directly into the scheme. This theoretically moves 'debt' between different parts of the employer balance sheet. Careful consideration needs to be given to the impact of such an approach on the employer's ability to borrow in future and the potential impact on share price.

If the scheme is invested in bonds and the sponsor pays corporation tax on its profits, a tax differential will potentially arise between the net coupon payments needed to service the debt and the gross coupons received on the scheme investments. Therefore, it may be considered more tax efficient to raise capital for additional contributions in this way. However, the relative tax positions need to be thought through carefully, taking into account the specific circumstances of the corporate sponsor, and consideration may need to be given to the spreading of tax relief.

## 2.3 Alternatives to cash funding

There are a wide range of vehicles and arrangements that have been and could be used to provide additional security without necessarily placing additional cash in the pension scheme. The main methods of providing contingent funding to pension schemes are as follows:

- Letter of credit – under a letter of credit the pension scheme would be able to claim from a syndicate of third-party banks (issuing the letter of credit) agreed amounts upon the occurrence or fulfilment of specified events and conditions, such as employer default or insolvency.
- Escrow account – an escrow account is a separate account held and administered by an independent third party. The sponsoring employer would pay funds into the escrow account and the funds would later, under the terms of the account, either be paid to the pension scheme or be released back to the employer.
- Fixed and floating charges – a charge over one or more unencumbered assets gives the grantee a prior ranking claim to that asset or pool of assets in the event of the insolvency of the employer, and so would provide additional security to the pension scheme while the assets remain employed in the employer. This may or may not be undertaken using a special purpose vehicle (SPV).
- Insolvency insurance/credit derivatives – insurance cover may be obtained against the insolvency of the company under specified conditions and over a given period of time. Credit derivatives, such as credit default swaps (CDS), are standardised market traded forms of credit protection. These instruments provide protection to debt holders against the risk of not recovering the full notional amount of the debt in the event of certain events (set out in the standard contract).
- Contingent loan – this is very similar to an escrow account, except the loan is paid into an SPV owned by the scheme, with repayments contingent on trigger events agreed in advance.
- Insurance solutions – solutions involving the use of a captive or third-party

insurer can be developed to avoid surplus building up in the pension scheme, especially as the scheme approaches full maturity.

- Structured solutions – other derivative solutions are currently being developed relating to some proxy for the scheme's financial position and trigger events related to some or all of the scheme's financial position, sponsor default or a substantial fall in the sponsor's share price.

## 2.4 Derivative investment strategies

There is an ever-changing range of investment options for pension schemes. Many schemes are now looking at investing in diversifying asset classes (eg, hedge funds, commodities, high-yield debt) that have low levels of correlation with equity returns in order to reduce risk. Similarly, some schemes have considered and implemented investment mandates that target an absolute return.

Other strategies involve the use of derivatives to reduce mismatching risk and/or increase efficiency of the scheme's investments as a means of eliminating deficits. The main areas of potential interest are as follows.

### *(a) Liability-driven investment*

Liabilty-driven investment encompasses a range of investment strategies that aim to ensure the assets respond to changes in the relevant liability valuation drivers in a similar manner. The main types of liability matching are:

- duration (protection against interest rate movements);
- inflation (protection against inflation movements); and
- full cash-flow matching (a combination of duration and inflation matching).

Pension schemes can broadly match liabilities by holding a portfolio of index-linked and fixed-interest bonds. However, swap contracts can be used to provide a closer match to liability cash flows. Using interest rate swaps, the scheme and bank agree to exchange cash flows. The scheme receives from the bank fixed interest rate payments and in return the scheme pays the bank floating interest rate payments independent of duration.

Using inflation swaps, the scheme pays periodic fixed cash flows to a bank in return for receiving periodic cash flows linked to the experienced rate of inflation. Effectively, this turns future inflation-linked pension payments into fixed pension payments.

### *(b) Other uses for credit derivatives*

As well as using CDS to reduce the risk of corporate sponsor default, pension funds can also use the growing CDS market to increase efficiency and diversity in their bond portfolios. They can sell protection to other corporate bond holders, and take on the credit risk in those bonds, in exchange for a regular premium. In this way, they gain exposure to the creditworthiness of the bond issuer without being materially exposed to currency and interest rate risk, as they would if they bought the bond itself. There could also be liquidity and transaction cost benefits. The CDS market therefore allows pension funds to gain diversified exposure to a large pool of international bond issuers, particularly in the United States.

Synthetic index-linked corporate bonds can also be created in this way. For example, allocating funds to a pool of CDS in combination with investment in long-dated index-linked gilts has the benefit of strong liability matching characteristics, with some expected added return from the exposure to credit.

*(c)* ***Option strategies***

A combination of call and put options on equity indices and bond indices can be used to gain exposure to out-performance and remove exposure to under-performance. For example, simple strategies might be to hold bonds or cash and buy equity call options or hold equities and buy put options. Such strategies can be used to address pension deficits.

**2.5 Considerations**

There is no simple answer: it depends on the type of employer, the nature and size of the pension commitments, and whether these are viewed from the perspective of risk, reward or cost. In reviewing different strategies, an employer would consider the following:

- Impact on key financials (eg, balance sheet, earnings, net cashflow) – injecting substantial cash into a pension scheme and how the contribution is financed will have different impacts on the employer's key financials. Similarly, contingent funding methods will have different reporting impacts.
- Impact on risk for the employer – different strategies (particularly in relation to investment strategy) will impact on the volatility of future pension disclosures and future scheme cash requirements.
- Tax implications – there will be different tax efficiencies and implications for corporate tax relief.
- Impact on the PPF levy – this will influence the cost comparison of different strategies.
- PR impact/market views – is the strategy expected to have an impact on the employer's share price or on the credit rating, which will affect the cost of borrowing?
- Market practice – what approaches are other employer sponsors taking? Are there any precedents? What has been the reaction?
- Impact on funding requirements – how will this interact with the existing and future funding requirements to be agreed between the employer and trustees?
- Recovery of future surplus – if the scheme were in surplus in the future, it is likely to be very difficult to take a refund, and even then, at penal tax rate of 35% and potentially at the cost of benefit improvements. Does this strategy increase the risk of future irrecoverable surplus and subsequent leakage of shareholder value?
- Impact on relationship with trustees/workforce – a strategy that increases the security of members' benefits is likely to be viewed favourably by the trustees and members. It may be easier to obtain the trustees' agreement to any changes that the employer might like to make to the pension scheme (benefit

design, powers, investment strategy) if this is combined with a large cash contribution or improvement in security. Conversely, how might the strategy (eg, a substantial cash contribution) be perceived by employees that are not members of the defined benefit scheme?

# Scheme benefit changes

**Camilla Barry**
Macfarlanes

---

So you've talked to the actuary, the auditors and the investment consultants. You've talked to the finance director of the company. There is a significant deficit in the scheme whichever way you look at it and the company, it appears, can't contribute any more. Once you've looked at all the investment strategy and funding options, it's time to look at liability management.

When we look at liability management, we have to start from the assumption that there are no effective and legal means of lowering mortality for the membership. A substantial redundancy exercise or the disposal of one or more of the employing businesses can have a significant impact on the liabilities. It can cut future benefit accrual and, unless future salary inflation is expected to be low for the particular workforce, a saving can arise from converting active member liabilities linked to future salary inflation to deferred member liabilities which are linked to lower price inflation. Clearly, these strategies may also have an impact on the sources of funding. So, short of selling the business or sacking the workers, you will need to consider benefit changes.

It makes sense to divide benefit changes by reference to future service benefits and past service benefits. This is because the legal and regulatory environments deal differently with benefits relating to past and future service, and because in most cases trustees and employers may reasonably take a different view of their responsibilities and duties according to whether the benefits have already been 'earned'.

This chapter sets out various options for scheme benefit changes which may assist in reducing a scheme deficit, and reviews the key legal and regulatory considerations relevant to trustees and employers separately according to whether they affect only future service benefits or past service benefits as well. Some of these legal and regulatory considerations are considered in more detail in other chapters.

## 1. Options for scheme benefit changes

Set out below are some common types of benefit change that might be considered. There can be many variants these and the list is not intended to be exhaustive, but rather to enable a discussion of the types of issue that arise with the various options. From the modest to the bold (but not necessarily in order), the range includes the following:

- Reducing future service benefits –
  - lowering rates for increases on pensions in payment in relation to future service accrual;

    - restricting early retirement provisions in relation to future service accrual;
    - reducing contingent benefits such as ill-health and survivors' benefits;
    - increasing normal retirement age for future service;
    - introducing or increasing member contributions;
    - reducing the future pension accrual rate;
    - restricting the pensionable salary basis for future accrual;
    - changing to a career average revalued earnings basis for future accrual;
    - changing to a money purchase basis for future accrual;
    - closing the scheme to new entrants; and
    - terminating future accrual under the scheme.
- Reducing past service (and future service) benefits –
    - increasing pension commutation availability and take-up rates;
    - lowering rates for increases on pensions in payment;
    - restricting early retirement provisions;
    - increasing normal retirement age;
    - restricting or holding down pensionable pay;
    - converting to a career average revalued earnings basis; and
    - converting to a money purchase basis.
- Other means of reducing liabilities –
    - encouraging members to transfer their benefits out of the scheme; and
    - bulk buy-outs of benefits with an insurer

Naturally, many of the options listed above may be combined. Some of the options may be combined to create a flexible benefit package where members choose either to maintain their current rate of benefit accrual by paying higher contributions or to lower their rate of accrual without increasing contributions. A defined contribution option can be run alongside defined benefit options.

Many schemes are reviewing their commutation rates for converting pension to lump sum so that they more accurately reflect the value of the pension. Nevertheless, high levels of commutation can still reduce the liabilities in a scheme and reduce the risks (primarily mortality, investment and inflation) associated with those liabilities. Many schemes have taken up the opportunities under the Finance Act 2004 of providing members with scope for commuting more of their pension.

Increases to pensions in payment can be costly, but most of all they are very long-term liabilities which fluctuate in value and therefore carry a significant amount of risk and volatility. Minimum increases required by statute have been reduced to the lower of price inflation or 2.5% per annum for benefits accruing from April 6 2006.

Early retirement provisions may vary for different groups and according to the circumstances of the retirement. The value of any early retirement enhancements, including early provision of pension on an unreduced basis, can be very significant. Withdrawing or changing such provisions or practices is likely to be an option only either in respect of future service or where the enhanced early retirement terms are subject to a discretion. This may limit the impact of such changes on the deficit.

Increases to normal retirement age will not affect funding significantly if members are given the right to draw their pensions unreduced before normal retirement age, but such a right may need to be granted in relation to past service benefits. Increasing normal retirement age may also increase risk benefits based on prospective service.

It may be possible for an employer to redefine elements of pay so as to limit increases in future pensionable pay without actually making changes to the scheme provisions. For instance, if pensionable pay is defined as basic pay, a greater portion of total remuneration could be paid as bonus. This can affect benefits payable in respect of all service, but only for active members. Changing pensionable pay for past service under the scheme provisions is unlikely to be an option for most schemes.

Converting past service benefits to a different basis such as a career average basis or a money purchase basis can be achieved in the same scheme or by a transfer to a new scheme. It can be achieved with cash incentives, enhancements or other favourable transfer terms, provided care is taken in the communication exercise to reduce the risk of 'mis-selling' claims. There is no need for such changes to apply to all members to have an impact on reducing a deficit or reducing the investment, inflation and mortality risks associated with final salary benefits. These options are discussed in more detail in other chapters.

Closing a scheme will result in a gradual increase in the age profile of the membership and the proportion of pensioners.

Terminating accrual under a scheme may in time result in a divergence of interest between the employer's business and the scheme as the overlap between the membership and the employees engaged in the business reduces. This may affect the approach the trustees take in exercising their powers in relation to funding. Once there are no members accruing benefits, trustees may be more inclined to trigger the winding-up of the scheme where they have power to do this and the employer either is able to meet the deficit or is not likely to meet a larger proportion of the deficit if the winding-up is deferred.

## 2. Reducing future service benefits

Reducing future service benefits will not reduce the current scheme deficit. However, such changes can help to stop the deficit increasing. Where employers are having to spend more on funding past service benefits, reducing future service benefits may also help manage the overall pension budget.

Changes to future service benefits are far less controversial than changes affecting past service benefits. Insofar as pensions are to be treated as deferred pay, whether or not the members pay contributions to the scheme, it is reasonable to treat pension benefits relating to future service as not having yet been earned. In that sense, future service benefits do not yet belong to the member. A change to future service benefits is effectively a change to the terms of employment, even where not covered by the contract of employment, but not a withdrawal of a financial benefit which the member already owns.

For this reason, trustees will generally be far more easily persuaded to agree to scheme amendments changing future service benefit terms. Many trustees indeed take the view that redefining benefit terms for future service is properly a matter for the employer and employees to agree upon, and not a matter for the trustees. On this basis, provided the power of amendment in the scheme rules allows them to make the changes, they will often be agreeable to making changes, particularly where these have been negotiated or consulted on with the membership or their representatives.

Other trustees take the view that even in relation to changes affecting only future service benefits, they cannot agree changes which are detrimental to their members unless the affordability of the scheme on its current terms is genuinely in question. An employer may well be called upon to provide financial information to justify the changes. The trustees may undertake their own employer covenant review, unless they have already done so in connection with scheme funding, to determine what level of benefit is in their view sustainable.

Some trustees will also be concerned about changes adversely affecting prospective members – such as closing the scheme to new entrants or providing lower benefits or benefits on a different basis, such as money purchase, for employees joining the scheme after a certain date. It is probably fair to say that prospective members already employed by the sponsoring company, who would be able to join the scheme subject to completing a period of service or 'waiting period', do come within the scope of the trustees' duties, but it is questionable whether the interests of any other possible future members can be considered at all. In any event, it is reasonable for trustees to favour the interests of current members (including deferred and pensioner members) over prospective members. Their primary duty is to ensure the scheme is administered in accordance with its provisions and that benefits which have been promised are paid.

Trustees may, in considering benefit changes, take into account the members' interests in continued employment and pay rises and other benefits. The trustees also need to consider the interest of the scheme in the continuation of the employer's business as its principal source of funding. There is also case law such as *Lock v Westpac Banking Corporation* [1991] PLR 167 and *Edge v Pensions Ombudsman* [2000] Ch 602 that trustees may take account of the employer's interests, although not so as to override the members' interests.

Since changes to legislation introduced with effect from June 13 2003 requiring employers to meet any deficit in the scheme on a buy-out basis (ie, a basis enabling all liabilities in the scheme to be bought out with annuity contracts), in considering proposed changes to benefits, the trustees should be less concerned about the willingness of the employer to fund the scheme as opposed to its ability to do so.

Whatever the attitude of the trustees in relation to such changes, the terms of the power of amendment in the scheme rules will need to be considered. The drafting of powers of amendment varies. The need to comply strictly with any requirements of the power of amendment has been emphasised in *Bestrustees v Stuart* [2001] 55 PBLR and in *Trustee Solutions v Dubery* [2006] 36 PBLR.

A number of cases provide guidance on the interpretation of powers of amendment. To some extent, they also illustrate the difficulty of such interpretation. In *Re Courage Group's Pension Schemes* [1987] 1 All ER 528, a provision that the trustees "shall concur in executing" any deed of amendment was construed as giving the trustees a discretion whether to concur. The case also contains comments from the judge that suggests restrictions protecting "benefits already secured by past contributions" mean the link to future salary for past service accrual cannot be broken. Provisions protecting benefits already "accrued" or already "secured", or using other terminology, therefore need to be considered carefully and in context in each case. In *Lloyds Bank Pension Trust Corporation Limited v Lloyds Bank Plc* [1996] PLR 263 the court held that the restrictions on reducing benefits contained in the scheme provisions protected not only accrued benefits, but also accruable benefits.

Given the often restrictive interpretation that has been placed on the terms of powers of amendment, some comfort can be drawn from the decision in *Capital Cranfield v Sagar* [2001] 54 PBLR that where express restrictions apply, it is wrong to imply additional restrictions unless plainly necessary and obvious.

In addition to any restrictions expressly provided in the scheme's power of amendment, there are statutory restrictions that may apply. Section 67 of the Pensions Act 1995 has been amended by the Pensions Act 2004. The provisions of Section 67 do not override scheme restrictions and the terms of the scheme's power of amendment also need to be complied with.

In revising Section 67, it was the government's intention that changes to Section 67 will

> *provide schemes with the freedom to adapt to changing circumstances, while continuing to provide security for their members. In particular, they will allow schemes to avoid escalating funding costs in the future, if the assumptions underlying the scheme change over time. They provide that the actuarial value of members' accrued rights must be maintained at the point of any change, which is an important safeguard that was widely endorsed in the responses received.*

The new Section 67 of the Pensions Act 1995 provides that where a modification is being made to a scheme (other than a public service or prescribed scheme) which might result in:

- a member's (or their survivors') 'subsisting rights' (see below) under the scheme becoming money purchase benefits; or
- a reduction in the prevailing rate of pensions in payment under the scheme rules

the trustees must give the affected member a written explanation of the proposed modification and its effect on him, tell him he is entitled to make representations and give him a reasonable opportunity to do so, and obtain his written consent to the modification.

In the case of any other modification which might detrimentally affect a member's or his survivors' subsisting rights, either the member's consent must be obtained as described above or the trustees must:

- give the member written notification explaining the modification and its effect on him and allow him to make representations;
- take steps to satisfy themselves that the actuarial value of the member's benefits after the modification will be equal to or greater than the value of

their subsisting rights immediately before it; and

- within a reasonable period from the modification taking effect, obtain a statement from the scheme actuary that the actuarial value of the member's subsisting rights has been maintained.

'Subsisting rights' are defined as accrued rights to future benefits under the scheme or any other entitlement at the relevant time to benefits under the scheme rules (and in the case of active members they are determined as if they had just left service at the relevant time). This means that the section does not protect the link to future salary increases for past service benefits.

After complying with the above requirements, trustee consent to the modification is also required (even where the scheme rules give the amendment power solely to the employer). The trustees must also notify all affected members that they intend to exercise their powers to make the modification.

As can be seen, these provisions are still restrictive. If the changes reduce the actuarial value of past service benefits calculated as if the member left service on the date of the change – that is, disregarding future salary inflation but taking into account limited price indexation – the changes can be made only with the consent of every member. Even where the actuarial test can be satisfied, the member must be given advance notice of the proposed change and an opportunity to make representations.

This still allows changes to be made for future service benefits. This also adds weight to the general notion that changes to future service benefits are legitimate and should generally be permitted.

It is also worth noting that the powers of the Pensions Regulator available to it where the trustees and the employer cannot agree on matters relating to scheme funding under the statutory scheme-specific funding regime or in respect of other breaches of those provisions allow it to make changes to future service benefits. This supports the approach that where funding is a problem, future service benefits should be the first to be considered for reduction.

Where changes are being made affecting current members, the terms of the contracts of employment should also be checked. Where detail about pension scheme benefits is included in the contract of employment, an employer may need to consider employment law aspects of changing the employment contract terms and this may require employee consent.

In addition, under the Pensions Act 2004, employers are now required to consult for at least 60 days with active members or their representatives before making a listed change. These requirements apply from:

- April 5 2006 to employers with at least 150 employees;
- April 5 2007 to employers with at least 100 employees; and
- April 5 2008 to employers with at least 50 employees (in each case regardless of the number of active members in the scheme).

The listed changes are:

- increasing the normal pension age;

- closing the scheme to new entrants;
- terminating accrual;
- reducing the rate of future accrual;
- terminating employer contributions; and
- introducing or increasing member contributions.

Introducing member contributions where the scheme was previously non-contributory will also require express written agreement of the members to ensure the deduction of contributions from pay is not an unlawful deduction contrary to Section 13 of the Employment Rights Act 1996. Any increase to member contributions may require similar agreement depending on the terms of the original agreement.

The obligation of employers to consult with employees over benefit changes may alleviate some trustee concern over agreeing detrimental changes to future service benefits.

Both trustees and employers will need to consider the application of age discrimination legislation.

### 3. Reducing past service (and future service) benefits

While future service benefits are likely to be the first candidates for change in response to a deficit or funding difficulties, there will be many cases where such changes are not sufficient to rescue the scheme or the employer's business. It is then time to consider the options for reducing liabilities which have already accrued. These options are limited.

Section 67 of the Pensions Act 1995 (as amended by the Pensions Act 2004 and discussed above) requires the consent of every member affected to be secured if the overall value of their accrued benefits is being reduced. Restrictions on the scheme's power of amendment may also apply and may make it impossible to reduce past service liabilities under the scheme. This is, in a sense, not surprising. If pensions are deferred pay and past service benefits are benefits which have already been earned by service or the payment of contributions or both, a reduction in past service benefits is effectively a cancellation of members' pay due in respect of services already provided. The counter-argument that the cost of the members' benefits has been underestimated will be unconvincing to many: the fact that the employer may have struck a bad bargain may not be reason enough to allow it to renege on the bargain.

The fact that the powers of the Pensions Regulator under the Pensions Act 2004 in relation to scheme-specific funding allow it to make changes to future service benefits but not past service benefits (as mentioned above) is indicative of the priority given to past service benefits in the view of the government.

The message is clear: only in limited cases can past service benefits as a whole be reduced, and then only with the consent of members.

Even then there is a doubt: Section 91 of the Pensions Act 1995 prohibits assignment, commutation and surrender except in specified circumstances. In particular, except as provided, any agreement to assign, commute or surrender benefits is unenforceable. There is some doubt as to how Sections 67 and 91 interact, and whether Section 91 applies only to cases where Section 67 does not apply. This would mean that, provided the requirements of Section 67 have been complied with, Section 91 does not apply so that any arrangement which satisfies the requirements of Section 67 will not be unenforceable.

There is a view, however, that the two provisions are not mutually exclusive. In other words, where members agree to reduce their benefit entitlements under a scheme, such amendments will be unenforceable so that the member will retain the same benefit rights.

Because of uncertainty over the scope of Section 91, it is not possible to answer with any certainty whether it is possible for members to agree to reduce their past service benefits at all.

Assuming for present purposes that members may effectively agree to reduce their past service benefits, in what circumstances might members consider it to be in their interests to do so?

Active members have an interest in the continuation and success of their employer's business, and increasing pension costs may be to the detriment of pay rises and may even result in redundancy exercises.

All members will also have an interest in the continuation of the employer's business as a source of funding for the scheme. However, members may not be easily convinced that a reduction in past service benefits will enable the employer to fund fully the remainder of the benefits.

If a scheme gets into winding-up in an insolvent state, where the employer is also insolvent, it is very likely that the scheme will be transferred to the Pension Protection Fund (PPF) if it is funded below the level required to secure benefits at the level of compensation that would be provided by the PPF. If a scheme is being wound up outside the PPF, benefits which would be covered by compensation under the PPF will take priority over other benefits under Section 73 of the Pensions Act 1995 (as amended by the Pensions Act 2004).

The PPF does not provide full scheme benefits for most members. If the member has reached normal pension age before the employer's insolvency, the member will receive his full scheme pension but increases are limited to the lower of price inflation or 2.5% per annum, and only in respect of pension accrued after April 5 1997. Survivors' benefits are also limited. Members under normal pension age get 90% of their pension subject to the compensation cap (£29,928.56 at age 65 from April 1 2007).

The availability of the PPF is a disincentive to members who are above pension age to agree to any reduction in benefits. Their concern about the scheme's funding level is limited as their current level of pension will be covered for compensation. If the scheme is funded above the PPF level, their benefits – again with the exception of pension increases – will rank first in an insolvent winding-up outside the PPF.

The PPF is, on the other hand, an incentive to members under normal pension age to transfer out their benefits or agree to benefit changes which affect benefits which would not be protected by compensation from the PPF. These benefits are also the first cut on an insolvent winding-up and are therefore payable only if the scheme is ongoing or is fully funded when they become payable. Members may reasonably be willing to agree to such a change even where it results in a net reduction to the overall value of their entitlements.

The PPF liabilities on which the scheme's PPF levy is paid would increase, but the amount of benefit being protected would also increase.

It has been argued that, on public policy grounds, trustees should not take into account the availability of the PPF in exercising their functions. This argument is untested in this context in the courts and is certainly open to debate. However, if such a remodelling of benefits were proposed by the employer, and the trustees were satisfied either that there was no reduction in the overall actuarial value of benefits (so that the change was effectively neutral) or all affected members had consented, or that there was some other benefit in the change possibly related to the employer's business or to the scheme's funding, arguably they could agree to the change without taking into account the availability of the PPF.

## 4. Other means of reducing liabilities

Transfer-out exercises and bulk buy-outs are not strictly scheme benefit changes. Transfers out with cash incentives are discussed in detail elsewhere in this book. However, it seemed appropriate to mention them in the context of this chapter as they do, in a sense, affect benefits and may, in some cases, require scheme changes.

In some schemes trustees may be permitted to buy out members' benefits and many schemes routinely buy out pensioners' benefits. Bulk buy-outs are sometimes raised as a means of addressing a scheme deficit. It is unlikely that buying-out liabilities will reduce a scheme deficit, although it may reduce some of the administrative burden related to those liabilities. The options for and the value of bulk buy-outs are discussed elsewhere in this book.

Deferred members are entitled to transfer out their benefits under the provisions of the Pension Schemes Act 1993. A transfer-out exercise can be undertaken without cash incentives either from the employer or from the trustee.

The statutory transfer value is calculated on a statutory basis (as the 'cash equivalent transfer value') and may be reduced where the scheme is underfunded. This will clearly mean that the member receives less than the value of his full benefit entitlement under the scheme. Cash incentives are therefore likely to enhance take-up. However, there may be members who, for instance, have benefits that would be significantly reduced on an insolvent winding-up or a transfer of the scheme to the PPF, and who prefer to take a reduced transfer value while the scheme is still ongoing. Other members may sometimes choose to take a transfer because they expect to earn higher returns by investing the transfer payment in a defined contribution arrangement.

The principal risk with any kind of transfer-out exercise is that members who take a transfer-out following an announcement encouraging them to do so may bring 'mis-selling' claims at a later date. The communications therefore need to be handled with care.

Other issues for consideration, particularly for trustees, are the appropriateness of paying transfers above the statutory level or buying out benefits in full where the scheme is underfunded and the transfer or buy-out is therefore likely to reduce, even marginally, the funding available for other members' benefits. It is therefore generally advisable to ensure the funding of any enhancement or cash incentive or any buy-out exercise is therefore met by the employer. The only exception may be where the scheme is significantly underfunded on the PPF basis. Where it is unlikely that the scheme funding will ever rise above the PPF level, any further weakening of the funding of the scheme may not have a material effect on the security of other members' benefits: assuming the scheme later transfers to the PPF, they will receive the same level of compensation.

## 5. Conclusion

The options for scheme benefit changes are theoretically extremely wide. They include changes to scheme benefit design and practices and changes to pay policy, as well as transfer-out exercises. In practice, given the protections applying to past service benefits, implementing scheme benefit changes as a means of deficit reduction is not straightforward from a legal perspective.

# Career average revalued earnings and other alternatives to final salary

**Danny Tsang**
K&L Gates

---

The history of why pension schemes in the United Kingdom are in deficit is covered elsewhere in this book. In recent years, rather than the traditional switch from final salary to money purchase benefits, many UK employers have considered and introduced alternative benefit structures.

The more traditional switch from final salary to money purchase benefits is examined in detail elsewhere in this book. This chapter considers other alternatives to final salary benefits and, in particular, career average revalued earnings (CARE) benefits.

Alternatives to final salary benefits other than money purchase benefits have been around for decades. They originated in different forms with the traditional average salary benefits seen in the United States back in the 1960s. Over the last several decades since then, other forms and alternatives such as cash balance plans have also been implemented by employers.

## 1. Why CARE?

Pension fund deficits became common ground in the United Kingdom during the late 1990s and early 2000s. This occurred after a sustained period of significant surpluses during the 1980s and 1990s which saw many employers enjoying the benefit of contribution holidays. However, the deficits of the last seven to 10 years have been one of the main reasons leading employers to explore ways of reducing deficits and containing pension costs.

A significant number of employers resisted the switch from final salary to money purchase in the 1990s, money purchase being the option adopted by some not only to contain costs and to provide certainty, but also to avoid the need for compliance with the requirements of the Pensions Act 1995. However, they found themselves sponsoring pension funds with sizeable deficits only a few years later. Over time, some of these employers decided to join the many that had already switched from final salary to money purchase benefits, while others continued to resist the traditional switch, preferring instead to consider a switch to another alternative to final salary, CARE.

CARE benefits have been seen by employers and employees alike as being a good alternative to final salary. Providing CARE benefits is cheaper for employers relative to final salary benefits. The volatility of costs for employers in terms of contributions is also significantly reduced. From the employees' perspective, CARE benefits are still 'defined benefits' where the employer continues to bear the investment risk. By contrast, employees being provided with money purchase benefits bear not just the investment risk, but also that of the annuity market.

This chapter examines some of the designs of CARE benefits, explains the main ways of implementing such designs and analyses some of the key legal and human resource issues and considerations. Other alternatives to final salary benefits besides CARE are also outlined.

## 2. What is CARE?

CARE benefits can probably best be described as pension benefits which are calculated for each year (or part year) of service which are then revalued from the end of that year until retirement. For each year of service, the amount of pension benefit in respect of each employee is calculated by multiplying the chosen accrual rate by the 'pensionable salary' of the employee for that year. The amount of pension calculated for that year in respect of that employee is then revalued up to retirement.

A switch from final salary benefits to CARE benefits will necessarily involve giving consideration to both past service and future service benefits. What should happen with benefits that have accrued for service completed up to the date of the switch? What benefits should be provided from the date of the switch and how should these be calculated?

For the benefits that have accrued for service up to the switch, there are two main options:

- treating members as if they have become early leavers with deferred benefits calculated on the basis of service accrued up to, and salary as at, the date of the switch; the deferred benefits are then revalued in line with statutory requirements from the date of the switch to the date on which benefits are drawn; or
- calculating past service benefits on service accrued up to the date of the switch but taking into account future salary increases to retirement, death or leaving service.

Clearly, in most cases, from the employer's perspective, it would be preferable to adopt the first option and treat members' past service benefits as deferred benefits. However, the available option will depend on the circumstances and the issues which are present in individual cases. Some of these issues are examined later in this chapter. There will be circumstances where it may not be possible to adopt the first option, relying instead on the second.

What about future service benefits? In order to design CARE benefits, decisions will need to be made in relation to the following elements:

- the accrual rate – this is much the same as for final salary benefits (eg, 1/60th, 1/80th etc);
- the method of revaluation – there are different options that may be adopted but broadly they may be linked either to the Retail Prices Index (RPI) or to national average earnings;
- cap or no cap – whatever the method for revaluation chosen, a decision must

be made as to whether a cap should be used to limit the level of revaluation and, if so, by how much; and

- whether the method of revaluation should be the same for the calculation of benefits both while in service and after leaving service in circumstances where a member leaves before retirement; care must also be taken to ensure compliance with the preservation requirements.

## 3. How is CARE implemented?

Employers may introduce CARE benefits in one of two ways.

### 3.1 New pension scheme

Employers may introduce CARE benefits by providing these under a newly established pension scheme. There are advantages to this approach. It will normally enable the employer to set the terms and conditions of the new pension scheme, including the more important powers. However, there are also drawbacks. Establishing a new pension scheme, besides incurring set-up costs, will involve compliance and regulatory issues. Additionally, it may involve having to terminate the existing scheme under which final salary benefits have been provided. This will result not only in incurring the costs and expenses of winding up the existing final salary scheme, but more significantly, the possible need for employers to inject a significant amount of cash into that scheme to meet any deficit. When a pension scheme is being wound up, such a deficit will be calculated on a buy-out basis.

### 3.2 New section in existing scheme

An alternative and probably more attractive option would be to introduce CARE benefits by providing these in a new section which may be created under the existing pension scheme. There will be no additional costs of having to establish a new pension scheme. At the same time, it will avoid the requirement immediately to fund in full any existing funding deficit, a requirement that would arise on the termination of a pension scheme. While the advantages of this route include avoiding the substantial costs and other issues involved when establishing a new scheme and in terminating the existing one, there are various issues which may prove problematic when introducing the switch from final salary to CARE benefits under an existing pension scheme. It will normally necessitate the exercise of the power of amendment by the employer, by the trustees or, as is often the case, jointly by both parties. The difficulties encountered with this option are examined below.

## 4. What are the key considerations?

A switch from final salary to CARE benefits will involve a number of considerations, the more important of which are:

- trust provisions;
- Section 67 of the Pensions Act 1995, as amended;
- contracts of employment;
- the employer's implied duty to act in good faith;
- employer consultation;

- trustee consent;
- employee communications; and
- administration.

### 4.1 Trust provisions

If an employer chooses to introduce CARE benefits by using an existing pension scheme, this will usually involve making changes to the terms governing the scheme and therefore consideration will need to be given to the scheme's power of amendment. The amendment power may be vested solely in the employer or in the trustee, but in the majority of pension schemes, both the employer and the trustees will play a role in the introduction of changes to a pension scheme.

Quite often there are restrictions attached to the power of amendment. While the employer and the trustees may have the power to introduce changes, certain proposed changes may not be permitted. These usually concern benefits that have accrued before the date of the proposed changes. Care should be taken to ensure that the employer and the trustees are acting within their respective powers when deciding whether to exercise the amendment power to terminate future accrual of final salary benefits. In certain circumstances, it may be necessary to obtain members' consent before changes are introduced.

In limited circumstances, it may be necessary to introduce CARE benefits by establishing a new pension scheme. This is usually the case where the exercise of the amendment power in an existing scheme would give rise to significant difficulties or become unnecessarily protracted. However, as explained earlier in this chapter, the establishment of a new pension scheme is not without its drawbacks.

It is also conceivable that the scheme's other trust provisions are such that the trustees have considerable powers enabling them to negotiate a stronger position on behalf of members. Employers should investigate the scheme's trust provisions carefully before putting forward any proposals for change to the trustees. Some of the more important provisions include the power to trigger winding-up and the power to determine employer contributions.

### 4.2 Section 67 of the Pensions Act 1995

Where an amendment power is used to introduce changes to an existing pension scheme to switch benefits from final salary to CARE, consideration will also need to be given to the restrictions imposed by Section 67 of the Pensions Act 1995, as amended. Section 67 was introduced on April 6 1997 to protect "any entitlement, or accrued rights, of any member of the scheme acquired before the power is exercised" unless certain conditions were satisfied.

However, the original provisions were highly restrictive and led to difficulties in construction. This resulted in revisions being made to Section 67 which came into force on April 6 2006 pursuant to the Pensions Act 2004. The application of any restriction to the power of amendment depends on whether the amendment power is being used to make a regulated modification. A 'regulated modification' can be either:

- a protected modification – that is, a modification which would or might result in any subsisting right of a member or his dependant (not being a right

to money purchase benefits) becoming or being replaced with a right to money purchase benefits, or which would or might result in a reduction in the prevailing rate of pension in payment under the rules of the scheme; or
- a detrimental modification – that is, a modification which would or might adversely affect subsisting rights of any member or his dependant.

Section 67 now provides that a 'regulated modification' is voidable unless certain statutory conditions are met, namely:
- a consent requirement in the case of protected modifications;
- a consent or an actuarial equivalence requirement in the case of detrimental modifications; and
- a trustee approval requirement and a reporting requirement for both protected modifications and detrimental modifications.

As a protected modification concerns a switch to money purchase benefits, moving from final salary to CARE benefits would fall within the ambit only of a detrimental modification. The restrictions and conditions under Section 67 would be of significance only if the proposed changes were to impact on rights accrued before the change itself. This is likely to be rare. If any proposed changes are likely to be considered as a detrimental modification, it would be necessary to seek members' consent unless the actuarial equivalence requirement could be satisfied.

Broadly, the consent requirement will be satisfied if members have been consulted and subsequently give their consent in writing to the proposed modification. The actuarial equivalence requirement involves consultation with employees and the scheme actuary providing a certificate to the trustees that the 'actuarial value' of the accrued benefit has been maintained.

### 4.3 Contracts of employment

When considering whether changes to benefits should be made, it is important for employers to review and consider the terms of employees' contracts of employment. A switch from final salary to CARE benefits may require a variation to the terms of employees' contracts of employment. While considering contracts of employment, it may also be necessary to check explanatory booklets and announcements to assess whether employees have been provided with a promise of a particular level of benefits or whether changes to pension benefits may be permitted.

If contracts of employment reveal that some kind of promise has been given to employees or if there are restrictions to making changes to benefits, employers will need to consider whether the consent of employees will need to be obtained in respect of any proposed changes. Clearly, the larger the membership, the more problematic any proposed changes will be.

Quite often, the position is not clear-cut. The terms of employees' contracts of employment may refer to explanatory booklets which in turn make reference to the pension scheme's governing trust provisions and rules. However, difficulties can be encountered as more often than not employees will not have been provided with a copy of the pension scheme's governing trust provisions and rules. As such, even if the amendment power is sufficiently wide, employees cannot be deemed to be bound by the scheme's provisions as there was no 'meeting of the minds' of the parties in relation to the power to make changes.

Where the power to introduce changes has been communicated to employees, care should be taken to assess whether the power is expressed in terms which are too wide. If so, the power may not be enforceable under the Unfair Contract Terms Act 1977 if its scope is so wide as to be considered unreasonable.

If a decision has been made by the employer to vary contracts of employment, there are three principal ways of doing so:

- obtaining each employee's prior informed consent, which is the most attractive in terms of future risk and exposure and involves a consultation exercise that, since April 6 2006, is far more prescriptive than previously, because the requirements are now set out in the Occupational and Personal Pension Schemes (Consultation by Employers and Miscellaneous Amendment) Regulations 2006;
- terminating the employee's old terms and conditions on full contractual notice (also after full and proper consultation) and offering to rehire on new terms, which may be combined with the option to obtain the employee's prior informed consent; or
- unilaterally varying the contract – this is the least attractive and exposes employers to significant risks.

## 4.4 Employer's implied duty to act in good faith

Employers wishing to introduce changes to their pension schemes by switching from final salary to CARE benefits will need to consider their obligations to employees. In particular, employers have an implied duty to act in good faith which derives from the case of *Imperial Group Pension Trust Ltd v Imperial Tobacco Ltd*. Essentially, in the exercise of any power, an employer must not do so in a manner which is likely to destroy or seriously damage the relationship of confidence and trust between the employer and his employees and former employees.

In considering the implied duty to act in good faith, employers need not act solely in the interests of employees. They are entitled to take into account their own financial and commercial interests when deciding how to act. It is very difficult for employers to determine whether any particular act they are performing would be in breach of the implied duty, but care should be taken to ensure that claims are avoided. Actions such as those contained in the following list, while they cannot be guaranteed to work, will assist employers to do so:

- consulting with employees in connection with the proposed changes and obtaining their consent, if appropriate;
- seeking the approval of the trustees and considering alternative proposals which may have been put forward;
- giving employees and their representatives sufficient time to consider any proposed changes; and
- ensuring that no threats are made regarding consequences in circumstances where employees do not give their consent.

It is arguable that although the implied duty to act in good faith is owed to employees, trustees of affected pension schemes may be able to enforce the duty. Much will depend on what details concerning the amendment power have been provided in communications with employees, including contracts of employment, members' explanatory booklets and announcements. The ultimate question for trustees is how the implied duty to act in good faith is likely to affect the exercise of the amendment power.

### 4.5 Employer consultation

Sections 259 to 261 of the Pensions Act 2004 (together with the Employer Consultation Regulations) require employers to consult with employees in circumstances where certain changes are proposed to be made to pension benefits. This includes a switch from final salary to CARE benefits. One of the 'listed' changes requiring consultation is a change in the basis on which future accrual rates may be determined.

Details of the employer consultation requirements are provided elsewhere in this book. The process requires that:

- written information is provided to affected employees before the start of the consultation exercise; and
- the consultation is conducted with employee representatives including, where applicable, recognised trade union representatives, representatives under the Information and Consultation of Employees Regulations 2004 or representatives elected for the purposes of the Employer Consultation Regulations.

The impact of the Employer Consultation Regulations is far less than was at first feared. Employers making changes to pension schemes (including a switch from final salary to CARE benefits) have invariably conducted consultation exercises before the Employer Consultation Regulations were introduced. The effect of the Employer Consultation Regulations is that the process is much more prescriptive than was previously the case. As explained elsewhere in this chapter, a successful, well-managed consultation exercise can often greatly assist in lessening the risks of a successful claim for a breach of affected employees' contracts of employment or the employer's duty to act in good faith.

### 4.6 Trustee consent

The introduction of changes to a pension scheme will usually require the involvement of its trustees. Typically, this is due to the fact that even if the amendment power is vested solely in the employer, its exercise may still require the consent of the trustees or their execution of a deed to effect any changes. Even where trustees' consent is not required, employers will nevertheless need to tread carefully to ensure that the trustees cooperate, as they will have a role to play in implementing any proposed changes.

Trustees have a duty to act in the best (usually the best financial) interests of members. If they are requested by employers to consider and give consent to any proposals to change benefits from final salary to CARE, trustees will need to consider all relevant factors and ignore those that are not relevant. For instance, trustees will need to consider whether their actions may be assisting in a breach of the terms of employees' contracts of employment or of the employer's implied duty to act in good faith. Hence, trustees will normally insist on being involved in the employer's consultation and consent process to ensure that their actions do not encourage or facilitate any unlawful acts.

One important issue that will need early attention is that of potential conflicts. Although it is becoming more rare, many pension schemes in the United Kingdom still have trustee bodies comprising a large number drawn from the employer's board or management team. Quite often, it is the same members of management who are responsible for introducing changes to pension schemes such as a switch from final salary to CARE benefits. The issue of potential conflicts should be considered and addressed at an early stage in the process. Trustees should also seek legal, actuarial and other professional advice independent of that obtained by employers.

### 4.7 Employee communication

A key to success in introducing and implementing any proposed changes to pension benefits is good, simple and clear employee communications. Employers will usually work with trustees and their respective advisers to prepare written communications and deliver employee presentations. The communications exercise is critical to the success of the implementation process in any proposed changes to benefits. The reasons for the changes should be clear. Details of changes should be as simple as possible, with the use of examples whenever possible and appropriate. The format of the communications exercise is also very important.

### 4.8 Administration

Attention will also be required at an early stage as to the future administration of the pension scheme once the proposed changes have been implemented. Although it should be relatively straightforward once in place, difficulties may be encountered in the initial set-up and a smooth process and transition are therefore critical. Employers, trustees and administrators will need to work together to ensure this.

## 5. Alternatives to CARE

During the last several years, CARE benefits have been seen by employers as an alternative to money purchase benefits in the switch away from final salary benefits – they are seen as a middle ground between final salary and money purchase benefits. There are, however, other alternatives to CARE benefits and some of these are briefly outlined below.

### 5.1 Average salary benefits

Rather than CARE benefits, employers may wish to consider switching from final salary to a more straightforward average salary benefit structure. This operates in a way similar to that of a final salary benefit design, except that the average (rather than final) salary of each employee over the whole period of membership is used to calculate the pension benefit.

An average salary benefit design should be far simpler and cheaper to implement when compared with CARE benefits. However, some argue that benefits based on average salary can be a less attractive option relative to money purchase benefits. It is a design which has been more popular in the United States in the past and has seldom been implemented by employers in the United Kingdom.

### 5.2 Cash balance plans

An alternative 'middle ground' to CARE benefits are benefits under cash balance plans which have also been relatively popular in the United States. There are modified forms of cash balance plans, but the principles are the same. The idea is that the employer and the employee pay contributions into a money purchase vehicle. The employer effectively promises a particular level of 'cash' built up over the number of years' membership. On maturity, the promised 'cash' pot would be used to purchase a pension from the open market. The employer bears the risks of investment returns, the employee the risk of annuity rates.

This form of benefit design has been implemented by a small number of (mainly larger) employers in the United Kingdom, but its popularity in the United Kingdom has been far less than that in the United States. Only time will tell as to whether employers will choose cash balance plans as a relative 'middle ground' alternative to final salary and money purchase benefits.

### 5.3 Freezing future salary increases

Some employers have also explored opportunities of controlling future pension costs and simultaneously reducing past service deficits by freezing future increases to the salary used for calculating employees' future pension benefits. This may be achieved by freezing the salaries of members at the point of change; instead of allowing future salary increases to determine future service pension benefits, the salary would be linked to the RPI or some other chosen index.

The link to RPI may apply both to past service (subject to legislative and scheme restrictions) and to future service. As with CARE benefits, it would also be possible to apply a cap on the increase in the RPI when determining future service pension benefits. This method is arguably simpler to administer and should be less expensive to implement relative to CARE benefits.

# Defined contribution schemes

**Gary Smith**
Watson Wyatt

---

## 1. Introduction

Defined contribution (DC) pension provision has generally found itself with a bad name in the United Kingdom, in part fuelled by the media's portrayal of companies slashing costs as part of a move from defined benefit (DB) provision. But just because companies have shifted away from DB as a response to the financial risks and burdens it places on the sponsor, does this mean that the most common alternative and replacement, the DC pension scheme, is automatically the poor relation?

For most employees, the answer is probably 'yes'. This is primarily a result of the escalating cost of DB provision, rather than some sudden collective miserliness on the part of employers. It is increased life expectancy and the additional guarantees and burdens imposed on DB schemes in recent years which have pushed the cost of DB provision so high. Indeed, the cost to an employer of running a good-quality DC scheme today is not so very different from that of many DB schemes when they were originally set up.

The perception of DC as the poor relation has not been helped by the fact that many employers switched to DC for negative reasons – that is, it was not DB – rather than going into DC with a positive attitude and clearly defined objectives and success criteria. As a result, many DC schemes have spent the last few years in the wilderness, receiving little or no attention from employers. Neither has there been very much commitment and understanding from sponsors concerning the need to communicate, educate and support DC scheme members.

However, many employers are now waking up to the reality that their DC schemes are not the panacea which they were originally hoped and assumed they would be. In particular, they are generally not delivering what employers and employees want or need, and have introduced a new raft of issues and risks for sponsoring employers. As a result, and encouragingly, we are now beginning to see the emergence of 'quality' DC pension schemes. This improvement in quality is in terms of not only the contributions employers are making, but also the investment of time and resources that many are now putting into governance and member communications.

Many company pension DC schemes were set up five, 10 or even 15 years ago for new employees at the same time as existing DB schemes were being closed to new entrants. Initially, these DC schemes had few, if any, members and next to no assets. They were consequently often given a low priority by companies. But today, for many companies, the majority of their workforce are now in the DC pension scheme and so management priorities are shifting. Companies are increasingly looking to invest more in ensuring that the pension benefits they offer meet the needs and expectations of their employees. In other words, they are looking to make DC work better.

For the past three years Watson Wyatt has undertaken a survey of DC pension provision among FTSE 100 companies. This chapter looks primarily at the results of the most recent survey and the trends that are emerging, and outlines what DC pensions currently look like at Britain's largest companies. The FTSE 100 is far from a cross-section of UK employers and the DC pension provision offered by these companies cannot be taken as typical for companies generally. However, it is larger companies that have traditionally offered DB pensions in the past – smaller companies have typically favoured DC pensions or no pension provision at all – and so the results of the survey provide a good indication of what the most common alternative to a DB pension scheme looks like today.

Watson Wyatt's 2006 Defined Contribution Pension Scheme Survey was drawn from the responses of 84 companies in the FTSE 100 index as at March 31 2006 and covered 88 schemes in total (of which 65 were DC schemes).

## 2. DC structures

Over three-quarters of the DC schemes in the survey are operated as occupational, trust-based schemes – an increase on the 2005 survey from two-thirds, as well as an increase on 2004. Some 28% of the DC schemes in the survey were occupational DC schemes set up on a standalone trust basis, while 49% were occupational DC schemes that were set up as a section of an existing DB scheme – for example, where a DB scheme had been closed to new entrants and/or to future accrual.

So an occupational, trust-based scheme continues to be by far the most prevalent and popular DC scheme structure (compared to the alternative contract-based structure, which includes group personal pension and stakeholder schemes) within this sector of the market. There is also an upwards trend in this direction. Some of this may be attributable to the fact that the composition of survey respondents has changed, but it is still a fact that occupational, trust-based DC schemes seem to hold significant advantages to employers within this universe.

Other types of DC scheme reported are group personal pensions (12%) and stakeholder pensions (11%).

## 3. Membership take-up

Membership take-up rates reveal a similar pattern to the 2004 and 2005 surveys. The percentage of schemes with take-up rates of over 80% is now 57%. This is evidence of our experience with new DC schemes that employers are increasingly utilising automatic enrolment. We looked at the split between employers offering automatic enrolment and those requiring an application form. As might be anticipated, the trend shows lower take-up rates for companies requesting completion and return of an application form.

Some 18% of schemes still have very low take-up rates (less than 20%). This may be accounted for by low employer contribution rates, but is more likely to be due to low levels of employee awareness and engagement. There is also anecdotal evidence of a correlation between low take-up rates and a high proportion of female employees, part-time workers and/or high levels of turnover.

Two-thirds of DC schemes in the survey offer immediate access to new employees. A few stipulate either three or six months' waiting (often this is consistent with an employer's probationary period).

## 4. Rising contributions

The Watson Wyatt survey found the maximum combined – employer and employee – contributions to DC schemes for FTSE 100 companies, assuming employees take full advantage of employer matching, is on average 13.7% of salary. Moreover, employer contributions have risen by 10% in the last two years, from 8.5% of an employee's salary in 2004 to 9.4% in the 2006 survey.

Two-thirds of FTSE 100 DC pension schemes are structured with matching contributions, whereby the employer pays more in direct correlation to how much the employee contributes.

The average total employer contribution for schemes offering matching member contributions is 10.1% of salary, assuming the member takes full advantage of the employer match. Where no matching contributions are offered, the average employer contribution is 8.1% of salary.

Matching contribution structures offer the best possible overall level of contribution for employees. While the average total contribution rate – employer and employee – for all schemes, with or without a matching facility, is 13.7%, the average for matching schemes is 15.3%, with the average for schemes without matching just 10.8%.

However, what these numbers do not show is whether members are actually taking advantage of the additional employer contributions available on matching schemes. If members are not using this additional facility (where available), the average core employer contributions tend to be lower so that members of these schemes may find themselves worse off than those in schemes offering no matching contribution.

## 5. Contribution structures

There are three common types of contribution structure – service-related, age-related and flat.

The percentage of schemes with flat structures (by 'flat', we mean either one contribution rate for all members or a core rate with scope for additional matching contributions) is roughly the same as last year (71% in both 2005 and 2006). Service-related schemes account for 8%, and the number of age-related schemes has decreased from 25% in 2005 to 21% in 2006. This is probably due to the age discrimination legislation that was coming into effect at the time of the survey.

As previously mentioned, in 66% of schemes employers offer some form of additional matching contribution on top of the core contribution to those employees who choose to make additional contributions of their own. The matching bases are typically 1:1 or 1:2, up to a maximum limit. This reveals an increasing trend (42% in 2004 and 57% in 2005) of schemes that are offering matching contributions.

## 5.1 Flat contributions

In the table below we show the average contribution rates of those DC schemes that offer a flat contribution structure, both with and without employer matching of member contributions:

- 'Minimum member contribution' refers to the average percentage of pensionable salary that an employee is required to contribute as a condition of membership;
- 'Core employer contribution' refers to the average percentage of pensionable salary that an employer will contribute if the employee pays the minimum;
- 'Maximum matching member contribution' refers to the average maximum matched employee contribution that an employee could pay to gain the maximum employer contribution; and
- 'Maximum matching employer contribution' refers to the maximum matched contribution that the employer is prepared to pay if the member pays the maximum matched employee contribution.

| Average flat contributions | % |
|---|---|
| Minimum member contribution | 2.4 |
| Maximum matched member contribution | 2.1 |
| Core employer contribution | 6.8 |
| Maximum matching employer contribution | 2.7 |
| TOTAL | 14.0 |

The average structure in the 2006 survey shows a significant shift from the previous year. Core employer contributions have increased from 5.7% to 6.8%. Although some of this may be attributable to movements in the FTSE 100 index and the survey respondents, some is also due to the fact that companies are reviewing their core contribution structures and improving employer rates, without necessarily asking employees to increase their own contributions (average member core contribution rates have increased only marginally since last year from 2.2% to 2.4%). On the other hand, average employer and employee matching rates are lower than in the 2005 survey.

## 5.2 Age-related contributions

The survey also looked at the average age-related contribution structures, including any additional matching contributions.

| Average age-related contributions | Under 30 | 30-40 | 40-50 | Over 50 |
|---|---|---|---|---|
| | % | % | % | % |
| Minimum member contribution | 1.7 | 1.9 | 2.1 | 2.2 |
| Maximum matched member contribution | 0.7 | 1.5 | 1.9 | 2.2 |
| Core employer contribution | 5.0 | 6.7 | 7.8 | 9.1 |
| Maximum matching employer contribution | 0.9 | 1.8 | 2.3 | 3.1 |
| TOTAL | 8.3 | 11.7 | 14.1 | 17.5 |

The contribution structures for age-related rates reveal a similar pattern to flat rates, with employer contributions increasing from last year. For members aged under 30, the core employer contribution has increased from 4.1% in 2005 to 5%; for ages 30 to 40, the core employer contribution has increased from 5.7% to 6.7%; for ages 40 to 50 the core employer contribution has increased from 7.0% to 7.8%; and for those over 50, the core employer contribution has increased from 8% to 9%.

Average core employee contributions are roughly in line with 2005, with average maximum matching contribution structures decreasing slightly.

## 5.3 Service-related contributions

As would be expected, the pattern for average service-related contributions shows core employer contributions increasing with years of service. However, employees are not typically asked to commit to higher contributions to take advantage of the additional service-related core contributions. Average maximum matched contributions also increase in steps with years of service, for both employees and employers. To simplify the table below, we have divided the service periods into under five years, five to 10 years and over 10 years, although companies will have structures that differ widely from this. Also included are any average maximum matching contributions.

| Average service-related contributions | Under 5 years | 5 to 10 years | Over 10 years |
| --- | --- | --- | --- |
| | % | % | % |
| Minimum member contribution | 2.3 | 2.3 | 2.3 |
| Maximum matched member contribution | 2.0 | 3.5 | 3.8 |
| Core employer contribution | 4.8 | 5.5 | 6.0 |
| Maximum matching employer contribution | 2.4 | 4.3 | 5.0 |
| TOTAL | 11.5 | 15.6 | 17.1 |

## 6. Value of contributions

As increasing numbers of employees join DC pension schemes, the total contributions are becoming significant. The Watson Wyatt survey analyses contributions in terms of value and the table below shows the distribution in tranches of £5 million for the 48 companies that were able to provide data. Contributions to DC schemes are still significantly smaller than to their DB counterparts.

| Annual contributions – combined employer and employee | % of schemes |
| --- | --- |
| Up to £5m | 52 |
| £5m to £10m | 23 |
| £10m to £15m | 10 |
| £15m to £20m | 0 |
| Over £20m | 15 |

In terms of assets, DC schemes are still very immature in comparison to DB schemes and the vast majority have assets under management of less than £50 million. However, as the table opposite shows, there is a small number of schemes with assets now in excess of £100 million.

| Assets under management | % of schemes |
|---|---|
| Less than £50m | 74 |
| £50m to £100m | 8 |
| £100 to £200m | 14 |
| Over £200m | 4 |

## 7. Investment options

Investment is another key area where we have seen significant evolution of best practice and substantial innovation continues.

In terms of the range of choice, there is a significant difference between the number of investment funds offered by occupational, trust-based DC schemes and contract-based schemes, with stakeholder schemes and group personal pensions tending to offer a much wider range than occupational schemes – many contract-based scheme providers over in excess of 100 investment fund options.

The data indicates that most (61%) of occupational, trust-based schemes continue to offer between six and 15 funds. This presents a similar picture to the survey in 2005. Some schemes offer limited choice – 14% offer between one and five investment options.

Four out of five schemes now offer a range of active and passive funds. A relatively low percentage of schemes (18%) offer only passive funds, while just one scheme in the survey offers active investment options only. Some schemes (18%) continue to offer a with-profits fund, probably due to legacy issues and the presence of market value adjustments.

## 8. Default options

Some 77% of schemes offer a default investment option (including stakeholder schemes where providing a default is mandatory). Where a default option is available, the majority of members, between 75% and 100%, will typically be automatically enrolled, be defaulted into it or have selected the default.

Of those offering a default fund, 86% use a Lifecycle strategy. A fund with a Lifecycle strategy is designed automatically to switch members out of higher return-seeking but more volatile assets such as equities and into lower return-seeking but more stable investments in progressive steps as retirement age approaches. The idea is that this provides a risk-managed approach to member investments, reflecting the changing risk dynamics of a typical individual as he progresses through his working life.

Of the schemes offering Lifecycle, 69% make only one strategy available. The remaining 31% of these schemes offer more than one Lifecycle option. Trustees and contract-based scheme providers are increasingly moving towards offering multiple Lifecycle options, with different funds and/or different switching periods, thereby giving members more flexibility.

The two most popular switching periods are five years and 10 years, but there has been a shift from the 2005 survey, with 10 years now more popular than five years. The table below outlines the percentage of schemes using the various switching periods.

| Lifecycle switching period | % of schemes |
|---|---|
| Less than 4 years | 5 |
| 4 to 6 years | 38 |
| 7 to 9 years | 6 |
| 10 to 12 years | 50 |
| 13 to 15 years | 2 |

## 9. Administration

Participants in the survey were asked whether their administration services are provided by a third-party administrator, in-house or through a 'bundled' arrangement with an insurance company or pension provider. Of the occupational, trust-based schemes covered by the survey, only 25% are administered in-house, with some 75% of schemes' administration being carried out by either a specialist third-party administrator (57%) or a bundled provider (18%).

This may reflect the fact that FTSE 100 companies are offering DC schemes at the top end of the market and have sufficiently high numbers of members, cash flow and assets under management to make this a cost-effective method. Those companies providing in-house administration services typically do so as they have historically operated such an administration capability, typically in respect of a DB scheme.

## 10. Retirement options

Some 20% of schemes offer a pension from within the scheme. This is typically through the main DB fund where the DC arrangement is a section of the same trust. All schemes, regardless of whether they also offer an in-house pension, offer an open-market option, as required by legislation. Just one scheme surveyed offers income drawdown. This is despite the fact that companies can now offer this facility from within their scheme (including an occupational scheme). Most companies prefer to avoid the complexity.

## 11. Death-in-service and ill-health benefits

DC pension schemes offered by FTSE 100 companies offer a wide range of lump-sum death-in-service benefits to employees. The most popular option by far is four times pensionable salary, with nearly 60% of schemes providing this. However, two times or less (11%) or more than four times (6%) also exist – in the latter case, this is where companies have taken advantage of the simplification rules introduced in April 2006 to permit multiples higher than four times. In addition to the lump sum, there will also be the return of the member's DC fund value.

Other types of benefit are provided on death-in-service by some schemes. Some 35% offer a spouse's pension ('spouses' now also includes civil partners) and 9% provide a children's pension.

Incapacity benefits are offered by 66% of employers with DC schemes. Some 35% of those in the survey offer a permanent health insurance (PHI) policy and 15% offer a limited term income replacement policy providing for payments for between two and five years. Seventeen per cent of survey respondents offer provision that takes an alternative form (eg, additional lump sums). The remainder of the respondents (34%) make no provision.

| Incapacity benefits | % of schemes |
|---|---|
| Permanent health insurance | 35 |
| Limited term insurance | 15 |
| Other provision | 37 |
| No provision | 34 |

The provision of private health insurance among employers with DC pension arrangements is likely to be higher than for the FTSE 100 as a whole, as those organisations which still provide DB benefits would typically provide incapacity benefits within the pension scheme rather than through a separate private health insurance arrangement. Of the respondents offering some form of incapacity benefit, 50% offer a replacement of 50% of salary on either a permanent or temporary basis.

## 12. Conclusion

This chapter provides a snapshot of the structure and extent of DC pensions among the United Kingdom's largest companies. It reveals that while DB schemes may provide the bigger financial issues for companies, for the many which have closed their schemes to new (and increasingly, going forward, existing) employees, there is a growing realisation that DC brings its own – not necessarily less important – issues and risks for sponsoring employers and trustees. As a result, increasing management attention is now being focused on DC schemes.

A marked result of this appears to be rising contribution rates, smarter approaches to investment choices within schemes, more robust and efficient scheme administration and greater commitment to, and stronger delivery of, member communication and support.

Companies are realising that while DC does not carry the obvious financial risks of DB, what might be termed the 'HR risks' of DC pensions are real and significant.

The HR risks largely concern employee engagement and expectations and, in particular, companies' ability to manage employees who are unable or unwilling to retire because they do not have enough money to do so. With the investment risk sitting with the employee, external events, such as stockmarket collapse, could cause significant workforce management problems.

Managing a workforce under such circumstances could prove difficult. While experience is kept within the company, there may not be suitable jobs available for younger employees. An alternative option is to enhance the pensions of these employees to a level where they can afford to retire. But as well as setting dangerous precedents, the cash may not be available in any case. Either way, not managing this situation proactively could lead to expense volatility, which brings us back to the reason why many employers have replaced DB with DC schemes in the first place.

This is one of the key reasons why many companies are now looking to make DC work better; they are doing so by up rating the management and governance of their DC schemes.

# Transfers with cash incentives

**Ian Gault**
**Susanne Wilkins**
Herbert Smith LLP

One way for an employer to reduce its pension liabilities is to offer members cash incentives, either to transfer their benefits out of their defined benefit scheme or to give up some aspect of their pension benefits within the scheme.

Where the cash incentive is offered in return for the member agreeing to transfer his benefits out of the scheme, the incentive typically takes the form of a lump-sum payment directly from the employer to the member or is made by way of an enhancement to the member's transfer value.

However, this approach is not without difficulties and employers should be especially careful to minimise the risk of mis-selling claims. The issue of offering cash inducements to members has experienced a high profile recently, with Her Majesty's Revenue and Customs (HMRC) and the Pensions Regulator publishing guidance on the treatment of such schemes in January 2007.

## 1. Different classes of member

In addition to actives and deferreds, it is possible for employers to use cash incentives to make 'deals' with pensioner members. For example, where pensioners are entitled to pension increases which go beyond the statutory requirements, employers may ask those pensioners to give up their right to the additional increases in return for a cash sum. Likewise, a similar offer can be made to deferreds where, say, they are entitled under the scheme rules to a revaluation of benefits which is more generous than the statutory minimum. There are thus a variety of schemes or proposals, based on the concept of offering members cash incentives to give up or transfer their pension benefits, which can form part of the employer's deficit management strategy.

The employer has considerable flexibility in the overall design of a cash incentive scheme or schemes. It is possible to implement different arrangements for the different classes of member at the same time or at different times; and the value of the proposals may differ as between the different classes of member. It is not necessary (or always possible) to treat the actives, deferreds and pensioners equally, or to offer them equal value. However, care should be taken where different offers are made to different categories of member within the same class. There is a risk that the difference in treatment may be directly or indirectly discriminatory – for example, on the grounds of age or sex.

The common thread is that the member is being offered cash, in some form, in return for which he chooses to give up some aspect of his pension entitlement or benefits or to transfer his benefits out of the scheme altogether.

## 2. Form of cash incentive

The cash incentive will usually take the form of an enhancement to the member's transfer value or the offer by the employer of a cash lump sum directly to the member. However, employers can also offer the cash incentive in the form of a pension contribution into the member's new defined contribution pension arrangement.

## 3. Tax implications

It is essential for employers which are considering a cash incentive scheme to obtain specialist advice on the tax implications of the proposal, for both the employer and employee. The extent and nature of the tax relief available to both parties will depend on the structure and mechanism of the incentive and on the status of the member.

Previously, it had been difficult to be definitive about the tax treatment of the cash incentive programmes, especially as the trend towards operating cash incentive schemes is relatively recent and employers usually made confidential approaches to HMRC for clarification before proceeding. However, the position was made clearer by HMRC in guidance published in January 2007. This notwithstanding, if there is any doubt as to the likely tax treatment of a particular cash incentive proposal, the safest course of action is still to approach HMRC for confirmation in advance, especially in relation to the employer's tax position where it proposes to make direct cash payments to its employees.

## 4. Employer tax

### 4.1 Pension scheme contribution

Where the cash incentive takes the form of an additional contribution to a new or existing pension arrangement, the normal tax principles which relate to employer pension scheme contributions, in terms of corporation tax deductibility and relief, apply.

The payments will be tax deductible for the employer only if they are assessed as being "wholly and exclusively" for the purposes of the employer's trade.

While the issue of tax deductibility is ultimately a matter for the employer's tax inspector, following the HMRC guidance there is a strong argument that a payment made to facilitate the reduction of a company's pension liabilities meets the 'wholly and exclusively' criterion.

### 4.2 Enhancement of the member's transfer value

Where the employer offers to augment the deferred (or active) member's transfer value in the defined benefit scheme through making a special contribution to that scheme, this will be tax deductible under the 'wholly and exclusively' test.

### 4.3 Cash lump sum

Where the cash incentive is in the form of a lump-sum payment to the active or deferred member, the position on employer tax relief is not entirely clear and will hinge on HMRC's interpretation of the payment. The January 2007 HMRC guidance makes it clear that the cash lump sum will be liable to both national insurance contributions and income tax in the hands of the employee (even though, as HMRC acknowledges in its guidance, such payments were often treated differently in the past). It would seem to follow that the payment would therefore be deductible for corporation tax purposes; however, the HMRC guidance is not entirely conclusive on this point.

One interpretation is that the payment will be deductible for corporation tax purposes, on the grounds that the company is acting to reduce its future liabilities. This was the conclusion reached in one analogous case, where the company was attempting to rid itself of the obligation to make further deductible expenditure.[1] On this basis, it seems likely that HMRC would allow the cash lump sum to be deducted from the employer's corporation tax liability.

However, analogies can also be drawn with other cases where the opposite conclusion was reached. For example, in a case concerning an initial distribution to a fund, it was held that expenditure is normally capital in nature if it is made "not only for once and for all, but with a view to bringing into existence an asset or an advantage for the enduring benefit of the trade".[2] Parallels can be drawn between these facts and those of a cash incentive programme.

The 2007 guidance draws parallels with the tax treatment of employer-financed retirement benefit schemes (ie, unregistered pension arrangements usually set up for the benefit of executives). Employer contributions to such schemes are deductible for corporation tax purposes when the benefits are paid out. This would suggest that the cash lump sum paid to the member would be deductible when it is paid out by the employer, although the position is not addressed explicitly and the position is complicated by anti-avoidance provisions applicable to employer-financed retirement benefit schemes but which do not sit well in the context of cash inducement schemes.

In conclusion, although there remains a risk that HMRC would deem the payment to be non-deductible, the preferred view is that the payments are likely to be deductible for corporation tax purposes.

### 4.4 Spreading of tax relief

The normal rules on the spreading of tax relief, set out in Section 197 of the Finance Act 2004, will apply. Broadly, the effect of these rules is that the total employer contributions to a registered pension scheme in one chargeable period cannot exceed 210% of the contributions in the previous chargeable period if full tax relief is to be secured in that tax year. Additional relief may have to be deferred.

This may be an issue where, under the cash incentive programme, the employer makes additional contributions into a pension scheme, either as extra contributions (not linked to a transfer of benefits) or in order to enhance members' transfer values.

1 *Vodafone v Shaw* [1997] 69TC376.
2 *Atherton v British Insulated Cables* [1926] AC 205.

## 5. Employee tax

### 5.1 Pension scheme contribution

The employee or deferred member will not be taxed on any payment made into a registered pension scheme on his behalf.

### 5.2 Enhancement of the member's transfer value

Likewise, where an employer makes a payment into its own pension scheme and that payment is applied to increase the member's transfer value, the employee will not be taxed on the enhancement. This was confirmed by the January 2007 HMRC guidance.

### 5.3 Cash lump sum

The January 2007 guidance provides that cash payments made by employers to employees in order to encourage employees to take a reduction of their pension benefits or to transfer them to a defined contribution arrangement are taxable as employment income[3] and are also 'earnings' within the meaning of social security legislation,[4] with the result that they are liable for Class 1 national insurance contributions.

### 5.4 Unauthorised payments

One of the reasons that cash lump-sum incentive payments are made by the employer and are not made directly out of the scheme is in order to avoid bringing the payments within the unauthorised payments regime.

The concept of 'unauthorised payments' was introduced by the Finance Act 2004 and applies to benefits paid out of a pension scheme which are not 'authorised payments', as defined under that act. Unauthorised payments will give rise to a 40% tax charge on the payment in the hands of a member and an additional 15% scheme sanction charge.

A contribution into an employee's pension scheme by a current or former employer will not count as an unauthorised payment under this; neither will the payment of an enhanced transfer value or cash directly from the employer. However, cash lump-sum incentives paid directly from the scheme (instead of by the employer) will fall foul of the unauthorised payments provisions and give rise to the punitive tax charges outlined above.

## 6. Mis-selling

Given that the cash incentive offered to the member will usually be significantly less than the value of the pension rights given up or transferred in return, many are concerned that the whole approach bears the hallmarks of a burgeoning mis-selling scandal. Recent press on some high-profile cases has been negative in tone, suggesting that employers are in effect discharging liabilities on the cheap. There is

---

3 Section 394 of the Income Tax (Earnings and Pensions) Act 2003.

4 Sections 3(1)(a) and 6(1) of the Social Security Contributions and Benefits Act 1992.

certainly a significant risk of mis-selling claims if the employer does not ensure that the member is making an informed decision when opting to take the cash incentive.

It is essential that the employer takes all reasonable steps to ensure that the member fully understands the consequences of transferring out of the scheme and the value of any rights given up. To this end, the employer should ensure that both active and deferred members have access to independent financial advice. In fact, it is good practice for employers to go one step further by obtaining written confirmation from members that they have indeed obtained independent financial advice before agreeing to the cash incentive offer.

The employer should also give careful consideration to the value of the cash incentive compared to the value of the rights given up. A substantial discrepancy would naturally affect the take-up rate, but would also increase the risk of mis-selling claims. The employer should take advice on a fair value offer for the rights exchanged for the lump sum, while taking account of the added value to the member of an immediate cash payment (if that is the cash incentive offered) and the employer's own objectives (specifically, the need to manage and reduce the pension scheme deficit).

The government, in consultation with the actuarial profession, is reviewing the requirements as to the basis and calculation of members' transfer values. In its most recent official statement on the issue,[5] the Department for Work and Pensions indicates that future legislation will provide that the calculation of a member's transfer value will be based on the cost to the scheme of providing the pension (and not on the (greater) cost of buying out the benefit with an insurance company). In other words, the current approach will be maintained.

In January 2007 the Pensions Regulator issued guidance on how employers, trustees and members should deal with inducement offers.[6] It lists the items which should be included in communications to employees. In addition to being "clearly expressed", the inducement offer should:

- explain the nature of the benefits being given up and, in particular, where reductions in pension increases are involved, the potential loss in inflation protection;
- where a transfer-out from a defined benefit scheme is involved, explain that the scheme which accepts the transfer may not provide the same level of benefits; and explain the risks inherent in (and the guarantees offered by) the defined benefit scheme (including the risk of employer insolvency, the protection offered by winding-up legislation and the Pension Protection Fund (PPF)). The guidance also suggests that it would be "helpful" if members were given an indication of the likely cost of replicating the PPF level of benefits;
- where a rule change leading to a reduction of benefits is involved, explain the likely cost of making good the lost benefit;
- explain that there may be tax implications for the member if the inducement payment is accepted;

5 "Approaches to the calculation of pensions transfer values: response to the consultation", January 2007.
6 The Pensions Regulator, "Inducement offers", January 2007.

- recommend that the member takes independent financial advice before agreeing to a transfer-out from a defined benefit scheme;
- specify the amount of the inducement offered to that individual;
- specify the nature of the inducement – that is, state whether the inducement is a cash payment (and, if so, how and when it will be paid), an increase to the transfer value or a combination of the two (and the extent to which the member is able to pick and choose from the options);
- state how long the offer will be open for;
- state why the employer is making the offer. The guidance states that it would be "helpful" if the impact of acceptance by the individual member on the employer's accounts could be quantified; and
- make it clear that the member does not have to accept the offer and that the member may retain his or her entitlement under the scheme. The guidance also states that the communication might usefully mention that there is very little consumer protection available to the member under the law with this type of financial transaction.

Although the guidance does not have the force of law, it is good practice for employers to follow it when communicating the terms of their inducement proposals. However, it does not affect the ability of the employer to include other additional statements in relation to the offer.

The Pensions Regulator's guidance also provides that pension scheme trustees should apply a high level of scrutiny to all inducement offers (see below).

Employers owe a duty of good faith to their employees, which underpins the whole employment relationship, including the exercise by the employer of its powers in relation to any pension arrangements. Specifically, case law provides that "there is an implied provision in [a pension scheme] that [the employer] will not, without reasonable and proper cause, conduct itself in a manner calculated or likely to destroy that relationship [of trust and confidence]". How this would be interpreted in the context of cash incentive offers is not entirely clear, but the more persuasive view is that the employer should be reasonable in its dealings with the member and should not do anything which might mislead the member.

## 7. Practical considerations

It is advisable for employers to undertake a comprehensive feasibility study before launching a cash incentive scheme. This should set out the options available and compare potential structures for the scheme. It should cover legal and tax implications and also detail the potential reduction to the deficit. The projected take-up rate will be a crucial determining factor.

Depending on the structure of the proposal, it may be necessary to check members' contracts of employment, to ensure that member consent is effective to implement the agreement and discharge any separate contractual liability.

It may also be necessary to check the rules of the pension scheme; there is an (albeit unlikely) possibility that some restriction in the rules might affect the ability of the trustees to make enhanced transfers, for example. Any restrictions on the trustees' transfer-out powers can be amended, subject to the scheme's power of amendment and Section 67 of the Pensions Act 1995.

## 8. Moral hazard, forfeiture, surrender

The power of the Pensions Regulator (derived from Section 38 of the Pensions Act 2004) to issue contribution notices applies, broadly, where a party has acted (or failed to act) and one of the main purposes of the action (or failure to act) was to avoid pension scheme liabilities. This power does not apply to a typical cash incentive programme, as such a programme is concerned with liability reduction rather than avoidance or reduction of a Section 75 debt.[7]

However, a cash incentive scheme must avoid infringing legal rules which prevent the surrender or forfeiture of benefits. Broadly, statute provides that where a person is entitled to a pension under an occupational pension scheme or has a right to a future pension under such a scheme, the entitlement or right cannot be assigned, commuted, forfeited or surrendered (subject to certain exceptions).[8] Where a member is being asked to give up certain pension rights in exchange for a cash sum, there is a clear risk that this could be interpreted as a 'surrender' in violation of the statutory prohibition.

However, there is a counter-argument which relies on the distinction between a reduction in benefits on the one hand and a surrender on the other; namely, that a member who accepts a reduction in benefits in return for a payment is not actually surrendering benefits within the meaning of the legislation.

In order to avoid the anti-forfeiture provisions of the 1995 act, many cash incentive programmes are implemented by way of a pension scheme amendment. Section 67 of the 1995 act allows members to consent to the reduction of their accrued pension rights. A strong argument can be made that Section 67 overrides the anti-surrender/forfeiture provisions in the same act, where a scheme amendment is made. This has the effect that members can lawfully consent to give up aspects of their pension entitlement – whether or not they accept a cash incentive in exchange.

Nevertheless, it will be necessary to consider these issues in the context of the particular arrangements proposed in each case. It may be that employers and trustees are advised to make an amendment to the rules to give effect to the cash incentive scheme, as a way of invoking the protection of Section 67, even though an amendment might otherwise be unnecessary.

## 9. Role of trustees

Where the cash incentive is a lump-sum payment paid directly from the employer to the member, it was thought that the trustees would have a limited role. However, the guidance issued by the Pensions Regulator in January 2007[9] goes further than many in the industry had predicted in encouraging the trustees to become involved in the process.

---

7 That is, a debt payable by virtue of Section 75 of the Pensions Act 1995.
8 Section 91 of the Pensions Act 1995.
9 The Pensions Regulator, " Inducement offers", January 2007.

Naturally, the trustees will have power to determine the basis of any transfer value, subject to legislative requirements. However, members have a statutory right to a transfer value, which should not (and in most cases cannot) be frustrated by the trustees. In fact, trustees may well be supportive of the cash incentive programme, as they may take the view that a reduction in the pension scheme's liabilities is in the interests of the members as a whole.

Where the employer proposes to augment the member's transfer value through the transfer scheme, the trustees will have more involvement, in that they will have to administer the receipt and allocation of the monies.

Throughout, the trustees must act within the terms of the scheme rules and in accordance with their usual fiduciary and trustee duties.

They must also be satisfied that the scheme's funding position is not worsened by, say, payments from the employer which are insufficient to meet the cost of the proposal. It is highly likely that they will also ask the employer to fund any enhancements to the transfer values in full. Again, their approach will be governed by the scheme rules, underpinned by their duties to act in the best interests of the beneficiaries of the scheme.

However, the Pensions Regulator's guidance (issued in January 2007) encourages trustees to "question or challenge the appropriateness of an inducement offer" when they become aware that the employer is contemplating a cash incentive programme. Emphasis is placed on the need for members to be able to make an informed decision.

The guidance highlights three areas in which the trustees may have particular involvement:

- in the modification of scheme rules;
- in ensuring compliance with data protection requirements; and
- in ensuring that the members receive independent financial advice.

The guidance states that the trustees must ensure that statutory provisions are complied with if scheme amendments are required in order to give effect to the inducement proposal.

With regard to data protection requirements, the guidance states that the trustees must consider whether to make members' contact and benefit details available to the employer. According to the guidance, the trustees should ask why the employer is asking them to release the information and, on becoming aware of the inducement exercise, they should also ask to see details of the proposed inducement offer. The trustees should then form their own view about whether the offer represents good value and whether they will cooperate with the employer. The guidance even goes so far as to suggest that the trustees might want to take their own legal and financial advice about the merits of the inducement offer and potential legal exposure before providing information to an employer to facilitate the inducement exercise.

Where an inducement offer proceeds, the guidance states that the trustees should ensure that members are made aware of the importance of taking independent financial advice and that this message comes out "strongly" in the inducement offer. The trustees may also try to persuade the employer to meet the cost of the provision of the advice.

Where the trustees take the view that the inducement may not be in the best interests of members, the trustees should, according to the guidance, "think seriously about issuing their own announcement to those members to whom the offer was made to highlight the risk for those members".

The upshot of the Pensions Regulator's guidance in its current form is to place a scrutineer's burden on the trustees, which does not seem to flow from the legislation. In light of this, it is possible that trustees will feel compelled to take a paternalistic approach to their new role in this area, and perhaps consider intervention by issuing their own member communications or by withholding their cooperation from the employer. Employers should therefore be aware of these risks and of the potential effect of trustee involvement on the timetable for implementation of the proposal.

## 10. Conclusion

Employers that wish to institute a cash inducement programme must give careful consideration to their proposals in light of professional advice, particularly on employee communications and tax issues.

From the trustees' perspective, they may seek their own legal advice on any cash inducement programmes, given the emphasis on the trustees' role in the Pensions Regulator's guidance and the fact that the guidance seems to go beyond what is commonly understood to be the law as it relates to trustee legal responsibilities.

# Escrow accounts

**Mark Alexander**
**Julian Jones**
Lane Clark & Peacock LLP

## 1. Introduction

Companies are coming under increasing pressure to better fund their pension schemes. However, money paid into pension schemes is normally irrecoverable. Putting money into escrow instead of the pension scheme can achieve the same aims, while allowing for the possibility of funds being released to the employer under specific circumstances – thus removing the risk of a trapped surplus.

Historically, escrow accounts have been used in relation to pension schemes only in very particular circumstances. Recently, however, changes to legislation and the pensions environment mean that escrow is now a much more suitable match for many of the wide range of pensions problems that companies face.

This is good news not only for the sponsor of a scheme, but also for the trustees, who can negotiate greater security as long as there is a route for the employer to recover excess contributions in the future.

This chapter explains how escrow accounts work in practice, considers the reasons for their increasing good fit with pension schemes and highlights some of the practical issues and potential pitfalls involved in relation to escrow accounts.

It also provides a real-life example of escrow in practice, for the Ericsson Marconi transaction.

## 2. What is an escrow account?

In its simplest form, escrow is an arrangement between two parties where an asset is placed in trust with an independent third party. This asset is passed to one or other of the two parties once a specific condition has been satisfied, or once it is clear that this condition will not be satisfied.

As escrow accounts are used in a myriad of financial transactions, a generic description of this sort is not always illuminating. However, a very simple example of escrow – and one which most people will experience during their lifetime – should help to explain how they work in practice.

When purchasing a residential property, it is usual for the purchaser to lodge a deposit with his solicitor when contracts are exchanged. If a certain condition is met – in this case the property sale going ahead – these funds will pass to the vendor. However, if the transaction falls through, this money is passed to one party or the other, depending on the reason for the sale stalling and the precise wording of the contract.

It can be seen from this example that the purpose of escrow is to reduce both parties' potential for loss in relation to a financial transaction.

In practice, the money is normally held in the solicitor's segregated client account, but this is an escrow arrangement in all but name.

In a typical residential property transaction, the period from exchange of contracts to completion (and payment) is normally short and there is only a small degree of uncertainty. However, it is easy to extrapolate from this example and see how complexities can be built in to cover any situation in which escrow could be used.

This can range from having a number of parties who benefit from the proceeds of the escrow under given circumstances to complex conditions relating to who receives the moneys.

The normal reason for using escrow is to act as a buffer to allow for uncertainty, where the amounts to be paid or the actual timing of the payments is uncertain. For example, it is common for the owner of a nuclear power station to set aside considerable funds for decommissioning in escrow. This provides certainty to the government when granting the operating licence that the decommissioning costs will be covered, while allowing the operator to profit from an efficient decommissioning process. In this example, funds could be tied up in escrow for several decades and the true costs are very difficult to predict in advance.

In addition, as in the property example, escrows can be used whenever there are issues of trust – a good example of this is on internet auction sites – where the purchaser's payment is normally released to the vendor only once the goods have been received.

## 3. Pensions and escrow

As set out above, escrow accounts can be used to provide security against future events that are uncertain. As the cost of meeting a final salary pension promise is uncertain (payments of an uncertain amount are to be paid to individuals at an uncertain time), escrow is, in principle, a good fit for pension scheme.

Due to the legislative environment in the past, escrow accounts have been used for pensions only in certain niche circumstances – for example, in the corporate transaction example set out below. However, things have changed and, going forward, the scope for using escrow appears to be increasing.

Rather than tie up cash in an escrow account, with the associated opportunity costs to the employer, other assets can instead be held, such as shares or property. Using these assets could provide a cash-poor, asset-rich company with a much more flexible approach to funding a pension scheme.

### 3.1 An example of how escrow has been commonly used

This example sets out a particular instance of where escrow has often been used in the past and continues to be used in relation to corporate transactions.

Let us consider a company being sold with a pension scheme in deficit. In these circumstances, the purchaser may seek to secure a reduction in the purchase price to compensate for the pension shortfall. The seller may agree to the reduction, depending on other wider commercial considerations.

The price reduction may be calculated by reference to the financial position of the scheme at completion and so will change on a daily basis to reflect changes in market conditions. The adjustment will therefore not be known with certainty until after the transaction has completed – resulting in risks for both parties.

The risks can be reduced if the buyer initially pays the full purchase price for the business, but with some of the funds set aside in an escrow account. The amount paid into the account would typically reflect both the purchaser's and seller's best estimate of the purchase price adjustment plus a margin, and would be subject to negotiation.

The funds in escrow would be released only once the purchase price reduction has been calculated and agreed. Once agreed, the pensions deficit adjustment is paid from the escrow account to the purchaser, with the balance being returned to the seller.

This arrangement should suit both buyer and seller; in addition, the trustees of the pension scheme are likely to appreciate having the comfort of funds being set aside in escrow for this purpose.

However, it is clear from this example that there are many potential difficulties that could arise. For example, it may be difficult for the purchaser and the seller to agree on the amount that should be placed in escrow.

In this case, though, both parties will be keen to see the matter of the purchase price adjustment resolved as quickly as possible. As the funds that are held in escrow are usually there only for a relatively short period, agreement can usually be reached, provided the process goes smoothly.

This example mirrors our example of the residential property sale, where the funds are held in escrow only for a relatively short period of time. However, this is only one example and the scope to apply escrow to more situations is increasing in the new pensions environment, particularly in relation to issues that are unlikely to be resolved over the short term and where the pension scheme trustees may be party to the escrow agreement. The next section summarises how the pensions environment has changed before outlining how escrow could be applied to these issues.

## 4. Why things have changed

In years gone by, the uncertainties in pension schemes were not necessarily a cause for concern – after all, companies were prepared to support the scheme over the long term and with schemes open to new entrants, the costs of benefits could be smoothed over successive generations of members.

**Projected cash-flow payments from an open defined benefit scheme**

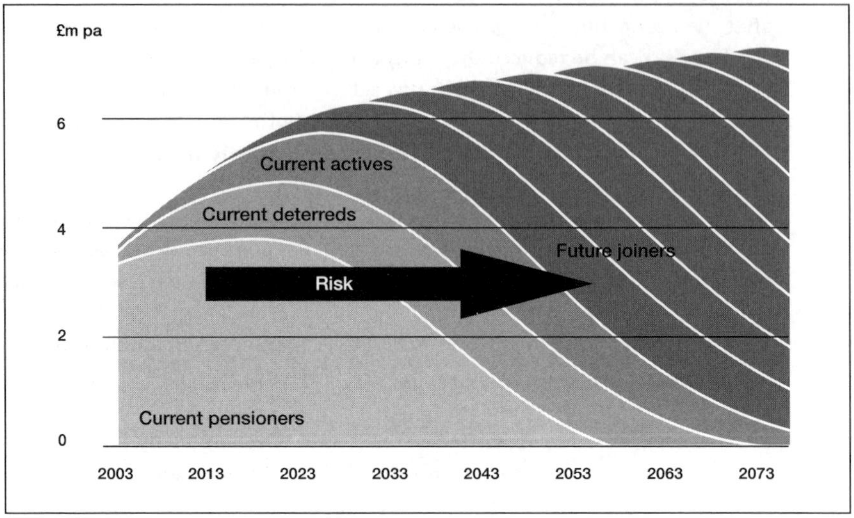


Any 'bad news' (eg, a fall in asset values) would hopefully be overcome with future 'good news'. And if things did not work out in the long term, the cost of walking away from the pension scheme was not significant, provided it had sufficient assets to cover the minimum funding requirement.

However, things have changed. Over recent years, there has been considerable pressure on company sponsors to improve the funding level of their defined benefit pension funds. Today, employers need to balance the need for additional contributions against the possibility of trapped surpluses in future.

**Projected cash-flow payments from an open defined benefit scheme**

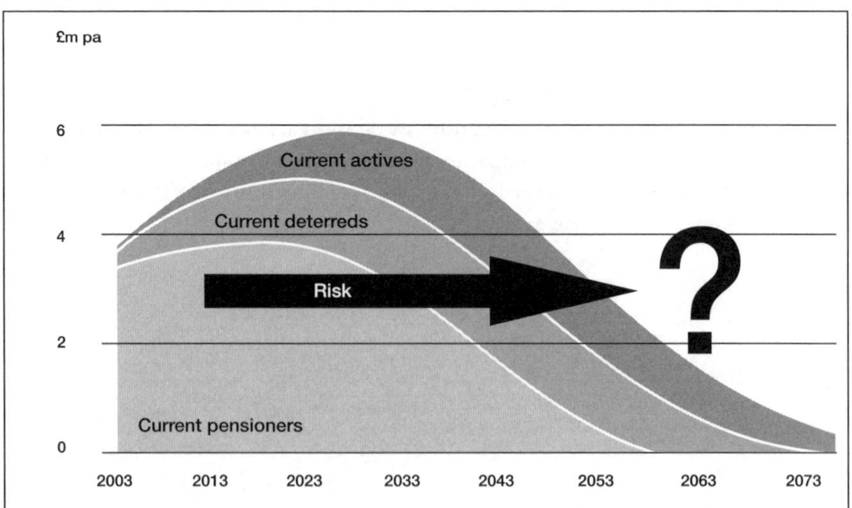

These issues are highlighted by considering various ways that pension scheme liabilities are measured, as illustrated by the following graph.

**Assets required under key funding measures**

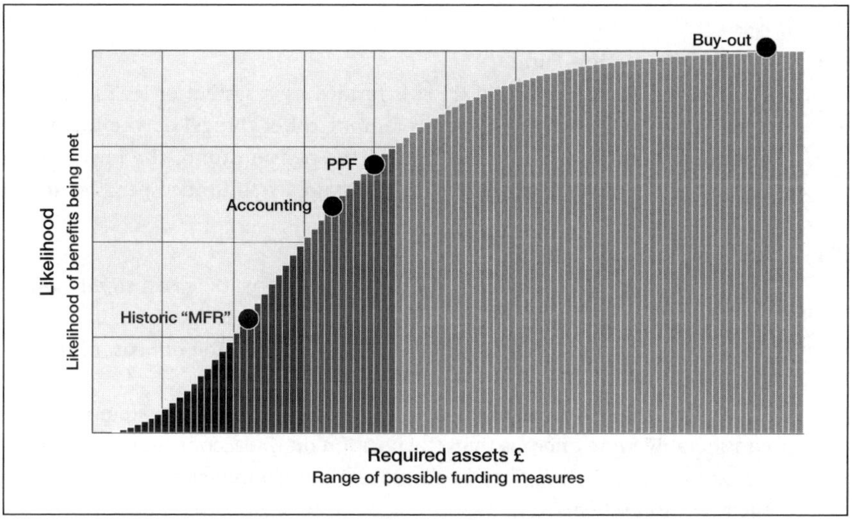


The graph shows that the assets required for pension scheme to be fully funded relative to a particular funding target will depend on how the liabilities of the pension scheme are measured. For example, a shortfall relative to the buy-out cost may still remain for a scheme that is fully funded on an accounting basis. However, as the graph shows, the better funded the pension scheme, the higher the likelihood that it will be able to meet the promised benefit payments without requiring future contributions.

In the following sections we consider the increasing relevance of the various measures in more detail.

### 4.1 Accounting for pensions

In recent years, the accounting treatment of pensions both within and outside the United Kingdom has become more prescribed. For example, liabilities are now discounted with reference to bond yields, with the scope to take advance credit for potential future equity out-performance removed.

In many cases the assets and accounting liabilities of a pension scheme appear on the company balance sheet. The scope to smooth any 'bad news' is limited, as the accounting deficit must be recognised immediately.

By contrast, once funded beyond a certain level, it will not be possible for a company to recognise fully the scheme's assets on the balance sheet.

The position is often highly sensitive to changes in market conditions and so companies are often walking a tightrope between over-funding and under-funding. The situation is particularly sensitive for mature pension schemes.

**4.2 Scheme-specific funding**

The Pensions Act 2004 introduced a new funding regime: scheme-specific funding. The principal effect of this legislation is to increase significantly trustees' power to set contributions to their scheme – resulting in upward pressure on cash contributions to pension arrangements.

**4.3 Pension Protection Fund**

The Pension Protection Fund (PPF) is funded by a system of levies. Part of the levy that is paid by the scheme depends (among other things) on the financial position of the pension fund. The better funded the pension fund, the lower the levy. This acts as an incentive for employers to maintain a well-funded pension arrangement.

**4.4 Buy-out/Section 75 debt**

The potential corporate risks in relation to pensions increased significantly on June 11 2003. Since this date, solvent employers have no longer been able to walk away from their pension scheme liabilities without meeting the full cost of the benefits on a buy-out basis (ie, a 'Section 75 debt' must be paid).

As the graph on the previous page illustrates, the buy-out position is usually considerably more onerous than the position on the accounting or funding measures – meaning that the majority of employers can no longer afford to walk away from their pension scheme.

In September 2005 this requirement was widened to cover employers that cease to participate in a multi-employer pension arrangement, as the departing employer must generally meet its share of the Section 75 shortfall or alternatively provide an open-ended guarantee to the scheme which is sufficient to satisfy the Pensions Regulator.

**5. Over-funding risks**

In recent years many pension funds have closed to new entrants and an increasing number are closing to future benefit accrual for existing members. Closure will naturally push pension scheme trustees to reduce risks and so demand higher funding levels, perhaps in excess of the accounting liabilities.

While such accounting surpluses are expected to arise, employers can recognise them on their balance sheet only to the extent that they could lead to a reduction in future contributions. Thus, once schemes are closed to future accrual, it is unlikely that any surplus can appear on the balance sheet.

However, the sponsoring employer will be eligible for a refund of surplus only once a scheme is fully funded on a buy-out basis, which is normally a much more stringent target – so preventing the employer receiving any value for the accounting surplus which exists, either in cash or in accounting terms.

In such cases it is likely to be preferable from the shareholder's point of view for these funds to be held outside of the pension scheme so that the company can take credit for them on the balance sheet.

## 6. Escrow is now a much better fit

Contributions to pension schemes may therefore be viewed as a one-way valve. Employer cash can flow in, but unless there is a substantial surplus, any excess will not flow back out to the employer.

One advantage of escrow is that cash can flow either to the pension scheme or back to the employer.

For example, if pension assets experience favourable returns over a sustained period, the risk that the benefits will not be met reduces and funds could be transferred back to the employer. Conversely, if assets under-perform or longevity improvements worsen the financial position of the pension scheme, the emerging shortfall can be made up from funds held in the escrow account.

Because pension scheme trustees are forced to take a prudent view of investment returns and longevity improvements, they will generally require a larger reserve than a 'best estimate' of the true liabilities. Because escrow can provide a security blanket for trustees, they should be happy with less cash now, on the basis of the additional security they have been given if things go wrong in the future.

In this context, escrow is being used as a long-term solution to pensions problems.

Let us return to our example of a property sale, but this time take a commercial property where there are questions over, say, previous subsidence which would lead to a reduced purchase price. Instead of accepting less money now, the seller may offer to place part of the sale proceeds into an escrow account. These funds would be released to the buyer if the house started to crumble in the next 10 years (for example), but would otherwise pass back to the seller.

## 7. How escrow is used in practice for pensions

This section examines how escrow accounts can be used to resolve some of the issues that relate to the different funding measures that were highlighted in section 4. These measures are examined in turn below.

### 7.1 Accounting for pensions

In certain circumstances, placing funds in escrow is a neat way to ensure that the funds are recognised on the balance sheet by structuring the arrangement appropriately. This would usually be preferable to cash contributions disappearing from the balance sheet into an unrecognised surplus on the balance sheet.

### 7.2 Scheme-specific funding

Where a pension scheme is in deficit, the Pensions Regulator has made it clear that trustees should aim to recover the funding shortfall as soon as possible. As such, there is considerable pressure for a company with a pensions deficit and cash reserves to make an injection into the scheme.

However, contingent assets – such as an escrow account – can be used to support a 'back-end loaded' deficit recovery plan. As such, an escrow account could be used by an organisation as a mechanism for reducing the contributions that are paid into the pension scheme in the short term, while it has other uses for the assets.

This would allow the company to monitor the development of the scheme before committing contributions – preventing funds from being locked into a well-funded pension scheme for the long term. It could also prevent an irrecoverable surplus developing on the company balance sheet.

Similarly, escrow would enable an asset-rich, cash-poor company to provide assets to the pension scheme to provide the trustees with security. This could delay the need for immediate cash funding, so enabling the company to pursue other opportunities for investment.

## 7.3 PPF

Improving the financial position of the scheme is one way to reduce the levy payable to the PPF. The PPF has issued specific (and complex) guidance which sets out the requirements that must be met before an escrow account can be considered as a pension scheme asset and so reduce the calculated PPF levy.

However, the funds in the escrow account can be taken into account by the PPF only if certain conditions are met. For example:

- the third party holding the escrow account must be domiciled in an Organisation for Economic Cooperation and Development country and be regulated by the Financial Services Authority (or an equivalent regulator); and
- the credit rating of the body must meet specified standard.

The potential PPF levy saving depends on many factors, including the financial position of the scheme and the Dun & Bradstreet rating of the sponsoring employer, but can be substantial in some circumstances.

## 7.4 Settlement of Section 75 debt

On ceasing to participate in a pension arrangement, employers are required to pay a 'Section 75 debt'. Since September 2005, this debt is calculated as the buy-out deficit in respect of the participating employer.

Due to the cost of securing pensions with an insurer, the debt is often onerous, particularly where the pension scheme is large in relation to the size of the employer.

If the company ceases to participate because of a corporate sale, the purchaser will want assurance as to responsibility for the debt. The seller would therefore need to provide some form of indemnity against the debt.

This indemnity may take the form of cash paid by the seller into an escrow account for the purpose of settling the debt. The debt is calculated by the actuary to the pension scheme and, once calculated, the funds are released from the escrow account for the debt to be settled. Any balance that remains within the escrow account would be passed back to the seller.

The employer will need to pay particular attention to the tax treatment of the funds and the view of Her Majesty's Revenue & Customs (HMRC) to the transaction, in order to avoid losing out on tax relief on the pension contributions. This issue relates to whether HMRC would support the deductibility of tax on the basis of the business activity being "wholly and exclusively" for trade purposes. The position will often depend on the individual circumstances of the companies involved.

## 8. Case study – Marconi

Marconi sold its Telecommunications Equipment and International Services businesses (and name) to Ericsson in January 2006. Following the transaction, the remaining business was renamed Telent.

As part of the transaction, Telent retained responsibility for the GEC 1972 Plan ('the Marconi Plan'). Marconi reported an accounting deficit in its UK pension scheme of £109 million as at March 31 2005; but the buy-out deficit might be around £1.3 billion.

The liabilities of the Marconi Plan are very significant when viewed in the context of the businesses that were retained by Telent. The pension plan has about 64,000 members, whereas Telent currently has only about 2,100 employees. This situation may become increasingly common in future as an increasing proportion of pension scheme liabilities relate to former employees and legacy liabilities.

In the case of Telent, roughly 75% of the business was sold to Ericsson. The sale generated proceeds of £1.3 billion (a similar figure to the buy-out deficit in the scheme), but the covenant of the new sponsoring employer to the pension fund was reduced as part of the sale.

As part of the transaction, agreement was reached with both the pension scheme trustees and the Pensions Regulator that £185 million of the proceeds of the sale should be paid into the pension fund.

In addition, £490 million was paid into an escrow account for the potential benefit of the pension scheme. A statement issued at the time of the transaction by the chief financial officer of Telent included the following observation: "Our estimates, and we have done quite a lot of detailed work on this in the last few weeks, are that the eventual cost of running the Marconi Pension Plan falls into a range of between plus/minus 20% of the FRS17 valuation of liabilities of £2.6 billion."

The escrow account was set up to cover the considerable uncertainty that exists with regard to the eventual cost of providing the benefits of the scheme.

The annual report and account for Telent for 2006 states: "The cash in the escrow, which is secured in favour of the UK Pension Plan, is available to meet any funding plan agreed between Telent and the Trustee to meet a deficit on an IAS19 or Pension Protection Fund basis. Cash can only be released from the escrow to Telent if, in the future, the UK Pension Plan achieves a funding level of in excess of 105% on a buy-out funding basis."

As the final benefit payments are not expected to be made until many decades into the future, there is considerable uncertainty as to whether the funds that are held in escrow will be required or whether the funds will be released for the benefit of the shareholders in due course.

For the time being, the funds remain in escrow and it is likely that they will do so for a considerable period of time.

## 9. So why isn't everyone doing it?

In the past, placing funds in escrow to meet future pension obligations has been used as a relatively short-term solution, or under very particular circumstances.

## 9.1 Long-term issues

Funds are now being placed in escrow to meet future benefit obligations. This is a long-term solution which is potentially more complex and could well result in disputes arising in the future.

Returning to our example of the property sale, there are significant differences between the short-term strategy of placing funds into an escrow account for the period until the sale is completed and the situation where funds are tied up in escrow for 10 years.

First, the opportunity cost of the money that is placed in escrow for the relatively short period up to the point of completion is considerably lower than the opportunity cost of tying up funds for 10 years.

Second, the opportunity for disputes to arise is much greater over the long term than the short term. All parties are usually fairly clear about why the funds have been put into escrow at the start of the period. However, the uncertainty increases over time, as does the possibility that the escrow agreement does not cover all future eventualities.

For example, what happens if there is exceptionally dry weather that affects the foundations of all properties in the area? The property may be resold many times over the next 10 years – does the escrow account automatically pass back to the original vendor in all circumstances or does it remain intact for the remainder of the 10-year period? To what extent do works carried out on the property affect the validity of the original agreement? Clearly, the potential for conflicts arising over a drawn-out period is significant.

The position for pension scheme trustees and their sponsoring employer may be considerably more fraught and sensitive, as these parties will need to continue to work together. The escrow agreement plays a vital role here and it is essential that it is comprehensive while being as clear as possible.

## 9.2 Tax issues

In addition to the potential complications that can arise, the company that pays cash into the escrow account will need to be mindful of tax considerations.

Contributions that are paid directly into a pension scheme by a company should be exempt from corporation tax. Tax relief is often viewed as a valuable incentive by companies that are making a profit. However, this tax relief is not available for funds that are placed into the escrow account.

Further, if funds are placed in escrow by a sponsoring employer for the future benefit of a pension fund and these funds are paid directly into the pension scheme from the escrow account, it is unlikely that the company will receive tax relief on the contributions or return achieved on these contributions at the future time that the payment is made.

This is likely to be a key concern for companies. The tax implications therefore need to be reviewed carefully. One possible solution would be for the funds to pass back from the escrow account to the company before they are paid into the pension scheme – although pension trustees will clearly be wary of such arrangements as the funds are less secure from their perspective. To get around this and some of the other potential issues, new types of escrow are being developed to meet the needs of the market.

### 9.3 Opportunity cost

In general, funds that are held in escrow are held on deposit with a third party. The potential to make returns on the funds is therefore limited to the interest rate that the funds attract while held in the escrow account and this interest will not be subject to tax relief (unlike in the pension scheme). This is another concern that may make companies reluctant to go down the escrow route – that is, the loss of control over the assets held in escrow. Clearly, there are potential opportunity costs associated with tying up any assets in this way.

This would affect the trustees, too, if the cash would otherwise have been paid into the pension scheme, as the trustees would be unable to change the assets held in escrow as part of regular reviews of investment strategy.

### 9.4 Attitudes of the trustees

From the perspective of the trustees of a pension arrangement, the priority is likely to be to secure funds into the pension fund rather than an alternative third-party arrangement. As such, the value placed by the trustees of £1 in the pension scheme is likely to be greater than £1 in an escrow account, so weakening the company's negotiating position. However, the attitudes of different trustee boards and the circumstances of individual companies will vary.

## 10. Conclusion

The scope to use escrow accounts to resolve pension issues is increasing, being driven by legislative changes, the increasing maturity of pension funds and the growth in the size of pension funds in the context of existing businesses.

As the scope for using escrow accounts increases, we expect companies to try to exploit these new opportunities; there is already early evidence of schemes taking this new route to funding schemes and using escrow to reduce PPF levies.

The choice of whether to place funds in escrow over the long term should be considered very carefully before a commitment is made. However firm you believe the foundations to be, you never know what can happen.

# Other types of contingent asset

**Mark Catchpole**
Stephenson Harwood

A contingent asset is not an asset of a pension scheme in the sense that legal ownership resides with the trustees of that scheme, but is one where, in certain circumstances, the trustees may nonetheless obtain the benefit of that asset. The circumstance or the contingency usually relates to the insolvency of the person who is otherwise obliged to fund the scheme – normally the participating employer or principal employer. From the employer's point of view, it does not have to transfer ownership of the asset to the trustees such that, in the event that it is not needed, it becomes difficult to get it back. The trustees may take account of the availability of the asset when assessing the strength of the employer's covenant and, consequently, the period over which any deficit should be amortised. If the contingent asset arrangement is one of the types specified by the Pension Protection Fund (PPF) and in the required form, the contingent asset may also reduce the amount of the risk-based levy paid each year.

In the previous section, one type of contingent asset was considered in detail: namely, escrow accounts. In this section, we look at the other main types of contingent asset used in connection with pension schemes, as follows:

- parent company guarantees:
- security over land;
- security over securities;
- security over a bank account; and
- letters of credit and bank guarantees.

First, we consider some of the issues that trustees face when they are asked to accept such arrangements. We then look at the guidance issued by the PPF and the Pensions Regulator in relation to such assets.

## 1. The position of trustees

### 1.1 Understanding the context

The motivation for entering into a contingent asset agreement may be solely to receive the benefit of a reduction in the PPF risk-based levy. This levy payable by the trustees and based on the relative risk of failure of the employer as assessed by Dunn and Bradstreet is, after all, 'dead money': it is money which diminishes the assets of a scheme but does nothing to reduce its liabilities. Therefore, it is a worthwhile aim in itself to minimise this cost to a scheme. However, in many cases, once one has weighed the amount of reduction in the levy to be obtained by entering into the contingent asset agreement against the cost of doing so, the benefits relative to the time and effort involved may not seem worthwhile. As will become apparent from a look at the guidance below, a number of requirements must be met before a contingent asset agreement will qualify for levy reduction purposes. For example, it will be necessary to secure a legal opinion which basically requires the lawyer to assume responsibility for the veracity of any such agreement. Valuations and, where appropriate, certificates of title will be needed which, depending on the type and number of assets involved, will also cost money to provide. Therefore, a wish to reduce the risk-based levy may not of itself be the sole or main motivating factor behind a contingent asset agreement.

In practice, the main motivating factors behind such arrangements are cash flow and control. Employers will wish to limit the amount of cash they need to pump into their schemes, because this diverts a precious resource from other areas of the business and, once it has been paid into the scheme, they lose control over it. Employers must effectively accept that once paid in, the trustees become responsible for investing those contributions and, if the contributions prove to be more than is needed, the employer is unlikely to see them returned. In many cases, employers think that with the increasingly 'safe' investment advice being provided to trustees and growth of liability matching, they are more likely to achieve a better return on any assets than the trustees. In addition, with most schemes in deficit, many employers wish to pay off that deficit over as long a period as possible. Add to this the gradual introduction of the scheme-specific funding requirement and the result is that employers are increasingly involved in a commercial negotiation with trustees involving the actuarial assumptions used, the amortisation period of any deficit and the investment strategy to be pursued by the trustees. These are all key drivers of the contribution rate and it is in this context that employers are increasingly looking at contingent asset agreements to affect these drivers.

These driving forces should inform the trustees' perspective when they consider, first, whether they can enter in to such arrangements, and second, whether they should.

## 1.2 Can and should?

Generally, trustees are given broad powers to make arrangements which are pertinent to their obligation to administer the trust and to carry its objects into effect. The first consideration is to check that the trustees have authority to enter into such agreements in the trust's governing provisions. When reviewing the trust deed and rules, and also the law relating to trustees' powers, it will be relevant to take a view as to whether the contingent asset agreement is itself a form of investment. Broadly, if one takes the view that it is an investment, it will be necessary to comply with the provisions of the Pensions Act 1995 relating to investments, including taking proper written advice that the investment is an appropriate one for the trustees to make. In addition, because the contingent asset will commonly involve providing security over an asset which is owned by a participating employer, the question arises whether the contingent asset agreement is itself a form of self-investment and as such the value of the investment may not exceed 5% of the total assets of the scheme. A further complication arises because many schemes' rules have greater restrictions than those set by statute by providing for an absolute prohibition on any form of self-investment or limited to holding such investments only through units in a pooled fund. The guidance recognises that this issue exists and takes the line that in the view of the board of the PPF, presumably upon advice, contingent asset agreements do not qualify as employer-related investments for the purposes of the legislation. While this may be a reasonably safe position to take, trustees should obtain separate confirmation from their legal advisers that they concur with this view.

In relation to whether trustees should agree to enter into a contingent asset agreement, they need to balance the benefit of what is being received with what they could have achieved without imperilling the ability of the employers to fund their schemes. The trustees, given the choice between cash and a contingent asset, will prefer cash. However, where cash is not available to the extent the trustees would like, a contingent asset can provide the trustees with comfort that in a worse-case scenario, the pension scheme will be in a better position than it would have been but for the agreement. The trustees need to ascertain what it is that is being offered to them, that it provides the comfort they think it does and that it has effect in the circumstances it is intended. The remainder of this section considers these aspects in the light of different types of contingent asset and the guidance.

## 1.3 The impact of guidance

In most cases the trustees and the provider of the contingent asset will wish, where possible, to obtain the benefit of a reduction in the risk-based levy when they enter into a contingent asset agreement. This is on the basis that while the reduction may not be the main reason for the arrangement, one might as well get the benefit of it if one can. This has had the effect of making the PPF guidance and standard form agreements the starting point for many such arrangements. As a result, the emerging practice is to follow the PPF requirements and use the standard form documentation unless those requirements prove too onerous. This makes the PPF guidance a good place to start when considering these types of arrangement.

This is the case even where there is no intention of getting the benefit of a reduction in the risk-based levy. The Pensions Regulator has issued its own guidance in relation to contingent assets which may be taken into account for the purposes of the scheme funding requirement. The Pensions Regulator's approach is less prescriptive and requires trustees to consider the circumstances of the particular scheme and the employer. It does not approve or require the completion of standard form documentation, but any agreements which meet the requirements of the PPF guidance will qualify as appropriate agreements to be taken into account for scheme funding purposes.

While the parties may think that the administrative burden and cost of meeting all the PPF's requirements for a valid contingent asset agreement are not worth the reduction in the levy that will result, the PPF guidance is still likely to be an important starting point for trustees because they will need to assess the strength of what is being offered. In this respect, the guidance provides a helpful pointer for trustees. For example, what should trustees be looking for when accepting a charge over land? The guidance indicates that they should require, among other things, an up-to-date valuation and certificate of title. While this may seem like common sense, trustees often find themselves in a position where they are being asked to accept contingent assets without such verification of their provenance or worth. In such situations, trustees should be asking themselves why they would accept a contingent asset which does not meet the requirements of the guidance. In short, they will need to have a good reason why they should accept a contingent asset on terms that are less favourable than those envisaged by the guidance. In practice, therefore, any contingent asset agreement is increasingly likely to be checked against the PPF guidance, even if the parties are not concerned to meet the requirements for a reduction in the risk-based levy, but wish to take the asset into account when agreeing the scheme funding objective in accordance with the Pensions Regulator's guidance.

## 2. PPF guidance

The PPF's guidance for the 2006/7 levy year was issued in September 2006 and is available on its website at www.pensionprotectionfund.org.uk. The guidance covers existing contingent asset agreements which will require re-certification to be effective for levy period 2007/2008 and new contingent asset arrangements. The guidance splits out the various types of contingent asset into three types: A, B and C (not to be confused with the Pensions Regulator's guidance on clearance events, which refers to Type A, B and C events). Type A contingent assets are parental guarantees. Type B contingent assets are those involving security (ie, security over land, securities and bank accounts), and Type C contingent assets are letters of credit and bank guarantees. If the contingent asset is not within one of these types, it will fail to qualify as a contingent asset recognised by the PPF and, accordingly, no reduction in the risk-based levy may be obtained in respect of it. One example of such a contingent asset which is not included is an art collection.

The guidance operates on three levels:

- guidance that applies to existing contingent asset agreements;
- guidance that applies to all new contingent asset agreements; and
- specific guidance in relation to particular types of contingent asset.

### 2.1 Existing contingent assets

The basic requirement is that the trustees will need to re-certify previously PPF-compliant contingent asset agreements. Therefore, it is not sufficient to satisfy the PPF's requirements once, but they must be re-certified by the trustees each year. The certificates which need to be completed for validation in 2007/8 were published in November 2006. In relation to Type B contingent assets (eg, security over land), there are additional requirements relating to valuations and certificates of title which are considered further below.

### 2.2 New contingent asset arrangements – general guidance

The key requirements are as follows:

- The contingent asset agreement must follow the standard form.

- The contingent assets must be conferred upon the trustees in the circumstances specified (ie, the contingency).
- The trustees must certify to the PPF that the contingent asset agreement meets the requirements specified in the certificate.
- The trustees must obtain and provide a copy of a legal opinion which basically states that the agreement meets the PPF's requirements; this effectively puts the lawyer's professional indemnity cover on the line in the event that the agreement proves to be unenforceable (see further below).
- The agreement must cover the liabilities of all employers that participate in the relevant scheme which are associated (within the meaning of Section 435 of the Insolvency Act 1986) with the person who is providing the asset.
- In certain circumstances, the provider of the asset must, for reasons of enforceability, be domiciled in an Organisation for Economic Cooperation and Development (OECD) state or be regulated by the FSA or equivalent EU regulator.

## 2.3 Specific guidance

### *(a) Type A contingent assets*

As noted above, a Type A contingent asset for the purposes of the guidance is a guarantee provided usually by another group company. The practical effect of such a guarantee, depending on its extent (see below), is to reduce the insolvency risk associated with the scheme employer. The main requirements for a guarantor are as follows:

- The guarantor must be associated with the scheme employer for the purposes of the Insolvency Act 1986;
- The guarantor must be domiciled in the OECD;
- The insolvency risk of the guarantor must be less than that of the scheme employer at the beginning of the levy period; and
- The guarantor must agree to become subject to the notifiable events regime as if it were a scheme employer and also notify the trustees of any breach of the guarantee.

Where there are multiple guarantors, the PPF treats it as a single guarantee based on the guarantor with the lowest risk of insolvency.

The key drivers in determining the effect of a parent guarantee are the risk of insolvency associated with the guarantor and the type of liability cap chosen by the guarantor. The guarantor must pick one of five types of cap (an increase of two from the 2006/7 levy year). The different types of cap are:

- a fixed monetary amount;
- a specified percentage of the Section 179 funding basis;
- a specified percentage of the Section 179 funding basis subject to a fixed monetary cap;
- the full Section 75 debt amount; and
- the full Section 75 amount subject to a fixed monetary cap.

These caps have a deemed value calculated by reference to the Section 179 funding basis. For example, a full Section 75 guarantee would provide a deemed value of 125% of the Section 179 basis. The board then gives credit for the guarantee based on the deemed value of the guarantee, depending on whether that deemed value is:

- less than 104% of the Section 179 basis; or
- between 104% and 111%, or 111% and 118%, or 118% and 125%, or over 125%.

***(b) Type B contingent assets***

Generally, the provider of the security, referred to as the 'chargor' in the guidance, must be an associate of at least one of the participating employers in a scheme. In addition, the trustees must have a first charge over the assets. There must be no prior or equal interest or claim in the asset. The Type B assets which may qualify as recognised contingent assets by the PPF are:

- land in the United Kingdom;
- securities held by a custodian; and
- cash in sterling held in a bank account.

Before looking at each asset class, there are some aspects of the standard documentation which are common to each Type B asset.

*(i) Liability caps*

There are two variables which affect the value of a Type B contingent asset for the purposes of reducing the risk-based levy: the type of liability cap chosen by the chargor and the value of the underlying asset. A liability cap is, as the name suggests, the way in which the chargor limits its liability under the contingent asset agreement. The chargor must pick one of five possible liability caps, as follows:

- a fixed cap consisting of a specified monetary amount;
- an amount which, when added to the assets of the scheme, will provide a 100% funding level on the PPF (otherwise known as the Section 179) funding basis;
- an amount which, when added to the scheme assets, will provide a percentage of the PPF funding basis, but limited to a specified amount;
- an amount equal to the Section 75 debt (ie, the full buy-out basis); or
- an amount equal to the Section 75 debt but subject to a monetary cap.

While the chargor must generally specify one of the above caps in the contingent asset agreement, it is also possible to specify the higher of two of any of the listed caps.

The value of the contingent asset taken into account for levy purposes will be the value of the lower of the underlying asset and the maximum theoretical liability under the agreement based on the type of cap chosen. In relation to the latter, it is not simply a question of picking the amount of the relevant cap: one must calculate the deemed maximum liability which takes into account the assets and liabilities of scheme rolled forward to a specified date and the deficit reduction contributions certified as being due up to that date. For these purposes, the Section 75 debt is taken as 125% of the full PPF funding basis. However, this is merely for the purposes of assessing the value of the asset in the calculation of the reduction in the risk-based levy. It does not affect the actual liability under the contingent asset agreement if this is the type of liability cap that is chosen.

*(ii)* *Notifiable events*

It is a requirement of the guidance that the contingent asset agreement must contain a commitment that the chargor and any employer covered by the agreement must be subject to the notifiable events regime. Therefore, if any employer-related event occurs in relation to any such person, it has an obligation to inform the Pensions Regulator unless an exemption applies.

*(iii)* *Land*

There are three specific considerations or requirements which apply where land is the contingent asset:

- The trustees must provide a valuation which is dated no later than three months prior to the certification by the trustees of the contingent asset agreement.
- A certificate of title must be obtained, which must be dated no later than seven days prior to the contingent asset certificate.
- The charge over the property must be registered prior to submission of the contingent asset certificate

Valuations must be prepared using the correct basis. The PPF requires that a market value basis is used. Where the land in question is – as it frequently will be – occupied by the chargor or any other employer whose liabilities are also covered by the security, the valuation must assume that the property is valued on a vacant possession basis. The valuation must also take into account any material matters disclosed in the certificate of title. At a practical level, this means that the certificate of title will need to be produced first and then the valuation. This presents real timing problems, as the time limits given in the guidance seem to suggest that the valuation will be produced first (within three months) and the certificate second (within seven days).

Other than referred to above, there are no detailed prescribed rules as to how valuations are to be prepared. The trustees must be satisfied that they have been prepared on a basis which:

- is consistent with their obligations to the members;
- is in conformity with market practice;
- accords with relevant professional guidance;
- is appropriate for the market conditions; and
- reflects the size and type of property.

In practice, trustees will need to take professional advice to the effect that the valuation has been prepared on an appropriate basis, as it is highly unlikely that they will be in a position to take a sufficiently informed view without such advice.

In relation to certificates of title, the basic requirement is that they confirm the chargor's title to the property. Again, no prescribed rules are laid down in relation to the form or content of the certificate; however, the guidance indicates that the City of London Law Society's standard form should be used in most cases. Certainly, any searches upon which the certificate relies must be recent.

The requirement that the charge over the property must be registered prior to the submission of the contingent asset certificate again makes for potential timing difficulties. In practice, this aspect of the arrangements will need to be done prior to the valuation and the certificate of title; or it will be necessary to have an earlier valuation and certificate upon which reliance is placed in respect of the actual charge which are then subsequently updated for the purposes of submission to the PPF.

*(iv)* *Securities*

The core requirements are as follows:

- The securities must be held by an appropriately qualified custodian;
- The securities must be of a type which the trustees are permitted to invest in under their governing trust deed and rules; and
- A valuation of the securities must be carried out at least one month prior to the contingent asset certificate.

The custodian holding the securities must be:

- domiciled in an OECD country;
- regulated by the Financial Services Authority (FSA) or an EU equivalent regulatory body; and
- have the requisite credit rating (ie, Fitch AA; Standard & Poor's AA-; Moody's Aa3)

In relation to the type of securities, the trustees will require confirmation from their legal advisers that the security falls within their power of investment. For these purposes, one ignores any restriction on employer-related investments. Therefore, it is possible for the contingent asset agreement to relate to the chargor's or another associated employer's shares. In most circumstances, this will be the case. However, where the securities would in fact qualify as employer-related investments, their value is not taken into account for the purposes of the risk-based levy. Therefore, if all the securities subject to an agreement are employer related, the trustees will not get a reduction in the risk-based levy. It follows that they could enter a different form of agreement and not meet the requirements of the guidance. While this is correct, the trustees will nonetheless wish to ensure, purely as a matter of prudence, that there is a third-party custodian who is appropriately rated and regulated, and that the shares have been recently appropriately valued.

*(v)* *Cash in bank account*

The cash in question must be sterling and held in a bank domiciled in an OECD country, regulated by the FSA or an EU equivalent. The bank must have a minimum credit rating which is the same as that for custodians of securities (see above). For the purposes of the contingent asset certificate, it will be necessary to append a bank statement which is not dated earlier than seven days from the date of the certificate.

### (c) *Type C contingent assets*

Type C contingent assets are either guarantees or letters of credit provided by third-party financial institutions. The key difference between Type B and Type C assets is that Type B assets are provided by the charger, which is either a scheme employer or connected and associated with a scheme employer, while Type C contingent assets are purchased by an employer or an associated person from a third party.

Type C contingent assets have two distinct broad forms. 'Evergreen' letters of credit or guarantees are arrangements where, if the letter or guarantee is not renewed or is allowed to expire, the trustees may claim under the guarantee or letter of credit from the relevant third-party institution. Fixed-term arrangements expire on a specified date; however, during the period of the term of the arrangement, the amount of the deficit which is covered by the letter or the guarantee is eliminated on an agreed basis. Accordingly, the key difference between the two types of arrangement is that under fixed-term arrangements, there is a requirement to make deficit reduction contributions on an agreed basis. If a contribution is missed, the trustees must have the right to enforce the guarantee or claim under the letter of credit. It is not just contingent upon the insolvency of the employer. Under an evergreen arrangement, there is no such requirement to contribute, but it is possible for the level of coverage provided under a guarantee or letter of credit to reflect any improvement in the funding of the scheme.

It will come as no surprise that the provider of the guarantee or the issuer of the letter must meet the usual requirements – that is, be domiciled in an OECD country, FSA regulated and credit rated appropriately. The purchaser of the guarantee or letter must be connected or associated with a scheme employer.

## 3. Commercial transactions – a warning

A contingent asset agreement will include the list of employers which it is intended are covered by the agreement. Any change in that list as a result of a restructuring or a sale will effectively amount to an amendment to the contingent asset agreement and will require the agreement of the trustees to such an amendment. This may give unintentional leverage to the trustees in such circumstances. This is worth bearing in mind when negotiating an agreement, even if it is not one designed to comply with the guidance. The trustees will want to include provisions that deal with any change in the employers' group, which may affect the overall employment covenant.

# Sectionalised schemes

**Penny Cogher**
Speechly Bircham LLP

## 1. Introduction

Companies are increasingly using sectionalised schemes as a way of managing their pension deficits. A sectionalised scheme, for these purposes, is a multi-employer scheme where an overall holding company, national or multinational, with several subsidiaries controls all participating employers. The one scheme will have multiple sections and one or more than one employer participating in each section. It is also possible to have a sectionalised scheme which covers a number of separate employers. The scheme must be set up in such a way that it is divided into discrete sections so that:

- contributions paid by a section employer, together with those paid by any associated employer and by any active member in its employment, are allocated to that section employer's section;
- a specified part of the sectionalised scheme's fund is allocated to each section and the assets allocated to one section are not used for the purposes of any other section;
- each person who becomes a beneficiary of the scheme is allocated by the trustees to a section of the scheme and his rights to benefits are against, and only against, the assets allocated to that section; and
- any benefits paid are deducted from the assets allocated to the relevant section. All other moneys and assets received or accruing to or in respect of a section must be added to the scheme's assets allocated to that section. Similarly, any moneys or assets paid out of the scheme by the trustees will result in a deduction from the assets allocated to that section.

The trustees have responsibility for maintaining the scheme's sectionalised status. Legally, to be a sectionalised scheme, the scheme must comply with the sectionalisation requirements of Regulation 8 of the Occupational Pension Schemes (Employer Debt) Regulations 2005 and Regulation 19, as modified by Schedule 2, paragraph 1, of the Occupational Pension Schemes (Scheme Funding) Regulations 2005. The key requirements are set out in Regulations 8(1) to (4) of the Employer Debt Regulations and paragraphs 1(1) to (4) of the Scheme Funding Regulations. These require that there is a multi-employer scheme:

- which is divided into two or more sections; and
- whose provisions are such that the sections meet conditions A and B.

Condition A is that contributions payable to the scheme by an employer, or by a member in employment under that employer, are allocated to that employer's section.

Condition B is that a specified part or proportion of the assets of the scheme is attributable to each section and cannot be used for the purposes of any other section.

A scheme which does this is treated for the purposes of Section 75 of the Pensions Act 1995, and for the provisions of the Employer Debt Regulations and the Scheme Funding Regulations, as if each section of the scheme were a separate scheme.

## 2. Structure

A sectionalised scheme has a principal employer, but unless the principal employer actually participates in a section, the scheme can be set up so that the principal employer has no financial responsibility to the scheme. However, with the moral hazard provisions of the Pensions Act 2004, it is possible for the Pensions Regulator, in limited circumstances, to impose liabilities on the scheme's principal employer in any event.

The scheme also needs trustees. The new flexibilities allowed for by the Member-Nominated Trustee Regulations 2006 make it easier to ensure that the various sections are appropriately represented on the trustee body. This is important given the increased role which trustees have under scheme-specific funding in determining the employer contribution rate and so deciding how quickly any deficit is reduced.

Each section has a section employer – this will be all it has if the section is just a single-employer section, the equivalent of a single-employer scheme for funding purposes. If it is a multi-employer section – equivalent to a multi-employer scheme for funding purposes – then the section will also have other participating employers, usually those that are associated or connected with the section employer. In these sections, the section employer may have a similar role to perform to that of a principal employer of a multi-employer scheme. Each section will have its own employer contribution rate, determined on the basis of that section's assets, liabilities, membership profile and the employer's attitude to risk.

How the powers and discretions are divided between principal employer, section employer and participating employer will vary depending upon exactly what is required, taking into account how much autonomy or streamlining is required by the scheme's key sponsoring employer and how it wants to run its organisation as a whole, including its pensions arrangements. However, generally, the holding company will want to keep and exercise control of the sectionalised scheme as a whole by acting as its principal employer and having much wider powers over each section than the section employer. In any event, there should be clear channels of communication between all the relevant parties – principal employer, section employer, trustees and members.

A sectionalised scheme will contain additional powers and the flexibilities given can be extremely useful in managing a group of companies' pensions deficit. These are:

- power of appointment and removal of a section employer;
- power to close/terminate a section while keeping other sections open;

- power to close/terminate all sections;
- power to wind up a section while keeping other sections open;
- power to wind up all sections of the scheme;
- power to create a new section;
- power to make transfers of benefits and assets from one section to another – on an individual basis or a whole section basis;
- power to desectionalise a scheme (ie, turn the scheme into a normal multi-employer scheme). The inclusion of such a power is not critical. The scheme's own amendment power can be used as long as it does not contain a prohibition on desectionalisation. Alternatively, it is possible to desectionalise a scheme by making whole section transfer from one section to another. This may be used if sections become too small for it to make commercial sense to keep them as separate sections;
- power over the payment of expenses – this will be an expanded power to allow for the various permutations in how expenses should be divided between the various sections and the scheme as a whole;
- power of investment. The investments can be operated in the same way as a common investment fund, with each section being given units in that common investment fund representing the amount of assets initially invested. Investment returns and costs are then tracked and allocated depending on the returns obtained on each class of unit. 'Hybrid investment' arrangements can also be used so there may be, say, five unit trusts available and the trustees choose the relevant investment ratio between the trusts in respect of each section. It is also possible to set up a sectionalised scheme where separate investment powers apply in respect of each section and investments for each section are made accordingly. Another approach is for the trustees to allocate the correct part of the scheme's assets to each section. Then, where the assets of more than one section are invested with a common investment manager or held by a common custodian, the trustees must inform that investment manager or custodian of the section to which any moneys invested or disinvested are to be allocated. The investment manager or custodian must ensure that the assets allocated to a section remain allocated to that section, except where the trustees direct otherwise, and that any income, capital gains or similar relating to any part of the scheme's assets is allocated to the correct section. For each section, the fund manager must be required to provide statements of the assets under its control that are allocated to each section of the scheme. Errors (with the fund manager) may creep in, so it is essential that the trustees have the power to re-allocate assets which have been incorrectly allocated. The trustees will also need to ensure that each section's statement of investment principles is followed and must keep a separate bank account for each section of the scheme; and
- power to establish the rules of a sectionalised scheme – each section has its own set of benefits and so will have its own rules. These will refer to all the usual benefit provisions, including the member contribution rule. It may be that some streamlining of benefits or administrative provisions can be

achieved, in which case a sectionalised scheme may have a trust deed, some general rules that apply to all sections of the scheme and then section rules. Since each section will have its own section rules, the scheme's amendment power can contain specific provisions/restrictions which apply only to that particular section of the scheme. The same approach can be taken when setting out the other powers and discretions in the trust deed, such as the employer contribution rule. This makes it straightforward for special exemptions to apply to one or more of the sections, if necessary – for example, the trust deed can require the agreement of the principal employer and the trustees to wind up all sections except in relation to one particular section of the scheme, where the decision rests solely with the trustees.

## 3. Advantages

The attraction for groups of companies is that such structures provide a transparency of pension costs. Each section is separately funded. Unlike a standard multi-employer scheme, there are no cross-subsidies; so a group of companies which has distinct trading arms can have freestanding pension costs and also employees who are all members of the same scheme. This seems to have become increasingly important as companies focus on their pension deficits and how best to manage them. A sectionalised scheme makes it easy for each employer to know exactly what its pension costs are. Also, if disposals of businesses or companies are anticipated, a company may want to reorganise its pension arrangements by using a sectionalised scheme to facilitate such sales. Disposals can be much cleaner from the sectionalised scheme. A sectionalised scheme is also useful where a holding company has a diversity of business interests. For example, where a US multinational has several disparate business interests in the United Kingdom, sectionalisation could prevent cross-subsidies in the pension scheme between one type of business and another.

Sectionalised schemes can also be used to facilitate whole scheme transfers. It is easier to make whole scheme transfers to a sectionalised scheme and so have a multiplicity of schemes under the umbrella of one pension scheme. The introduction of a proactive Pensions Regulator, the high levels of regulation now imposed on defined benefit schemes and the corresponding costs of compliance, together with the ongoing issue of scheme funding, have provided an added impetus for employers to effect scheme mergers. There are stringent statutory and regulatory requirements to be satisfied if transfers are to be made without the consent of the members concerned. Often, the funding position of the various schemes concerned is so disparate that whole scheme transfers are not possible without a large cash injection and/or a company guarantee. Also, if trustee consent is required to effect the transfer, the trustees must be satisfied overall with the balance of powers between employer and trustees in the scheme which is to receive the transfers. It is more straightforward to satisfy all these requirements if the transfers are to be made into a completely new section of a sectionalised scheme. Also, with a sectionalised scheme, there is no need, on a scheme merger, for employers to feel an obligation to streamline benefits, although care must be taken as regards compliance with the pensions aspects of the Age Discrimination Regulations.

A sectionalised scheme, as against a multiplicity of smaller defined benefit schemes, should provide some scope for cost savings. The scheme can have just one scheme actuary, one legal adviser, one set of accountants, one scheme administrator and one investment adviser, all with a single set of terms and conditions. Cost savings should also be obtained for bulk service purchasing. However, as a counter to this, each document produced for a sectionalised scheme must reflect the fact that the scheme is sectionalised. It can therefore take more time and thus be more costly to produce the advice, policy documents, member communications and so on for a sectionalised scheme.

The larger the scheme, the less conservative it may be able to be with its investment strategy, subject to taking account of the group's overall attitude to risk, and some investment options may be open to it which would not be appropriate for a small scheme, such as the use of hedge funds. Hopefully this will result in better returns.

Companies prefer sectionalised schemes as against a number of smaller schemes because one larger scheme generally takes up less management time. Because of changes introduced on the back of the new Pensions Regulator, compliance with issues such as the notifiable events regime is more straightforward if the group has just one pension scheme. Similarly the free flow of information from sponsoring employer to trustee about the group's business plans and any significant company events which might affect the pension scheme is easier to manage if there is just one scheme and one set of trustees to consult with.

## 4. Potential disadvantages

However, other aspects of a sectionalised scheme will not lead to cost savings and can actually increase costs. In particular, each section needs its own separate set of accounts to be audited. These are then put together to form the scheme's accounts. Similarly, each section, because it is treated as a pension scheme in its own right, will need to comply with the new scheme-specific/section-specific funding rules. Each section will also have its own liability/risk profile and its own statement of investment principles. There should also be a statement of investment principles for the scheme as a whole. Both the Scheme Funding Regulations and the Investment Regulations require the trustees at least to consult with the relevant employer. However it is possible, in a sectionalised scheme, to use the nomination process allowed for in both sets of regulations. This allows the trustees to consult with/agree with whomever the sponsoring employers have nominated for this purpose – usually the principal employer or the section employer. The individual employer itself may be concerned about its lack of input into such issues as investment and funding, since it may be compelled to follow strategies which the group prefers rather than those which it prefers. This can also be the case with a normal multi-employer scheme, but the transparency of a sectionalised scheme may bring this type of issue to the fore.

Pensions legislation itself is not consistent about how it uses the term 'section' and exactly what compliance means for a sectionalised scheme. For example, different requirements and definitions of a 'sectionalised scheme' are contained in the Age Discrimination Regulations and the Cross-Border Regulations 2005. The Pension Protection Fund (PPF) recognises sectionalised schemes, although it calls them 'segregated schemes', and will regard normal multi-employer schemes effectively as sectionalised schemes. In doing this, it is perhaps just recognising the general legal trend that each employer should ultimately bear responsibility for its own pension costs and is following the thrust of recent changes to the Employer Debt Regulations and the Scheme Funding Regulations.

Finally, great care must be taken in drafting the trust deed and rules for a sectionalised scheme: if a mistake is made, it potentially calls into question the whole sectionalisation of the scheme. In a worse-case scenario the sectionalisation is lost, turning the scheme into a standard multi-employer scheme. This will have major funding consequences.

## 5. Sectionalisation of an existing multi-employer scheme

This can be appropriate if a group has two or more distinct trading branches, each of which must be financially freestanding, and its pension costs are to be included as part of that. It can be done as part of a corporate reorganisation – perhaps because this is how the group wants to organise its businesses, or as a precursor to the sale of one trading branch.

Sectionalising an existing scheme is done by amending the scheme's trust deed and rules to ensure that legally, the scheme operates as a sectionalised scheme. Changes must be made in accordance with the scheme's amendment power, so the sectionalisation must not breach any of the relevant restrictions. If trustee consent is required for amendment, the trustees need to go through their standard decision-making process and essentially be comfortable with what is proposed, and that it is in the interests of the scheme's beneficiaries. Given that the request for sectionalisation comes from the company, the trustees will probably be looking for some sweeteners for agreeing to it – whether in the form of additional lump-sum payments and/or accelerated funding of any deficit which a scheme might have and/or a company guarantee. In particular, from the trustees' perspective, the key concern should always be the security of members' benefits, since they will be secured only against the assets of a particular section in a sectionalised scheme. It is possible that the section employer may not be particularly strong and the trustees may refuse to sectionalise on the basis that the security of members' benefits would be weakened. This can be addressed by the provision by the parent company of a guarantee for benefits in some or all of the sections. Such a guarantee also has the advantage of reducing the risk-based element of the PPF levy, assuming that the parent company has a stronger Dun & Bradstreet rating than its subsidiaries.

The scheme's assets must be notionally allocated to each section. A clear formula and the mechanics for the allocation of both assets and liabilities between sections will be needed. This formula can be very complex, depending upon exactly what investments/assets the trustees hold and whether any weighting should be given to the particular asset classes, the membership profiles and other liabilities of each section.

Also, the scheme's liabilities (its members and beneficiaries) need to be allocated to each section. It is fairly straightforward to allocate those active, deferred and pensioner members, and related contingent beneficiaries, whose employment relates to one of the companies which is still participating in the scheme and for whom records are available. However, it is quite common to find that the records are inadequate and do not show which company employed which members, and/or that the companies which did employ the members no longer participate in the scheme. Members and beneficiaries who cannot be readily allocated to a section are 'orphan' members. They (and the assets and liabilities which relate to them in the scheme) must be divided, on an agreed basis, between the sections and the section employers (and other participating employers) which are still paying contributions to the scheme.

Practical decisions must be taken as to who is to be the section employer of each section, whether any section needs to have participating employers, what contracting-out arrangements need to be put in place and so forth. Post-sectionalisation compliance issues will also have to be considered, such as a review of the member-nominated trustee arrangements to see whether they remain suitable. Each section then needs to review its own funding position and comply with its own scheme-specific funding arrangements, statement of investment principles and so on. Her Majesty's Revenue & Customs will also need to be informed.

Sectionalising a scheme is not *prima facie* a notifiable event under the Notifiable Events Regulations 2005, although there must always be a query as to whether sectionalising a scheme could be regarded as an action by the trustees/employer which will or is intended to result in a debt that is or may become due to the scheme not being paid in full. Nor is it something which is specifically referred to in the Pensions Regulator's April 2005 guidance note on clearance. This means, therefore, that each case needs to be reviewed on its own merits. However, clearance should be obtained from the Pensions Regulator when sectionalising a scheme, since there is clearly scope for potential avoidance of Section 75 liabilities when a multi-employer scheme is being sectionalised so that each employer gets its own single-employer section. The Pensions Regulator will want to know whether the trustees agree to the sectionalisation and what is in it for the members. There is an argument that without sectionalisation there would be a withdrawal event, so the trustees should be looking for funding paid into the scheme which would satisfy the new withdrawal rules.

Member consents are not required for a scheme to be sectionalised. However, members do need to know that the sectionalisation has occurred and it can be quite difficult to explain to them what sectionalisation means. Obviously, trustees/employers must comply with the disclosure requirements under the Occupational Pension Schemes (Disclosure of Information) Regulations 1996.

## 6. A case study

The most recently publicised example of a scheme being sectionalised is that which occurred on WH Smith plc's restructure and demerger, as a result of which the company split into two separate companies, with the retail business remaining WH Smith and the news distribution business becoming Smiths News. A key part of the restructuring was the agreement of the trustees of WH Smith's pension scheme to the sectionalisation of the scheme where the size of WH Smith's pension scheme deficit scuppered earlier attempts to sell WH Smith.

On the sectionalisation, the scheme split into two sections – one section for WH Smith and one section for Smiths News – and the fund's liabilities and assets were split 35% and 65% between the two sections, with each company bearing its own share of the WH Smith group's pension obligations. As a sweetener, a lump-sum payment of £50 million, raised from borrowings by Smiths News, was paid into the scheme to reduce its deficit of £159 million. Employees' pension benefits were unaltered. By sectionalising the scheme, the deficit was split into two, more manageable, chunks; plus there was the additional top-up payment. Part of the rationale was to make each new group more attractive to the market. In this scenario, the change was made possible by 'A-Day' changes which removed the previous requirement that all employers participating in the same pension scheme should normally belong to the same corporate group. WH Smith obviously preferred this approach to demerging its pension scheme completely into two separate pension schemes.

## 7. The future

Companies are increasingly waking up to the possibilities offered by sectionalised schemes as a way of managing all their defined benefit pension liabilities – be they legacy schemes or fully open schemes, all can be catered for under the umbrella of sectionalisation. Sectionalisation provides the flexibility required and its worth is being noted by many commentators and advisers. Post 'A-Day', it may even be possible to have a sectionalised scheme with some sections that are registered and some which are not registered for the purposes of Chapter 2 of Part 4 of the Finance Act 2004, and so a sectionalised scheme could include an employer's senior executives' pension liabilities in a separate section, as well as different defined benefit sections and a defined contribution section.

Sectionalised schemes will retain their popularity even as all schemes begin to be funded at more uniform funding rates with the introduction of scheme-specific funding where the Pensions Regulator's goal is for schemes to be 100% funded on the Financial Reporting Standard 17 level within 20 years of the scheme's first scheme-specific funding valuation. This may gradually result in surpluses being generated again, rather than deficits. But even so, how many schemes will have surpluses on the only basis which really counts: the buy-out basis? And if they do, with a sectionalised scheme it is straightforward to decide which sections/benefits should be bought out. So sectionalisation will help with companies' final exit strategies from defined benefit occupational pension schemes.

# Asset allocation: the drive to bonds

**Daniel Peters**
Aon Consulting

---

## 1. Bond basics

Although often considered complex financial instruments, a bond at its core is nothing more than a loan to a company, institution or government. The investment consists of lending a sum (the principal) and in return receiving a promise to be paid interest on the loan, with a return of the principal at the end of the term of the loan.

Bond investments can be classed as follows:

- By type of loan – are the interest payments fixed or do they depend on some measure of inflation? The latter are referred to as 'index-linked bonds'. Generally, this is debt issued by governments, as it is not usually an advantage to companies to link their loan repayments to the rate of inflation.
- By type of borrower – is the borrower a company/institution or a government? The former are known as corporate bonds. Loans issued by the UK government are referred to as 'gilts' and can be either fixed-interest or index linked.

All of these classes of bond can play their part in the portfolio of assets of a pension scheme. Bonds have long been considered the natural 'matching' asset for pension scheme liabilities, and rightly so. Pension payments are known (to a great extent) each year and when these are valued in an actuarial valuation, they are discounted at a fixed rate of interest. A fixed-interest bond, whether government or corporate, provides cash flows that share these characteristics. For pensions that increase with inflation, an index-linked bond can also share the dependency on inflation.

For schemes seeking a higher return than that available on government bonds, they may also invest in corporate bonds. Corporate bonds will tend to promise a higher rate of interest (or yield) in return for the investor taking on an element of default risk – this being the possibility that the issuer of the bond defaults on its promise of interest and/or capital repayments. A key consideration for actuaries and trustees is whether they will allow for some of this additional return from corporate bonds in the expected rate of return they use to discount the liabilities of the scheme. (Note that most accounting bases take corporate bond yields as a starting point without further consideration.)

## 2. Changes in asset allocation over recent years

The chart below shows how asset allocations have changed over the last 40 years.

Noticeably, average bond allocations were around 50% in the 1960s, before declining to less than 10% in the early 1990s as the cult of the equity took root. As at the end of 2005, the average allocation to bonds and cash was back to around 27%. As defined benefit pension schemes close and subsequently mature, the allocations to bonds is expected to increase.

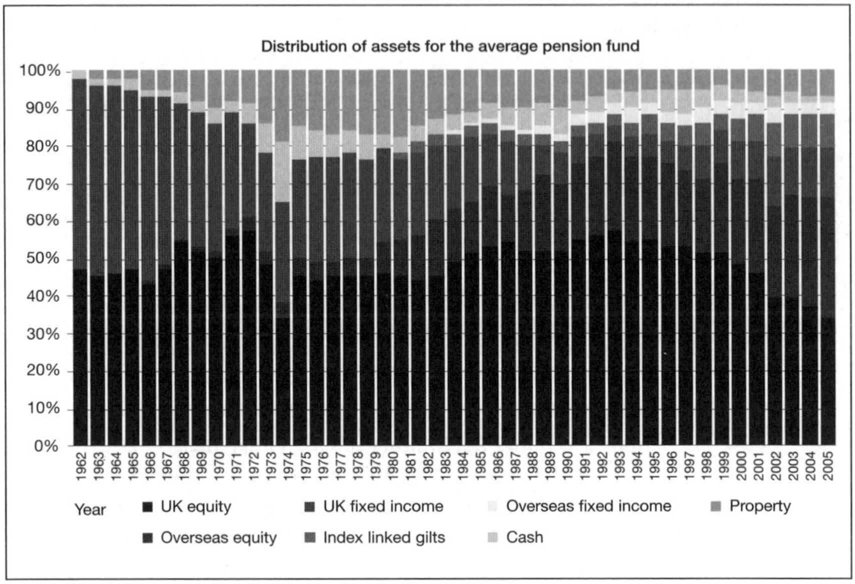


Pension schemes have recently buying bonds faster than ever before. During 2006, prices of long-dated bonds were driven to levels that almost all commentators viewed as unsustainable in the long run; the shape of the yield curve at that time demonstrated the distortions that this demand had in the market.

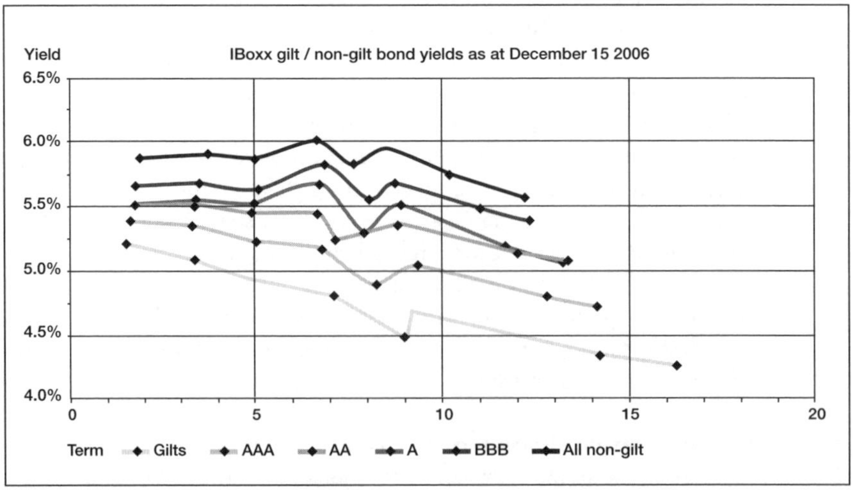

In this context, many trustees are taking a step back and reconsidering the reasons for investing in bonds – namely, to provide some matching against their liabilities. A key question is how much matching you can, or want to, achieve.

But before answering that question, it is worth asking why, in a book dedicated to dealing with deficits, bond investment is relevant. Surely investing in bonds does not reduce deficits? Other than the additional return you might seek from corporate bonds (dealt with later in this section), this is correct; where bonds add value is not in deficit reduction but in deficit stabilisation, to enable other measues to improve the position.

## 3. Considerations – how matched should you be?

Traditionally (in the minimum funding requirement (MFR) days), pensioner liabilities would be backed by bonds and the liabilities in respect of active and deferred members would be backed with equity assets. The rationale behind this was that whereas pensioner liabilities can be predicted with relative certainty, active and deferred liabilities carry much more variation – due to their dependence on future salary increases and inflation, as well as length of service with the employer. In addition, the active and deferred liabilities would not be realised in terms of pension payments until members retired, which could be some time away, while pensioner cash flows were soon enough that they could be better matched with bond investments. Therefore, a longer-term investment in the form of equities was adopted for non-pensioners. The MFR basis for valuing the liabilities also made specific allowance for equities being used to back non-pensioner liabilities. However, following the abolition of the MFR and the introduction of new accounting rules governing actuarial valuations for company accounts, the debate over how best to match pension scheme liabilities has been flung wide open.

If the aim is to protect the funding level of the scheme against all possible scenarios, then critically, just investing in bonds is not the answer. Instead, it would be necessary to implement a strategy incorporating the following elements:

- swaps/bonds whose interest rate and inflation sensitivities are exactly the same as those of the liabilities;
- some form of protection against improvements in mortality – one such development in this area is the introduction of mortality bonds, similar to an insurance contract paying out in the event that people live longer than expected; and
- knowledge of exact future salary increases and retirement dates for non-pensioner liabilities.

Mortality bonds are still very much at an embryonic stage and it is rarely possible to know with certainty the future benefits that will be payable to non-pensioners. Increasingly, though, pension schemes are implementing strategies that aim to reduce interest rate and inflation risks as far as possible – these are often referred to as 'liability-driven investment'. However, there are also schemes which have considered such an approach and rejected it. The primary reasons for this include the following:

- For schemes with liabilities stretching out 30 years and beyond, generally bonds of a sufficiently long maturity do not exist.
- A fully matched strategy (like that described above) can be adopted only by schemes that are fully funded. If a deficit exists, by definition there are insufficient assets to match fully the liabilities.
- Often a funding position will be determined on the assumption that the assets of the scheme will be partially invested in equities. If a switch to a full bond/swap position were adopted, this could impact on the actuary's assumptions and could increase the deficit.
- The cost of purchasing assets with the necessary interest rate and inflation sensitivities may be deemed prohibitive.
- Just reducing the sensitivity to fluctuations in interest rates may not have a significant impact on reducing volatility of funding level if the assets of the scheme are not diversified.

There are investment managers who have developed solutions to address some of the above issues, in particular providing the assets with the appropriate sensitivities to interest rates and inflation. In addition, some have developed solutions that enable schemes in deficit to hedge fully their interest rate and inflation exposures – in order to overcome the problem of insufficient assets, these funds will typically employ a level of gearing to provide the required exposures. Many investment managers can now offer such solutions in pooled funds, thereby making access possible for smaller schemes. However, the technical ability to invest should not be confused with the extensive training and governance requirements that these approaches will entail; often this can be the most significant barrier to entry.

Whether or not a sophisticated solution is adopted, an important decision facing trustees (especially for schemes in deficit) is the extent to which they should invest in bonds/swaps to match their liabilities. Even a scheme wishing to adopt a traditional approach and match pensioner liabilities with bonds must decide whether the percentage of pensioner liabilities should equal the percentage invested in bonds, or whether the amounts should be the same. Depending on the size of the deficit, the two possibilities will differ to a greater or lesser extent.

Generally, investing in bonds will bring with it greater certainty of future funding levels. However, for all schemes not fully funded on a bonds basis, this could mean greater certainty of preserving a deficit position. Schemes in deficit will inevitably need to take some investment risk in order to return to a fully funded status. The one exception to this is where contributions will be paid into the scheme in order to bridge the funding gap – in such cases it may be that minimising investment risk is a priority.

For schemes with a significant deficit the dilemma will be even more difficult. Adopting a mismatched position means that if interest rates (specifically long-dated interest rates) fall, then the funding position would be impaired further. Conversely, a rise in interest rates could improve the funding position without the need for additional contributions. Ultimately, the decision as to the extent that the scheme will protect itself against falling interest rates will be a combination of risk appetite on behalf of the trustees and sponsoring employer, and perhaps a subjective view on the level of interest rates and the respective probability of the above two scenarios.

Further, interest rates affect only the reported funding position – that is, the liabilities remain the same, although their present value may change. The extent to which the trustees can take a long-term perspective and overlook short-term fluctuations will also be a factor in this decision. As discussed below, legislation and government initiatives are driving trustees and employers to focus increasingly on the short term.

In some cases, there may be a divergence of views, with trustees being prepared to take a long-term view but the employer focusing on short-term volatility. In such cases, it may be the employer which is willing to cover the costs of any such matching exercise.

## 4. Getting more buck from your bond

Over the last few years the bond market has developed tremendously and continues to do so. Whereas as recently as the late 1990s it was uncommon for a pension scheme to make a strategic allocation to corporate bonds, nowadays this has become the norm; the corporate bond market has evolved into a huge global market.

In addition to the corporate bond market, pension schemes now have access to investment in swaps and other derivative instruments. The swap market has also expanded over recent years and is now over three times as large as the bond market.

All this means that while pension schemes will predominantly invest in bonds and gilts for matching purposes, it is now possible to generate some additional return from these matching assets. For a scheme in deficit, this can be crucial. It means that risk can be minimised by matching to a degree considered appropriate, while at the same time these assets can be used to generate additional return to clear the deficit.

As mentioned above, the view of the actuary and the trustees will be important here as well. For example, if a scheme were to adopt a bond portfolio targeting a return above gilts of 1% (net of fees), would the trustees (having considered the advice of the actuary) be prepared to allow for any of this additional return when carrying out the valuation? If the answer were yes, this could immediately reduce the reported deficit by adopting a higher discount rate. However, the trustees could take the view that this would be imprudent and prefer a lower discount rate, with any additional return accruing as an item of surplus to the scheme.

In seeking this extra return, trustees and companies should be aware of the potential increase in risk that the use of active management and different financial instruments may bring.

Despite this, a bond manager with the appropriate skill, experience and resources should be able to manage effectively the use of a wide variety of bond instruments to create a diversified portfolio of assets that seeks to generate a return above that on government bonds with a relatively small increase in risk.

## 5. The cult of the equity – on the wane?

### 5.1 Equity basics

An equity is a share in a company; the shareholders of a company are the owners of that company. As a part-owner of a company, a shareholder is entitled to the residual profits of the company after all creditors and bondholders have been paid. In addition, they will often have the right to vote at the company's general meetings.

A shareholder is in a different position from a bondholder in two principal ways:

- The potential profit from the holding is unlimited as the company may grow in value and in dividends paid; and
- The risk is greater, in that there is no obligation on the company to pay dividends (unlike bond repayments) and the eventual value of the shareholding may be worthless if the company deteriorates in value.

Equities have been considered an appropriate asset class to be held by pension schemes for a long time. The chart in section 1 indicates that despite the publicity of pension schemes shifting to bonds, the average allocation to equities is still in the order of 60% to 70% of total scheme assets. What is the rationale for equities playing this predominant role in pension scheme assets?

### 5.2 Equities – the natural long-term investment

In many ways, equities are the natural long-term investment. A broad-based equity portfolio should generate exposure to the key elements of the underlying economy and in this way can benefit from the natural economic growth that the economy can deliver.

Further, although equities tend to experience periods of high volatility in the short term, research has shown that over the long term (20 years or more), the returns from equities outstrip those of other major asset classes. For investors with this kind of time horizon, the argument for equities is certainly strong.

Historically, pension schemes could afford to take a long-term perspective. The majority of liabilities were very long term and generally linked to salaries. Equities were seen as an asset class that could be expected to deliver returns in the long term that would at least match salary inflation. In fact, in 1989, pension schemes as a group were the single largest owner of equities in the United Kingdom, accounting for over 30% of the UK market. This trend has changed, with insurance companies now taking the lead role and pension schemes owning around 16%.

Given that the above assumptions and justifications for investment have been borne out – equities have provided long-term growth and have outstripped wage inflation – why are trustees and employers reconsidering the dominance of equities as an asset class for pension schemes?

### 5.3 The changing environment in the United Kingdom

Whereas bonds can often be a good match for liabilities – mainly because they produce a stable income and react to changes in interest rates in a similar way to the liabilities – the same is not true of equities. Broadly speaking, the equity part of the portfolio of assets is not there to match the liabilities, but instead to beat them – that is, to generate a return greater than necessary to meet the liabilities in order to reduce the long-term cost of the scheme and to clear any deficit that may exist. As a result, the liabilities may define the overall goal of the equity strategy, but not the detail as to how this might be achieved.

Another way of referring to the above distinction is to refer to the bond assets as 'matching' assets and the equity assets as 'growth' assets. This reflects the fact that the aim is for the bond assets to match closely the liabilities, whereas the aim of the equity assets is to generate growth for the scheme so as to enable it to meet the longer-term liabilities.

The key questions to be addressed with regard to the growth assets are as follows:

- How much growth/return needs to be generated?
- What is the most efficient way to generate this growth?

On the first question, section 1 has already answered this to some extent. As schemes mature, the nature of liabilities becomes more known and less long term, and as a result the need for growth assets may reduce. The absolute level of growth that the assets will need to generate will depend on the funding plan for each individual scheme. The more interesting question, and the one which has come under most scrutiny in recent years, is how to generate that growth.

In the past, trustees of pension schemes relied almost entirely on equities for the growth part of their investment portfolio. It was always expected that the long-term return would be greater than the return on bonds, but accompanied by much greater volatility in the capital values. This volatility was managed in the funding of pension schemes in a variety of ways in the past – for example:

- for the purposes of the actuarial valuation, the value of equities was determined either by discounting the future dividends or simply by averaging the market values;
- the scheme actuary had a large amount of discretion when setting the valuation basis;
- as long as the employer paid contributions at the minimum required under the MFR, trustees could not legally demand higher contributions; and
- equity investment was spread across domestic and international markets, to provide some diversification.

However, for various reasons this model has broken down:

- In the new regulatory funding environment, the trustees (on the advice of the scheme actuary) have no discretion on how to value the assets, less discretion in setting the valuation basis and more power to demand higher contributions;
- Accounting standards now require the funding position to be shown on the balance sheet, with very little flexibility in interpretation;
- The powers of the Pensions Regulator mean that corporate transactions can be influenced by the funding position of a scheme on a particular date; and
- The globalisation of markets has meant that the correlation between international equities has increased.

Volatility in the 'growth' assets is therefore likely to make funding, accounting and corporate events more difficult for employers and trustees – any deficit caused by a reduction in market values could result in the need for increased employer contributions, deterioration in a balance sheet position or failure of a corporate transaction. It is considerations like these that are driving employers and trustees to reconsider their allocations to equities.

It is worth reminding ourselves, however, that other than the increased correlation between international markets, it is not the equity markets that have changed in nature – equity volatility is more or less what it has been historically. What has changed is the time horizon over which pension scheme trustees and sponsors are now looking.

### 5.4 The culprit of deficits or a convenient scapegoat?

Many would point to the stock market crash of 2000 to 2002 as the cause of the current deficit crisis in the United Kingdom. Equity markets fell by 37% over this period and left pension schemes in crisis. However, this is by no means the whole story.

What actually happened over this period was a combination of two factors, not just one. At the same time as equity markets were falling, interest rates and bond yields were also falling. This meant that the present value of liabilities as assessed in the actuarial valuation of a scheme was increasing at the same time as asset values were falling. Hence funding levels hit crisis point in many cases.

There are many lessons that can be learnt from this period. Protection against interest rate risk is one of them – this was discussed in the previous section. An arguably more important lesson is the danger of overexposure to a single asset class and the need to diversify away from reliance solely on equity markets. We will explore this idea in the next section.

## 6. Alternative investment – the new frontier

Conventional pension scheme investment has historically been comprised predominantly of equities and bonds. Asset classes or strategies that fall outside of this are often classed as 'alternatives'. However, studies have shown that trustee bodies of many schemes are already investing in alternative assets and many more are now considering them. Before considering the alternative asset classes on an individual basis and assessing their fit within a pension scheme portfolio, it is often helpful to analyse the motive behind the inclusion of alternative assets. This can help to focus attention on the asset classes that will be most appropriate for the particular circumstances of the scheme.

With the exception of certain 'alternative' assets which are considered for matching purposes (eg, those discussed in section 1), alternative investment is generally considered for two possible reasons:

- to enhance returns on the portfolio, often in order to bridge a funding deficit; and
- to reduce the volatility of returns, thereby attempting to stabilise funding levels.

## 6.1 Enhancing returns

### (a) *Motives*

For a pension scheme in deficit, the deficit can be bridged in one of two ways – either through increased contributions from the employer (and/or members) or through investment returns. For schemes where increased contributions are not a realistic possibility, by virtue of either a lack of ability or a lack of willingness, investment returns must achieve a certain target in order to bridge the funding gap. Properly constructed investment and actuarial advice should identify the return that is necessary and over what time horizon. Once the target is set, the aim should then be to achieve this target with as low risk a strategy as possible.

In many cases, the expected return from the equity portfolio will be sufficient to bridge the funding gap over time (provided that the Pensions Regulator accepts the recovery plan) – in these instances the focus will then be on reducing risk where possible without decreasing return.

However, there will also be some instances where the expected return will simply not be sufficient to bridge the deficit in the necessary time horizon. This could be as a result of a significant deficit, a very short time horizon or a combination of both. In these cases, it will be necessary to look for a strategy that is capable of delivering returns in excess of equity market returns. This kind of strategy may involve taking greater levels of risk in pure investment terms, but this may be deemed necessary as opposed to facing the risk of insufficient funds to pay benefits.

Another example of where a scheme might decide to look for increased returns may be where in fact the sponsoring employer is in a very strong position. Instead of simply shovelling valuable cash into the scheme, the trustees and employer may come to an agreement whereby the trustees are prepared to adopt a more riskier strategy that attempts to clear the deficit through investment strategy alone, in exchange for assurance that the employer will support the scheme if the investment strategy fails.

### (b) *Approaches*

One approach to targeting a higher return may be through investing more heavily in equities (as opposed to bonds) than would otherwise be the case. However, it may also be possible to maintain the allocation to bonds and instead seek to generate the extra return through targeting a higher return on the non-bond assets. In the past, the only practical method for pension schemes to achieve this would have been through active equity management.

In the last few years, many active managers have struggled to deliver the performance targeted and so trustees and employers alike are looking for other ways to generate this additional return.

Examples of alternative asset classes or strategies that could be employed to achieve this kind of objective are:

- commodities;
- active currency management;
- hedge funds (either individually or in funds of hedge funds);

- private equity;
- Private Finance Initiative (PFI); and
- tactical asset allocation strategies

A number of these have the potential to generate long-term returns at a greater level than equity investment, although not without commensurate risks. Some of these are explored further below.

## 6.2 Reducing volatility

For many schemes, the focus will be on reducing the volatility of returns, rather than increasing their absolute level. This can help to reduce the risk of volatile funding levels, which, as discussed above, can prove difficult for both trustees and employers. (This may also then permit a larger growth portfolio than would otherwise have been the case, as the risk in this portfolio is lower.)

At the heart of reducing volatility lies the concept of diversification: looking for the desired return in a variety of places. The advantage of a diversified strategy is that if one strategy underperforms for a period of time, it will not adversely affect other strategies. This will be true if the different strategies are truly uncorrelated – in other words, there is no strong link between the returns of one strategy and those of another. In practice, correlation exists between most asset classes and strategies to some extent.

### *(a) How can diversification be achieved?*

In order to understand how diversification can be achieved, it is helpful to consider first the primary sources of risk (and return) in the investment strategy of a scheme. These are:

- market risk – the risk that the market where the assets are invested performs poorly; and
- manager risk – the risk that the investment manager does not meet the targets set.

Although it is common for trustees of pension schemes to spend much time and effort monitoring the second of the above two risks – the performance of the active equity managers – there is generally far greater risk being taken with regard to the market than with regard to the investment manager. If the investment manager underperforms, this might be 2% below the index in a bad case; however, a market crash can give returns of -25%. Reducing market risk is precisely what diversification looks to achieve.

Looking for returns in a variety of markets goes some way towards protecting the pension scheme against the risk of one market crashing. A further level of protection can be reached by reducing the extent to which the scheme is dependent on any of the markets for return and increasing the expected return from the skill of the investment managers – that is, allocating the risk more evenly between the above two sources of risk and return.

As a result of the above considerations, there are three key criteria when considering investing in alternatives in order to diversify away from equities:

- A significant proportion of the growth assets must be allocated to alternatives in order to benefit from diversification. Simply allocating a very small proportion to an alternative asset class will not make a meaningful impact on the risk of the overall portfolio; essentially, any assets remaining invested in equities are exposed to the volatilities of those markets.
- A corollary of the above point is that the alternative class itself should not be excessively volatile. Since a significant proportion of assets will need to be invested, if the alternative is more volatile than equities, this could defeat that very objective. Ideally, the alternative asset should have lower volatility than equities.
- The alternative asset class should not be closely correlated with equities. Since the aim is to remove some of the dependency on equities, it is critical that the alternative itself should not be dependent on equities in a significant way.

Examples of alternative asset classes or strategies that could be employed to achieve this kind of objective are:

- property;
- funds of hedge funds; and
- PFI.

Some would also include private equity as a possible diversifier, although there may be a higher correlation with equity markets than with some of the other asset classes listed above.

Once the motive for the inclusion of the alternative asset has been explored, it is possible to assess how it might fit within the portfolio.

*(i) Property*

Property is a familiar asset class to most trustees, in both a domestic and a commercial sense. UK pension schemes have invested in property since the 1960s and earlier, although the average allocation has never been over 20%. The familiarity of property, together with the relative ease of understanding, makes it a natural possibility as a diversifier within a pension scheme. However, common concerns relate to costs, which can often be high, as well as views on the current position of the UK property market and its relative value.

UK pension funds invest to a very large degree solely in the UK property market. Although this may evolve in the near future, globalisation of property investment is still in its formative years.

Importantly, the income from property forms a significant part of the total return; this has historically proved more stable than capital returns. This not only gives greater stability in property returns than those of other investment classes, but also is a key factor to be considered when assessing property as an alternative asset. Even if the view is taken that growth in property values may not be what it has been over the last few years, the income component of return should nonetheless assist in preserving a consistent return from property.

Property can offer benefits both in terms of diversification – that is, as an alternative to equities – as well as income, to match liabilities. It is these characteristics that mean that schemes may allocate assets to property from a combination of both the equity and bond portfolios. This helps to overcome the justified concern that long-term returns from property may not be quite as high as those from equities.

Liquidity can sometimes be a concern when considering investing in property. Even pooled funds (in particular, closed-ended pooled funds) that tend to be very liquid can become illiquid at times of market stress. However, most pension schemes have far more liquidity than they are likely to need for many years to come, so such worries should not be a major concern.

Property is also a relatively management-intensive asset class and, consequently, the total costs of management are likely to be higher than for other asset classes. It is important, therefore, that property comparisons are made on a basis net of all transaction and management costs.

*(ii)* *Commodities*

The commodities market covers a wide variety of different commodities, including energy, livestock, agriculture, industrial metals and precious metals. Institutional investors will rarely invest in commodities directly, but instead will take exposure via commodities futures contracts. These contracts are standardised, exchange-traded agreements which give the holder an exposure to the market without needing to trade in the physical markets. There are now active and liquid futures contracts based on all of the major commodities. It is the widespread existence of these futures contracts that enables commodities to be considered as an alternative asset class providing an increased return.

Unlike equities, bonds and property, commodities offer no income-generating properties, but the way in which the futures contracts are set up allows the investor to earn interest on the cash held to back the contract and benefit from the commodity risk premium.

Commodity futures are still a relatively unknown investment for institutional investors despite trading for over 100 years in the United States. This may perhaps be attributed to the fact that investment in this asset class is an investment into derivatives rather than physical asset trading, which has historically been frowned upon or considered too risky by investors.

Various indices exist (including the Goldman Sachs Total Return Commodity Index, Dow Jones-AIG Commodity Index, Reuters Commodity Research Bureau Index and Standard & Poor's Commodity Index), and hence exposure to this asset class can be achieved through investment in pooled investment vehicles that are actively or passively managed. Minimum investments tend to be around $1 million.

One of the key drawbacks for most pension schemes when considering commodity investment is the volatility of prices inherent within this asset class; any investment would therefore need very careful management. Further, many investors believe that there is a significant level of commodity exposure within many of the large equity holdings, particularly with regard to oil and mining. This could lead to a doubling-up of exposure to a particular sector.

*(iii)* *Active currency management*

Because a large proportion of currency traders are not primarily in the market to make a profit, there are inefficiencies which active currency managers seek to exploit to make a positive return. There are those who claim that as a result, active currency managers are more likely to outperform their underlying benchmark than, for example, active equity managers.

Investment in currency is often a high-risk/high-return exercise and there can be some difficulty in maintaining the risk levels to an acceptable degree.

Both commodity trading and active currency management are strategies that would often be included as part of a fund of hedge funds framework. The fund of hedge funds approach may be preferred in this context as these high-risk investment strategies can be incorporated as part of a diversified portfolio, with the risk levels and exposure controlled in a professional manner.

*(iv)* *Funds of hedge funds*

Funds of hedge funds are an example of an alternative asset to equities that can generate similar returns but often with lower risk. Although this may sound surprising, given the public image of the hedge fund industry, 'hedge funds' is a term that spans a wide range of investment approaches, ranging from the very risky to the ultra-conservative. Pension schemes will typically be interested in the lower-risk approaches.

Hedge funds will typically rely on the skill of the manager rather than the performance of the underlying markets to generate returns, and this is a key factor in explaining the lack of correlation with the equity and bond markets that hedge funds tend to exhibit.

The following charts demonstrate the low volatility of returns that funds of hedge funds exhibit in comparison with the equity market. However, in any such comparison it is important to be aware that the existence of survivorship bias can undermine the extent to which hedge fund indices may be relied upon

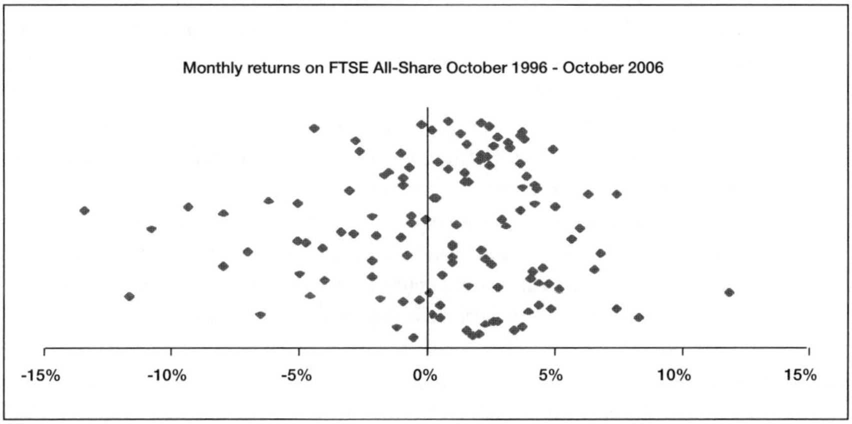


Source: FTSE, Aon

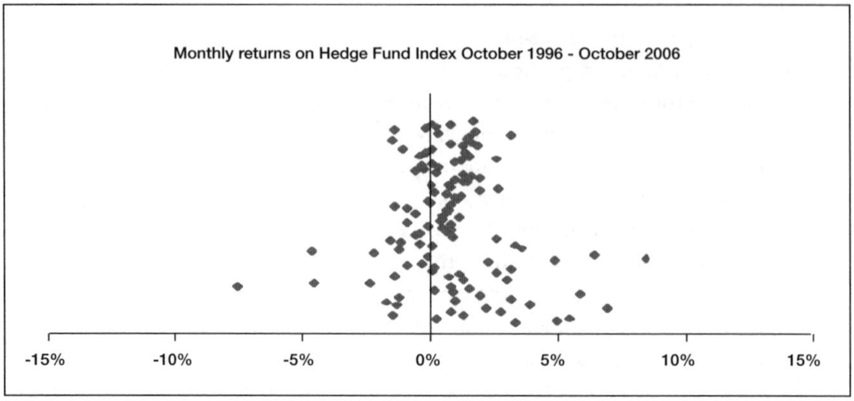


Source: CSFB /Tremont, Aon

The difference in the patterns of returns between the FTSE All-Share Index and the Funds of Hedge Funds Index is clear. The FTSE All-Share has historically exhibited far greater variation (ie, volatility) of return than the Funds of Hedge Funds Index. Further – and arguably of greater concern to trustees – the FTSE All-Share has sustained greater downside volatility: the number of negative months and the extent of the fall on the FTSE index during these months are substantially higher than on the Funds of Hedge Fund Index.

Investing in a single hedge fund carries with it other risks (eg, exposure to fraud and being heavily dependent on a few 'key men'), and therefore of specific interest to trustees are funds of hedge funds. A fund of hedge funds is a collective vehicle that invests in a number of underlying hedge funds. Extensive research is carried out by the fund of hedge funds manager before investing in any hedge fund and the risks are monitored in a thorough manner and on an ongoing basis. In fact, probably the most important aspect of any fund of hedge funds manager is the extent of the risk management systems that it has in place.

A fund of hedge funds will generally involve an exposure to active currency management, commodity trading and other strategies that are considered 'alternative'. The major advantage of the fund of hedge funds framework is that these strategies can be combined in an effective manner to maximise returns and reduce risk, without placing undue emphasis on any individual strategy or manager to perform consistently well. Further, the overall level of risk can be monitored closely by a dedicated and experienced manager.

For schemes seeking to diversify away from equities, funds of hedge funds can be an ideal solution. For those seeking to increase returns on the portfolio, it is also possible to invest in a fund that targets a higher return than might be expected to be achieved on equities, although this may bring an increase in risk.

*(v)* *Private equity*

Private equity is simply equity that is not listed on the stock market. Well-known companies such as Burger King, Homebase, Pizza Express and Weetabix are all now funded by private equity investors. Private equity involves real people and real companies, making real things or providing real services. This is one reason why private equity is attractive to investors – compared to other return-seeking assets such as hedge funds, private equity is tangible.

The Myners Review created a great deal of interest in this asset class by suggesting that all pension funds should consider investment in private equity. However, to date pension funds have been generally slow to react, often because of concerns about high risk, high fees and poor liquidity.

The private equity market is about the same size as the listed markets – so the opportunity set is not small. The biggest market by far is the United States (like the listed equity markets). The route often taken is through funds of funds: that is, a fund manager packages up a broader portfolio of private equity funds, thereby diversifying exposures across various sectors and types of private equity.

Where pension schemes have historically made an investment, the average allocation tends to be around 2% to 4%. Private equity is an asset class that is difficult to model and an optimal allocation is hard to define.

There is scope for good active managers to add real value in this asset class, as there exists significantly more inefficiency in the private equity market when compared against the major listed stock markets. However, there is a very wide dispersion in returns from private equity funds and some exhibit poor long-term returns. Further, accusations of survivorship bias exist in determining performance indices.

Commitments to private equity are illiquid and the secondary market for trading private equity funds of funds is limited. Trustees must therefore accept that this could mean an investment time horizon of perhaps 12 to 15 years, which may be too long for some schemes.

Private equity can provide some diversification from equities, as well as the possibility of additional performance. However the high volatility, difficulty associated with choosing superior private equity managers, illiquidity and relatively high correlation with listed equities mean that for many schemes this is not a realistic opportunity.

*(vi)* *PFI*

PFI is a form of private equity. It is characterised by government use of private sector capital and management skills to develop or upgrade public sector infrastructure and services such as schools, hospitals and roads. Private sector companies commit to providing a specific public sector asset and related services under a long-term concession contract from a government agency, in return for a performance-related payment.

There has been significant growth in PFI across Europe and in the United Kingdom (the most advanced European PFI market), and this substantial growth is expected to continue. For some schemes this represents an attractive investment opportunity.

However, the term of a PFI fund might typically be 10 years or more and there may not be a public market for the interests in the fund. This lack of short-term liquidity may be a concern for some schemes. Further, risk levels can sometimes be high and therefore it may not be possible to allocate more than a small proportion of the scheme's assets to the investment.

## 6.3 Practical considerations for alternative assets

In considering investing in alternative assets, it is important also to bear in mind the (many) practical obstacles that may need to be overcome in the process. In some cases it is the practical issues, rather than the theoretical arguments, that prevent a scheme from investing.

### *(a) Governance*

Before investing in a new asset class, it will be necessary for all but the very experienced to undergo a period of education to understand the nature of the investment. Further, there will inevitably be increased governance requirements with regard to the ongoing monitoring of the investment. Some of this monitoring may be delegated to advisers, although there will still be a residual responsibility with the trustees and/or employer.

### *(b) Change in behaviour and culture*

Another important feature of moving away from traditional asset classes is the perception of the investment, in the eyes of both the trustees and employer, as well as the members and others associated with the scheme. It is important that the investment strategy of a pension scheme fits with the collective culture of those involved within the scheme, and this may prohibit (or sometimes encourage) a deviation from the norm of pension scheme behaviour at the time. It is important that the advisers to the trustee and employer appreciate and understand this culture.

Further, when analysing these assets, both initially and on an ongoing basis, it is important that they are considered in the context of the overall strategy for the scheme. For example, a fund of hedge funds that is meant to generate a return of 9% per annum should not be monitored on a month-by-month basis against the returns of the equity markets. This may sound trivial, but it is something that for many requires a shift of mindset.

### *(c) Cost*

There will often be increased costs associated with alternative assets, in terms of both investment manager fees and fees for advisers. In addition, there is generally a limited budget of trustees' and employers' time to devote to such matters. These costs need to be weighed against the benefits that a revised approach may bring. Arguably, trustees should devote a significant amount of their time to investment matters.

The natural 'cost' of a diversified strategy that seeks to reduce volatility is that in protecting against the risk of significantly poor returns, it also sacrifices the possibility of significant positive returns – you will never match the returns of the 'best' asset class if you have exposure to a range of asset classes. This is also another element where a change of mindset can sometimes be required.

*(d)* ***Views of the employer***

Although investment strategy is the sole responsibility of the trustees of a pension scheme (trustees are required merely to consult the employer regarding strategy), it is generally important that the employer is supportive of the approach being taken. Here again, education is crucial, as well as close liaison and an understanding of the common objectives.

## 7. Integrated funding and investment

As we have seen in this chapter so far, the nature of pension fund investment has changed considerably in recent years and continues to do so. At the same time, there have been strong developments in the actuarial advice available to pension funds and the ability properly to integrate funding and investment advice.

Money to pay pensions comes, crudely, from one of two sources – cash contributions and investment return. Increase one and the other can decrease. Put investment return at risk and the contribution risk increases to compensate; put contribution income at risk (with a weak employer) and either the investments need to be capable of meeting any gap or you risk a deficit arising. It therefore makes sense for the questions of funding (through contributions) and investment to be considered together.

Historically, this has been dealt with on an *ad hoc* basis. A typical valuation result will show the contributions required from the employer based on a particular investment strategy and a set of assumptions that the actuary has defined (or more likely not defined) to be 'prudent'. It is a spot-rate answer to a complex question and might be represented graphically as outlined below.

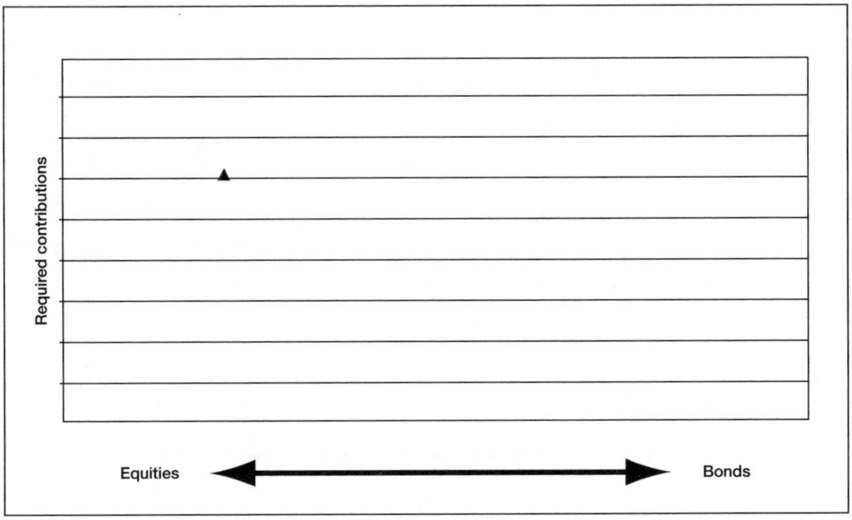

With new techniques, it is possible to expand this information considerably not just to show a single result, but to extend the results in two dimensions:

- First, allowing for investment strategy, how is the balancing contribution expected to change under different investment strategies? This might start with basic strategies such as equities and bonds (as shown above), but extend into more complex strategies including, for example, liability-driven investment and diversified growth portfolios.
- Second, looking at likelihoods rather than just at a 'typical' set of assumptions, what combinations of contribution and investment strategies result in different likelihoods of achieving a particular target?

The issue of targets and objectives could take up a whole chapter in itself and there are a number of possible things that such techniques might try to achieve. For example:

- there should be no greater than a 5% chance of having a Financial Reporting Standard 17 deficit above £5 million in the next three years;
- there should be no more than a 10% chance of contributions increasing above 30% of payroll in the next 10 years; or
- there should be at least a 70% chance that the scheme will be able to meet benefit payments as they fall due if the scheme is run to maturity

Whatever the particular target, integrating funding and investment allows a better understanding of risk than traditional techniques. The chart below shows such analysis in action.

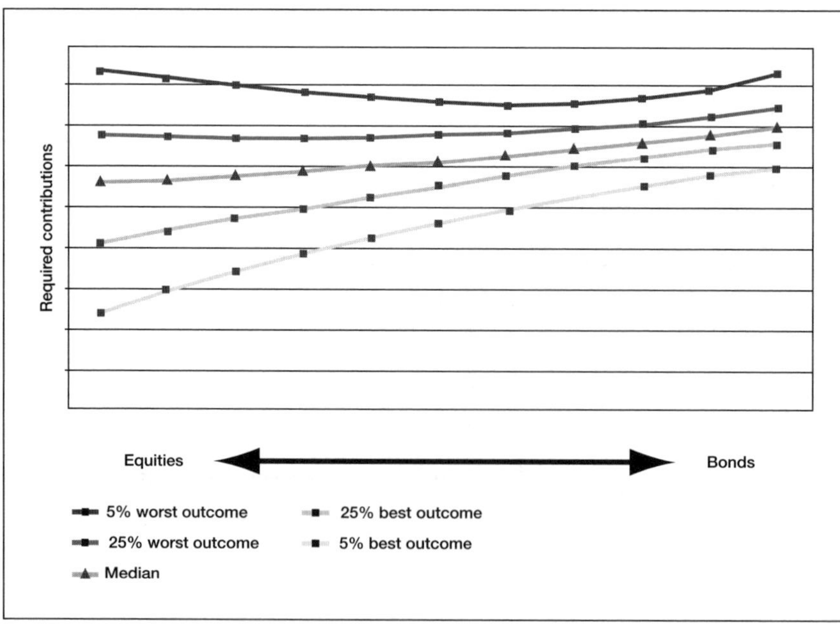

The key features of the graph are as follows:

- At the 100% equity end, the chart is characterised by lower median contribution rates, but a wide range either side, demonstrating equity volatility.
- At the 100% bond end, the chart has a higher median contribution rate but a narrower range.

In the above example, the range of outcomes at the 100% bond level is still significant and reflects the remaining inflation and interest rate risk that remains with a simple bond strategy. Better matching, as outlined in section 1, can improve this. At the 100% equity level, the range can also be narrowed through diversified growth strategies, as discussed in section 3, which maintain the median level but reduce the likelihood of extreme outcomes.

Using such modelling techniques, the investment strategies that have been discussed in this chapter can be truly brought alive so that trustees and employers can discuss and adjust their strategies to provide the optimal mixture of risk and return. No longer is it necessary to adopt an investment strategy simply because it sounds feasible. The tools now exist to demonstrate much more clearly the risks that you are running and whether your investment strategy is in reality likely to remove your deficit.

# The legal position of employers and trustees

**Diane Preston**
Trowers & Hamlins

---

## 1. Introduction

This part of the book is about practical considerations. What, then, in practice, are the legal duties of the employer and the trustees? The consequences of having a deficit in the scheme are that various legal duties or considerations will, or may, restrict the ordinary commercial activities of the employer. Similarly, the existence of a deficit will impact on various matters which the trustees will ordinarily need to consider in relation to their scheme. Due to the range and nature of the various legal duties of trustees and employers, it may also be the case that the legal duties of one party potentially conflict with those of the other. The existence or potential existence of a conflict creates a further layer of complexity and legal considerations.

No two schemes are exactly the same (except possibly some wholly insured arrangements), and the nature of the legal problems facing the employer and the trustees will depend on the specific circumstances and the relevant documentation.

## 2. Legal position of the employer

### 2.1 Commercial flexibility

The existence of a deficit in the pension scheme will impact on many aspects of the employer's (and its group's) ability to pursue its commercial and trading objectives. The impact of any commercial decision on the pension scheme and the deficit must be explored at the outset of any transaction. Corporate activity which may appear to have no impact on the pension scheme may turn out to be caught by legislation as a result of the existence of a deficit. An employer needs to understand:

- whether, while a deficit exists, certain action (or inaction) on its part will expose it to a legal liability to pay funds into the scheme;
- whether its financial standing (or that of other employers in its group) will make it vulnerable to scheme funding liabilities; and
- whether and to what extent it must try to reduce a scheme deficit in the context of its decision-making powers under the constitution of the scheme.

### 2.2 Financial support directions

It is often the case that when a number of employers participate in the same scheme, one or more of them may be companies which do not have a high net asset worth. Often, due to previous internal reorganisations, one or more of the participating employers, or even the principal employer, may have no assets at all. Where there is a deficit in the scheme, this scenario could give rise to new legal obligations. The employer should be aware of the Pensions Regulator's ability to impose a financial support direction. A financial support direction directs that another body must put in place financial arrangements to support an employer's pension liabilities. The Pensions Regulator may do this where it believes that an employer is:

- a service company (where turnover derives principally from providing employees to other group companies); and/or
- insufficiently resourced.

Legislation provides that an employer is insufficiently resourced if the value of its available assets is less than half the value of the deficit in the scheme, calculated on a buy-out basis. Thus, an employer whose scheme is in deficit must be aware that it is potentially exposing other group members to a financial support direction. It must also be aware of the ongoing possibility of having a financial support direction imposed on it in respect of any employer in its group.

Attention is most likely to be focused on this risk in the context of an internal reorganisation or an external transaction. However, an employer with a scheme in deficit is always potentially exposed to the issue of a financial support direction.

The Pensions Regulator issued its first determination notices in June 2007 against Sea Containers Limited, a company registered in Bermuda. These related to two UK occupational pension schemes of which Sea Containers Services Limited (a wholly owned subsidiary of Sea Containers Limited) was the principal employer. At the time of writing, it remains to be seen whether an appeal will be lodged or whether the financial support directions will be issued. It also remains to be seen what the impact of these determination notices will be on commercial transactions.

## 2.3 Section 75 of the Pensions Act 1995 and contribution notices

Section 75 of the Pensions Act has become a significant impediment to much commercial activity. Section 75 sets out the circumstances in which a statutory debt liability is triggered on an employer when a scheme is in deficit. This debt is nearly always onerous because the calculation is based on the cost of purchasing annuities to secure the pension benefits for the members of the scheme.

### *(a) Single employer schemes*

If a scheme is in deficit, the employer will want to avoid triggering a wind-up of the scheme and crystallising the Section 75 debt. This will be a relevant consideration in acquisitions as any potential purchaser will require assurances that a Section 75 debt will not be triggered by the transaction or by any predator protection provisions or at the discretion of the trustees.

Even when no transaction is contemplated, the existence of a deficit means that the scheme is a significant creditor of the employer and that it is impossible for the employer to walk away from the scheme.

### *(b) Multi-employer schemes*

If a scheme is in deficit, a statutory debt will be triggered under Section 75 if there is an employment-cessation event. That debt will be calculated at the full buy-out cost. Therefore, a scheme which is not funded to full buy-out will be subject to Section 75 if there has been an employment-cessation event. It is worth looking at the Occupational Pension Scheme (Employer Debt) Regulations 2005, which define an 'employment-cessation event' as an event that occurs "in relation to an employer if he ceases to be an employer employing persons in the description of employment to which the scheme relates at a time when at least one other person continues to employ such persons".

An employment-cessation event will often occur in a commercial transaction where a company or business is sold. In the case of the sale of shares of a company, the statutory debt will fall to the withdrawing employer and the purchaser of that withdrawing employer will usually expect the amount of the statutory debt to be reflected in the price of the company being purchased. If it is a sale of a business and the seller is left with a company with no employees, then the statutory debt will be a liability of the seller.

Where a scheme is in deficit, there are many other circumstances where a cessation event may occur and which may be less obvious. Where there is a pension scheme with several employers, an employment-cessation event may occur simply because one employer has gradually had fewer and fewer active members and suddenly finds that the last active member is about to retire; an employment-cessation event will occur and a statutory debt will be triggered. Similarly, a business reorganisation or restructuring may inadvertently be an employment-cessation event. A partnership which sponsors a multi-employer scheme and converts to a limited liability partnership would trigger an employment-cessation event. A registered social landlord merging with another registered social landlord (following Housing Corporation guidance) could find itself liable for statutory debt on the transfer of employees. Where there is a scheme with separate sections (eg, final salary section and money purchase section), there could be an employment-cessation event when employees move from the final salary section to the money purchase section if the scheme is in fact a 'sectionalised scheme' for the purposes of Section 75 of the Pensions Act. The legal position of the employer is clear: upon an employment-cessation event, a statutory debt is triggered and the employer must pay this pursuant to the legislation.

Any attempt to avoid the statutory debt or prevent it from arising could fall foul of the so-called 'moral hazard' provisions. Basically, the Pensions Regulator can impose a contribution notice where it considers that there has been an act or a deliberate failure to act which has, as its main purpose (or one of its main purposes), the avoidance or reduction of the debt which would otherwise be due from the employer. A contribution notice is a notice requiring an amount up to the full amount of the Section 75 debt (calculated on a buy-out basis) to be paid to the trustees of the scheme. If the scheme is in an assessment period within the meaning of Section 132 of the Pensions Act 2004, then the Pensions Regulator can issue a contribution notice requiring payment to the Pension Protection Fund (PPF).

An employer potentially subject to a statutory debt has some alternative avenues to consider. First, is it appropriate to seek clearance from the Pensions Regulator that a contribution notice will not be triggered? Second, will the Pensions Regulator (and the trustees) agree to a withdrawal arrangement? Third, do the rules of the scheme allow apportionment among other employers of any debt arising, and if so, will the trustees agree to an apportionment? Finally, continuing participation may avoid a statutory debt being triggered.

*(i)* *Applying to the Pensions Regulator for clearance*

If, on the facts, a statutory debt will arise, there is no point in applying to the Pensions Regulator. However, an application for clearance can be made in circumstances where the transaction has been structured such that the parties are concerned that they could be subject to a contribution notice in respect of the statutory debt which might otherwise have arisen. The Pensions Regulator refers to events requiring clearance as 'Type A' events. These are events which are financially detrimental to the scheme's ability to meet its liabilities. For an event to be measurably detrimental to the scheme's ability to meet its liabilities, the scheme must be in deficit. The Pensions Regulator will generally (but not always) regard Financial Reporting Standard (FRS) 17 as the appropriate measure of establishing whether a scheme is in deficit.

The effects of Type A events typically fall into any of the following three categories:

- changes in priority – a change in the level of security given to creditors which results in the pension scheme creditor receiving a reduced dividend in the event of a subsequent insolvency;
- returns of capital – a reduction in the overall assets of a company (eg, dividends or demergers); or
- changes in control structure – a change in the group structure of an employer which reduces the quality of an employer's covenant or a change in the parties that could be subject to a financial support direction.

However, any attempt to compromise the debt due to a pension scheme is both a notifiable event and a Type A event for which it is appropriate to seek clearance.

*(ii)* *Withdrawal arrangement*

This needs to be approved by the Pensions Regulator and, broadly, requires an agreement to which the trustees of the scheme and the cessation employer are party which provides that, at or before a time specified in the agreement, the cessation employer will make a payment (determined by regulations), and requires that persons act as guarantors and pay an amount (determined by regulations) on the occurrence of certain events. The amounts must be payable to the trustees of the scheme (or to the PPF if it has assumed responsibility for the scheme). Generally, the agreement will continue in force (subject to any revisions) until the winding-up of the scheme is completed or the Pensions Regulator issues a notice to the parties stating that it considers that the agreement is no longer required.

*(iii)* *Apportionment*

If the rules of the scheme so allow, a statutory debt which would otherwise arise on an employment-cessation event can be apportioned to the principal employer and/or the remaining employers. If the rules of the scheme do allow this, then trustee consent will probably be required. If the rules do not currently allow apportionment, it is possible that the rules can be amended – again, subject to trustee consent. In any event, it will be necessary to apply to the Pensions Regulator for clearance (because a Section 75 debt has arisen but is not being paid by the liable employer), regardless of whether the scheme is funded to a level above FRS 17.

*(iv)* *Continuing participation*

It was previously the case that in order to participate in a pension scheme, an employer had to be associated in business with the principal employer of the scheme (except in the case of certain 'industry-wide' schemes). Since April 2006 these requirements no longer apply and it may therefore be appropriate in some situations for an employer which has been sold out of the group to continue to participate and not trigger a debt. In these circumstances, consideration must be given to whether the scheme becomes 'sectionalised' and whether Pensions Regulator clearance is necessary.

## 2.4 Statutory funding objective

A new regime for scheme-specific funding applies to schemes where the effective date of the actuarial valuation is on or after September 22 2005.

This new funding regime imposes a new legislative framework on the employer in respect of funding the scheme and specifically in respect of funding a scheme which is in deficit.

The employer's legal position may be different once subject to the new regime. The Pensions Act 2004 provides that the trustees of defined benefit schemes are responsible for decisions on scheme funding. Any scheme rules which reserve contribution setting solely to the employer are overridden. The trust deed and rules may provide that the 'balance of power' rests with the employer. However, employers need to be prepared for the new regime and the fact that in future, the employer and the trustees must agree the basis for funding the scheme and managing the deficit.

For the legal position of trustees, see further below.

## 2.5 Reducing scheme benefits to improve deficit situation

Since June 11 2003 it has been suggested that trustees can resist requests from the employer to change future benefits because the employer has lost its 'bargaining' position, insofar as it cannot wind up the scheme without having to fund the scheme to full buy-out.

Whether trustees in this position could or should resist changes to future benefits is open to question. However, it is certainly now the case that trustees should consider the funding position of the scheme when asked to consider giving their agreement under the rules to any amendments. Therefore, if the employer wishes to amend the rules to reduce future benefits and requires the consent of the trustees to do so, it should be prepared for a request from the trustees – for example, to accelerate the timescale for funding any deficit.

The existence of a deficit combined with the new statutory funding regime has a direct impact on the employer's ability to change the benefits accrued under the scheme for future service.

If the extent of the underfunding is serious and there is no realistic expectation of a significant improvement, then the employer and trustees may have to consider reducing past service benefits. Any such amendment would be subject to the rules of the scheme and to Section 67 of the Pensions Act 1995.

### 2.6 Pension scheme as a creditor

The scheme is an unsecured creditor of the employer. This will be relevant in any discussions with the Pensions Regulator. This will also be relevant to any financial agreements which the employer may wish to enter into. The bigger the deficit, the greater the impact on the employer's flexibility to borrow money or give banking covenants or guarantees.

A parent company in a group may have given a financial guarantee to a subsidiary employer. The existence of such a guarantee may impact on the parent employer's ability to borrow generally and may also have an impact in other areas – for example, the existence of such a guarantee could prevent the parent from being able to give a further guarantee for the purposes of a withdrawal arrangement.

Employers – particularly small net worth employers with comparatively large pension scheme liabilities – should monitor the employer's financial accounting situation (in particular, its FRS17 liabilities) and ensure the employer is not at risk of insolvency in terms of its pension liabilities.

### 2.7 Employment contracts

Employees may have specific pension promises in their contracts of employment. An employer has a legal obligation and duty to comply with the contract and, depending on contract terms, will often have to take these into account when considering its legal obligation to employees in terms of pension benefits, especially in the context of any future benefit changes or perhaps termination of pension accrual altogether in order to attempt to control the deficit.

### 2.8 Duty of good faith

In 1997 the House of Lords in *BCCI v Malik/Mahmud*[1] recognised the existence of what it described as a term implied in all employment contracts that the employer should not "conduct itself in a manner likely to destroy or seriously damage the relationship of confidence and trust between employer and employee". Before this case there had been a number of decisions on the exercise of powers in a trust deed which are reserved to the employer as settlor, notably the landmark case of *Imperial Tobacco*.[2] A more onerous duty as a fiduciary arises regarding certain employer powers under pension schemes, in particular when a scheme is winding up.

It is beyond the scope of this chapter to analyse this duty in detail, but it is clear

1 1998 AC 20.
2 1991 1 WLR 589.

that an employer must act in accordance with its duty of good faith and its fiduciary duties. These duties are therefore another legal obligation for the employer to consider when taking decisions in respect of a deficit in the scheme.

### 2.9 What action should employers take in respect of their legal obligations?

- Identify whether a financial support direction could be imposed at any time and if so, how best to finance this.
- Carefully consider whether any transaction or movement of staff could trigger a statutory debt.
- Identify which employers participate in the pension scheme and how many employees they each employ. If only one employer has only a handful of active members, consider moving other members to that employer to avoid inadvertent triggering of Section 75 debt.
- Check that a scheme with different sections does not become a sectionalised scheme for the purposes of Section 75.
- Anticipate what the trustees may request under the new statutory funding regime.
- Remember that if trustee consent is required for any desired rule amendment, the trustees may use that opportunity to request greater employer contributions.
- Raise awareness of pension scheme accounting liabilities in the context of the employer's net assets.
- Understand contractual obligations to employees regarding pension benefits and how this fits with pension scheme rules.

## 3. Legal position of the trustees

### 3.1 Trustee as a fiduciary

Trustees must always consider and act in the interests of the members. If the scheme is in deficit, the accrued entitlements of the members are not properly secured. The trustees must therefore consider their legal responsibilities and what they can or should be doing to reduce the deficit. It is unlikely to be the case that the trustee can do nothing.

### 3.2 Specific legal duties

Based on trustees' fiduciary duties and their obligations under legislation, the main areas that will arise where a scheme is in deficit are:

- duty of care in respect of scheme investments;
- statutory funding objective and employer contribution rates;
- awareness of the strength of the employer's covenant;
- obtaining appropriate advice regarding trustee actions and decisions;
- conversance with duties under the constitutional trust deed and rules of the scheme; and
- trustee knowledge and understanding.

### 3.3 Gathering information

The trustees should take steps to obtain as much information as they can in respect of the scheme and the employer. In relation to the scheme, the trustees should understand the liabilities and why/how the deficit has arisen. For example, the trustees should ensure they understand the impact of the membership of the scheme on the funding liabilities – for example, is it a mature scheme and what is the history of the scheme?

### 3.4 Investment strategy

The trustees should also carefully review the investment strategy and take expert advice. The trustees should obviously be conversant with their legal responsibilities in relation to scheme investments generally. Trustees must act in accordance with any provisions in the trust deed and rules, with trust law in general and with additional requirements in the Pensions Act 1995, the Pensions Act 2004 and the Financial Services and Markets Act 2000. In summary, the trustees must exercise their investment powers:

- after obtaining and considering proper advice;
- with a view to securing quality and liquidity of the fund;
- where relevant, with a view to giving effect to the requirements of the statutory funding objective;
- having regard to the suitability of investments;
- having regard to the need for a spread of investments for the scheme;
- ensuring the scheme assets are invested mainly in regulated markets; and
- in line with the scheme's statement of investment principles.

One primary objective of the trustees is to manage the scheme's investments in order to meet the scheme's liabilities as those liabilities fall due. The existence of a deficit, by definition, means that the investments will not match the liabilities as they fall due unless additional contributions are made to the scheme and/or investments perform better than expected. The existence of a deficit therefore means that the trustees must manage the investments in the context of the deficit and must take and consider advice which is specific to their deficit and their scheme.

In recent times there has been a move towards diversification of investments, moving away from traditional investments in gilts and equities towards private equity, hedge funds and infrastructure. For example, the pension fund for the Railways Pension Scheme has moved 30% of its assets into alternative investments. Likewise, the BT Pension Scheme has increased its deployment of assets in this area from 7% to 15%. Although the potential for increased returns on this form of investment may seem tempting, there is wide variation in the yield of different funds and voices in the industry have advised caution. The PPF has issued guidance stressing the need to balance risk against potential returns. Trustees should ensure that they take regular advice from investment professionals to make sure that their strategy is appropriate for the particular circumstances pertaining to the scheme.

### 3.5 Statutory funding objective

As mentioned above, a new scheme-specific funding regime applies to schemes where the effective date of the actuarial valuation is on or after September 22 2005. This provides that every scheme is subject to a requirement that it have sufficient and appropriate assets to meet its technical provisions. A scheme's 'technical provisions' means the amount necessary to meet the scheme's liabilities.

The Regulatory Code of Practice 03 on Funding Defined Benefits, published in February 2006, sets out clear guidance for trustees in meeting the key statutory obligations. Trustees must understand the calculation of the technical provisions, the methods and assumptions to determine the funding target and the timescale for funding any deficit. The trustees must prepare a statement of funding principles as part of their compliance with the statutory funding objective.

In May 2006 the Pensions Regulator published its statement on how it will regulate the funding of defined benefit schemes. The Pensions Regulator has stressed that although it has set triggers for when it will consider intervention, these should not be seen as targets. It is expected that the Pensions Regulator's focus will be on ensuring that a scheme's technical provisions have been correctly calculated using the appropriate prudent assumptions and methods. The Pensions Regulator has also indicated that one of its triggers for intervention is where a recovery period is set for longer than 10 years.

### 3.6 Employer's covenant

It is of the utmost importance that the trustees understand the strength of the employer's covenant – this will be particularly important when negotiating the new statutory funding objective requirements. The Pensions Regulator has published guidance on this.[3] The trustees should consider appointing an independent financial adviser to assess the financial status of the sponsoring employer and must have a clear understanding of:

- the employer's ability to pay;
- the willingness of the employer to continue sponsoring the scheme;
- any potential future developments which may impact on the strength of the employer's covenant; and
- financial information.

Trustees should request such information that they reasonably require from the employer. In addition, the Pensions Regulator's code of practice advises trustees to consider using commercially available information or other sources of information including:

- credit-scoring institutions or rating agencies;
- credit specialist advisers;
- reports of industry regulators;
- information which may become available in connection with the risk band element of the PPF levy; and
- any new developments in the credit advisory services market.

---

3 Regulatory Code of Practice 03 on Funding Defined Benefits.

The trustees should, in particular, consider using investigative services in circumstances where the employer claims to be unable to afford the appropriate level of contributions.

The importance of trustees having a good knowledge of the employer's covenant has been demonstrated by the position of British Airways in 2006. The pension scheme has an estimated deficit of £2.1 billion and the trustees found that they could compel the employer to make additional contributions of funds. British Airways has (at the time of writing) pledged an additional £500 million and this figure is expected to rise. Although the company is asking the members of the scheme to make some sacrifices in return for the additional funds, the extra input of capital can certainly not be described as insignificant and provides a clear example of the trustees of a scheme making use of pressure they can legitimately exert on a sponsoring employer.

## 3.7 Trustee knowledge and understanding

Trustees of occupational pension schemes have always been required to have a certain level of conversance with their scheme and its constitution. The Pensions Act 2004 has created a statutory requirement for knowledge and understanding. Section 247 of the act states that a trustee must be conversant with:

- the trust deed and rules of the scheme;
- any statement of investment principles;
- where applicable, the statement of funding principles required in accordance with the statutory funding objective; and
- any other document recording policy for the time being adopted by the trustees relating to administration of the scheme generally.

Investment strategy and the statutory funding objective have been referred to above. The requirement to be conversant with the trust deed and rules and any other document recording policy is really a statutory modification of what was the case prior to April 2006. While the trustees should, of course, be conversant with these documents, there are specific provisions that the trustees should be aware of when a scheme is in deficit. Most notable are those relating to the balance of power between the employer and the trustees. For example, do the trustees have a unilateral power to trigger a winding-up of the scheme? If they do, then they should take advice as to whether it would be appropriate for them to do so. If there are provisions in the documentation of which the trustees are unaware, but which they should have considered in the context of a scheme deficit, they are at risk of a claim from the members.

The trustees must also be aware of the status of the scheme, including:

- the funding position;
- when the next actuarial valuation is due;
- any foreseeable issues which will affect the scheme; and
- the proportion of actives, pensioner and deferred members and the number of employers participating in the scheme.

If there is an employment-cessation event in a multi-employer scheme, the trustees must be aware of that in order to enforce the Section 75 debt.

### 3.8 Transfers

Trustees must carefully consider their position in relation to requests for transfers out of the scheme and any request to agree to allow transfers into the scheme. Where a scheme deficit exists, the issue of transfers of funds becomes more sensitive.

In relation to transfers out of the scheme, trustees should take actuarial advice on the calculation of cash equivalent transfer values and their impact on remaining benefits. Any request from the employer for a bulk transfer should also be carefully considered.

Trustees should carefully consider any request to transfer in to ensure that there is no dilution of existing assets.

### 3.9 What action should trustees take?

- Ensure conversance with relevant provisions in the trust deed and rules;
- Take advice in relation to the statutory funding objective;
- Consider the current investment strategy; and
- Take specific advice on the strength of the employer's covenant

## 4. Conflicts

It will be apparent from the above that when there is a deficit in the scheme, the interests of the trustees are likely to be different from those of the employer. For example, an employer may want to use available cash assets to improve the business but the trustees may – knowing the employer has available cash assets – want the employer to use the cash to help reduce the scheme's deficit.

If the same individuals are both executives of the employer and trustees of the scheme, those individuals have a conflict of interest. This is particularly apparent if the managing or finance director of the sponsoring employer is also a trustee. If trustees believe that they have a potential conflict of interest, they should obtain independent legal advice before making any decisions as a trustee. In a deficit situation such as that involving the British Airways pension fund in 2006, where the trustees were in direct negotiations with the company's directors over additional funding, a conflict would exist where a person is both a trustee and a director. In such circumstances, it would be impossible to serve the best interests of both roles and so it may be necessary to withdraw from discussions completely. The Pensions Regulator has encouraged trustees to take a firmer line in fighting their corner for their scheme in times of dispute with the sponsoring employer (eg, by making more effective use of the employer covenant) and so the potential for conflicts of interest is increasing, particularly where a scheme deficit exists. The trust deed for the scheme may address how trustees should deal with conflict situations and trustees should ensure that they are familiar with any procedure in place. The trustees (and/or the employer) should consider whether an independent trustee should be appointed where a conflict has arisen. If an independent trustee is not appointed, the trustees should make alternative arrangements to manage an existing conflict. If trustees act inappropriately in these situations, they risk committing a breach of trust and could find themselves liable for losses suffered by the scheme as a result. Given the risk of personal liability, the seriousness of a conflict situation is clear.

## 5. Conclusion

Both the employer and the trustees have a multitude of legal duties in relation to an occupational pension scheme. These duties are variously based on trust law, contract and statute. The existence of a deficit in the scheme perhaps puts the spotlight on many of these general duties. The existence of a deficit also creates new legal obligations and considerations. The legal framework is constantly changing, whether through new precedents or by new legislation. The economic circumstances which affect deficits are also unlikely to remain stable. No doubt there will be further problems, and possible solutions, in the coming months and years.

# Employment considerations: consultation and discrimination

**Sally Ling**
GR Comunications

## 1. Consultation with members

Since April 6 2006, private sector employers have been required to consult with pension scheme members before making certain changes to future service benefits. These new requirements – introduced under the government's 'A-Day' changes, one objective of which was to help improve understanding of pension benefits – also form part of the implementation of the EU Information and Consultation Directive. While the consultation requirements are not specific to deficit issues, they do relate to scheme changes, and in the current pensions environment these are most likely to arise out of an employer's/trustee's attempts to make good a current deficit or to avoid future funding problems and control ongoing costs.

The consultation regulations apply to employers rather than trustees, no matter who has proposed the changes. No change can be made until the consultation process has been completed, even if it is the trustees rather than the employer who are responsible for deciding upon and implementing any such change. In exceptional circumstances the Pensions Regulator may waive the requirement to consult on application from the employer.

The Department for Work and Pensions (DWP) has produced guidance on the practical application of the consultation regulations. In some places, its recommendations go further than what is required by law.

### 1.1 Who is affected

The new requirement applies to all UK employers which provide an occupational pension scheme or, in some cases, a personal pension arrangement. There are a number of exclusions to this, most notably employers whose employees belong to public sector pension schemes (where there are already statutory requirements to consult). Also excluded are small self-administered pension schemes, single member schemes and schemes administered outside the European Union. In addition, the requirements do not apply to employers where there are fewer than 50 employees, even if the employer is part of a larger multi-employer pension scheme.

From April 6 2006, the consultation requirements have applied to employers with 150 or more employees. The scope of the regulations is being extended over the following two years, to employers with 100 or more employees from April 6 2007 and to those with 50 or more employees from April 6 2008. The number of scheme members is not relevant, although they are the main target for the consultation.

Therefore, a company with a payroll of 200, but with just 45 individuals who are active or potential pension scheme members, will be caught by the consultation requirement. At the same time an employer with 45 employees, all of whom belong to its pension scheme, will not.

While the legal obligation to consult applies only to 'larger' employers, the government has made it clear that it would encourage employers of all sizes to consult with their employees. This is most likely to be an issue for multi-employer schemes which could include a mix of employers that are and are not covered by the statutory requirements. In this case it would be a matter of good practice for all employers to consult, especially if the outcome were to apply equally to all active and prospective members covered by the scheme.

## 1.2 When to consult

Consultation is triggered when an employer, trustee or other authorised person (as might be the case with a multi-employer scheme) proposes a significant change to the pension scheme that will affect the benefits of current and prospective scheme members.

These 'significant changes' are defined as follows:

- Applicable to all pension schemes (including money purchase schemes) –
  - increasing the scheme's normal pension age;
  - closing the scheme to some or all new members (existing members to continue accruing pension);
  - stopping accrual of pension for future service for some or all existing members;
  - removing the employer's liability to contribute to the scheme;
  - introducing contributions for some or all members who had not previously been required to contribute; or
  - increasing contributions rates for some or all members.
- Applicable to defined benefit schemes –
  - amending the scheme to provide some or all of the benefits on a money purchase basis;
  - changing the basis for determining future accruals such as changing from final salary to career average salary or to a mix of defined benefit and money purchase; or
  - changing the accrual rate for future benefits.

    (There are also some requirements that apply solely to occupational money purchase schemes and, in some cases, employer-sponsored personal pensions, but these are not relevant in the context of scheme deficits.)

The regulations also set out the instances where consultation is not required, which are as follows:

- changes notified to members before April 6 2006;
- a situation where an employer which originally proposed ceasing future accruals of pension benefits and has already consulted on this, in accordance

with the regulations, subsequently changes the proposal to one where the future accrual rate is reduced;

- a situation where an employer which originally proposed ceasing future employer contributions and has already consulted on this, in accordance with the regulations, subsequently changes the proposal to one where the future employer contributions are reduced (this is unlikely to occur in a defined benefit scheme);
- any changes made in order to comply with statutory requirements; and
- any changes resulting from a determination made by the Pensions Regulator in respect of the scheme

## 1.3 Who must be consulted

As mentioned above, while the extent of the application of the consultation requirement is based on the size of the employer's workforce, the consultation itself is based on scheme membership. Specifically, those who must be consulted are:

- active members (ie, employed members who are accruing pension benefits in the scheme) who may be affected by the proposed changes, or their representatives; and
- employees who have not yet joined the scheme but who are currently eligible to join the scheme or will be eligible at some point in the future, and their representatives.

'Representatives' can be

- recognised trade unions;
- information and consultation representatives (as defined by the Information and Consultation of Employees Regulations);
- existing pensions representatives; or
- if none of the above exist, representatives whom the employer has arranged to be elected to represent the members who will be affected by the proposed changes.

Where there are employee representatives already in place, the employer must involve them in the consultation. They employer is not allowed to bypass such representatives and consult direct with employees.

There is no obligation to consult with members who have left with a deferred pension and individuals who are in receipt of a pension. Employers may, however, wish to consider informing these groups of what is happening, in order to dispel any concerns about their own benefits. Alternatively, this could be done by the scheme trustees as part of any regular communications with members.

## 1.4 Form of the consultation

The consultation period must be no less than 60 days. If the employer fails to consult in accordance with the regulations, this should be reported to the Pensions Regulator. This complaint can be made by any employee or an employee representative who was entitled to be consulted under the terms of the regulations.

Where the employer already has a formal consultation procedure in place, this must be used. If there is more than one consultation process, the employer can choose which is the most appropriate. However, if there are any employees who are required to be consulted under the regulations but who are not covered by existing arrangements, specific arrangements must be put in place to consult directly with these members.

Where there are no existing arrangements, the employer can decide to put in place consultation procedures especially to deal with the proposed changes to the pension scheme, rather than consult directly with the members. In this case, the regulations set out how such representatives should be elected. However, the employer cannot set up a new arrangement where there are already appointed representatives who are able to deal with pensions issues.

Information must be provided in writing to all individuals who might be affected by the change – that is, to members and prospective members, and their representatives. This information must be provided before the start of the consultation process.

The regulations specify that consultation document must:

- state what changes are proposed and how these are likely to affect members' benefits;
- contain any relevant background information;
- set out the timescales for implementation of the changes; and
- state how employees and their representatives can submit their views and comments on the proposals. This must include the date on which the consultation period ends.

The DWP guidelines go into more detail on what should be disclosed than the regulations, stating that any communication should also indicate:

- how many members and prospective members are likely to be affected by the change; and
- any categories of member who are exempt from the change.

The DWP recommends that the consultation document should include an illustrative worked example showing how the proposed change will affect the employee's future pension arrangements. It should also provide basic information about the role of the Pensions Regulator and details of how the Pensions Regulator can be contacted.

According to the regulations, the consultation material must be "given in such fashion and with such content as are appropriate to enable, in particular representatives of affected members to consider, conduct a study and give their views to the employer on, the impact of the listed changes on such members". While the regulations do not specify exactly how this information is to be distributed, according to the DWP, "the employer should use a method that fulfils its obligation to ensure the widest possible coverage of all those affected". The DWP goes into more detail in its interpretation of this, saying that "any [medium] which only reaches some of the relevant parties is not acceptable on its own". As examples of unsuitable distribution methods, it cites emails to which not everyone affected has access and display of the information on a noticeboard with the expectation that everyone will read it. Therefore, it would seem prudent to send a printed copy of the consultation document directly to every member and potential member who is likely to be affected. The DWP also points out the need to include current or prospective members who are absent from work during the consultation period. The employer will need to decide whether to deliver the communication internally or by post to people's home addresses.

Simply distributing a consultation paper may not, however, be sufficient. In the course of the consultation, employers and those persons consulted are under a duty to work in "a spirit of co-operation, taking into account the interests of both sides." The DWP considers that this would generally involve an exchange of views between the employer and the people being consulted.

As well as making sure that the information is distributed in such a manner as to reach all the relevant people, employers would be advised to consider the tone and style of the content. Pensions are complex, especially when it comes to funding and calculating liabilities and deficits. Therefore, the employer will need to make sure that the consultation documents are not overly technical and can be understood by those likely to be affected. Where representatives are involved, these representatives should be able to explain the issues to the members.

### 1.5 Presentation and production

Another consideration is how the information is to be presented. This will, to a certain extent, be governed by budget and resources. Issuing the information in a letter will in many cases be the most straightforward approach, but it may not be the best way to present the information. Multiple pages of dense text are unlikely to be read by anyone who is not generally interested in the topic. If employers genuinely want their employees to understand the information they are providing and to engage in the consultation process, they may wish to consider a printed newsletter-style communication. This can use graphics, colour and photographic images to make an initial impact, highlight different issues and generally make the consultation document more user-friendly and easier to understand. Another approach which is becoming more popular as a method of employee communication is to produce a DVD. This is only really suitable for very large employers where there are economies of scale to be had. However, these approaches might be too costly: the employer might prefer to take a lower-key approach or might not want to appear to be spending a lot of money on a glossy communication – although one way to counter this would be to tell people how much it actually cost, as people will find it hard to object if they know that a DVD cost just £1.50 per member to produce.

A more 'home-made' approach would be to issue a short letter outlining the key points – the purpose of the consultation, timescales and how to respond, plus an accompanying factsheet setting out the details. This could be narrative, use simple factual bullet points arranged under headings, or use questions and answers to explain the issues and how members will be affected. The most appropriate approach will depend on the audience – in particular, their level of financial awareness and involvement with the pension scheme. It will, of course, also depend on whether the employer wants the consultation document to be read and responded to, or would prefer that it was ignored by the majority.

### 1.6 The role, rights and responsibilities of representatives

The consultation regulations give representatives employment rights and certain protections. These include the right to take reasonable time off to perform their role as representatives. Representatives are also entitled to payment "at the appropriate hourly rate" for time taken off work in performing these duties. Where the employer fails to comply, the representative will have recourse to an employment tribunal.

Employees acting as representatives and those who stand for election as representatives are also protected against being dismissed or suffering "other detriment" for performing their duties or for requesting time off to perform their duties. Any such claim would again be dealt with via an employment tribunal. In certain circumstances these protections may extend to other employees.

### 1.7 Outcomes

If no responses are received before the consultation period closes, the consultation process can be regarded as complete. If the changes were proposed by the scheme trustees or another authorised person or body, the employer must inform them that the consultation process has been completed and that there were no responses.

Where the employer has received one or more responses to the consultation, these must be passed on. This must include copies of any responses submitted in writing and a report of any views expressed verbally. It is up to the person or body that proposed the changes to make sure that the consultation process was conducted in accordance with the regulations.

The person who proposed the changes must then consider any responses received and decide whether to proceed with the changes. There is, however, no obligation for the views of those who have responded to be acted upon. In addition, any changes that have been made without the consultation process having been followed correctly do not have to be reversed. The Pensions Regulator may, however, impose penalties in such cases.

### 1.8 The role of the Pensions Regulator

The Pensions Regulator has a number of roles in relation to the consultation requirements. It has a policing role and can take action where it appears that the employer has failed to comply with the requirement to consult. It can also determine whether a trade union is recognised for the purposes of collective bargaining or whether an information and consultation agreement has been properly negotiated.

Where the Pensions Regulator considers that the requirements have been breached, it has powers to impose fines of up to £50,000 on companies and up to £5,000 on individuals

In exceptional circumstances the Pensions Regulator can waive or relax an employer's obligation to carry out the consultation process. To achieve this the employer must explain to the Pensions Regulator why delaying the change to the pension scheme for a minimum of the consultation period poses a problem and would be damaging to scheme members. An example of this could be that the employer fears that it will go out of business during that period. The Pensions Regulator will waive the consultation requirement only where it is deemed to be in the best interests of the members.

## 2. Discrimination issues

Addressing a pension scheme deficit by paying additional money into a pension scheme should not give rise to any discrimination issues. However, it is possible that some changes to benefits could be seen as discriminatory – whether directly or indirectly.

New requirements banning discrimination on the grounds of age were due to come into force at the beginning of October 2006. However, the implementation of those aspects that relate to pension provision was delayed until December 1 to allow for further consultation and clarification. The requirements will apply to young as well as older workers, and could therefore be a consideration when changing future pension scheme benefits. There is also potential for changes to be indirectly discriminatory on the grounds of sex – for example, where changes apply to only one category of employees and those employees are predominantly of one sex.

Employees, leavers with a deferred pension and pensioners can make a complaint to an employment tribunal if they believe that the terms of the pension scheme discriminate against them on the grounds of age. Alternatively, they can use their scheme's internal dispute resolution procedure or pursue their case via the Pensions Advisory Service.

The Age Discrimination Regulations set out a number of areas where pension schemes are exempt. These are explained in guidelines issues by the Department of Trade. According to the guidelines, some of these are changes that might be made to a scheme in order to reduce a deficit, including:

- setting minimum and maximum ages for joining, including setting different ages for different groups of workers;
- setting different member contribution levels according to age – as long as these reflect the increased costs of providing pensions to older workers and the accrual rate is the same for all members;
- closure of a scheme to new members, whether or not the employer offers an alternative arrangement for new joiners; or
- setting up a hybrid scheme with different levels of benefits and different minimum joining ages – for example, a defined contribution scheme for members aged 18 and over with the option to join a defined benefit scheme on reaching age 35.

In some cases an exemption applies to the employer but cannot be relied upon by the trustees. An example of this is where a scheme wishes to introduce a waiting period before which an employee is not eligible to join the pension scheme, in order to reduce future costs. Such a rule could be seen as indirect discrimination against younger workers and so would need to be objectively justified by the trustees.

Most employers will already have an equalities policy. In terms of consulting on scheme changes due to a deficit situation, this will set out what special adaptations need to be made to the consultation documents for people with special requirements. This could involve providing the material in a number of different languages or offering translation or interpretation services, large print, audio or Braille versions of written material.

## 3. Sample worked example of how members' benefits might be affected by proposed changes to a pension scheme.

**ABC Pension Scheme**

The following table shows future service pensions at different ages and different salaries according to whether:

- you continue to pay 5% contributions and your pension builds up at 1/70th of final pensionable salary a year; or
- you choose to pay 7% contributions and your pension builds up at 1/60th of final pensionable salary (as now).

These figures are for information only. If the change to the scheme goes ahead, you will be sent a personal statement showing how your benefits will be affected to help you make your decision. All figures are in today's terms and do not take account of any pension already built up in the scheme, any future salary increases or inflation.

| Years to retirement | 10 | | 15 | | 20 | | 25 | | 30 | | 35 | |
|---|---|---|---|---|---|---|---|---|---|---|---|---|
| | 1/60 | 1/70 | 1/60 | 1/70 | 1/60 | 1/70 | 1/60 | 1/70 | 1/60 | 1/70 | 1/60 | 1/70 |
| Salary | | | | | | | | | | | | |
| £15,000 | £2,500 | £2,143 | £3,750 | £3,214 | £5,000 | £4,286 | £6,250 | £5,357 | £7,500 | £6,429 | £8,750 | £7,500 |
| £20,000 | £3,333 | £2,857 | £5,000 | £4,286 | £6,667 | £5,714 | £8,333 | £7,143 | £10,000 | £8,571 | £11,667 | £10,000 |
| £25,000 | £4,167 | £3,571 | £6,250 | £5,357 | £8,333 | £7,143 | £10,417 | £8,929 | £12,500 | £10,714 | £14,583 | £12,500 |
| £30,000 | £5,000 | £4,286 | £7,500 | £6,429 | £10,000 | £8,571 | £12,500 | £10,714 | £15,000 | £12,857 | £17,500 | £15,000 |
| £35,000 | £5,833 | £5,000 | £8,750 | £7,500 | £11,667 | £10,000 | £14,583 | £12,500 | £17,500 | £15,000 | £20,417 | £17,500 |
| £40,000 | £6,667 | £5,714 | £10,000 | £8,571 | £13,333 | £11,429 | £16,667 | £14,286 | £20,000 | £17,143 | £23,333 | £20,000 |
| £45,000 | £7,500 | £6,429 | £11,250 | £9,643 | £15,000 | £12,857 | £18,750 | £16,071 | £22,500 | £19,286 | £26,250 | £22,500 |
| £50,000 | £8,333 | £7,143 | £12,500 | £10,714 | £16,667 | £14,286 | £20,833 | £17,857 | £25,000 | £21,429 | £29,167 | £25,000 |

# Issues in implementation: communications

**Sally Ling**
GR Comunications

---

## 1. Introduction

While employers are required to consult with employees on pensions matters, trustees are legally required to disclose information. Most go further, however, and set a programme of ongoing communication with their members which is designed to keep them informed and help them understand and value their pension benefits.

As with consultation, the legal requirements do not relate specifically to deficit situations. However, the Disclosure Regulations set out the general information that must be provided or made available to scheme members – including information about the scheme's finances. In addition, the Finance Act 2004 introduced a requirement to provide information, automatically to all members, about a scheme's funding position. Both of these legal requirements deal with information that must be made available to members no matter what the funding position of the scheme. Under the Disclosure Regulations, trustees must also inform members of any changes to scheme benefits.

As mentioned, many trustees will wish to go much further than simply complying with the basic requirements. It is much easier to deliver 'bad news' in an environment where members are used to receiving regular, clear information from the trustees about their scheme and feel confident about the way the scheme is being run. Trustees who do not have a regular dialogue with their members and find themselves having to communicate about a deficit will need to work hard to explain all the issues and why any proposed changes are required. They will need to plan carefully how to deliver the information so that members understand what is happening and why, and are equipped to make any necessary decisions.

There will often be cases where scheme members are receiving information from other sources and the trustees want to put across their side of the story. For example, where an employer is required to consult on proposed changes to a pension scheme, the trustees may wish to issue their own information. This could be because they have a different viewpoint which they wish to get across or simply wish to demonstrate that they are acting in the best interests of scheme beneficiaries. Once again, in organisations where there are active trade unions or other employee representation, the trustees might wish to issue information to members to ensure that they are getting the full picture and not just the union's angle on the issues. Often a union's initial standpoint will be to maintain the current benefit level at all costs. It might even go as far as to suggest that the deficit has arisen due to mismanagement. In such cases the trustees and, indeed, the employer may wish to join the debate.

In recent years, pension scheme deficits have gained extensive coverage in the national media. In particular, there have been some very high-profile company failures, leaving pension schemes with insufficient funds and long-serving employees with little or no pension. While a scheme's trustees cannot respond to every scare story, they may well wish to clarify the extent to which the problems discussed apply to their scheme. It is important to remember, however, that it is possible to over-communicate. Scheme members will not appreciate being swamped with communications that tell them nothing new. If they feel that the trustees have been open and honest with them so far, they will in most cases prefer to wait until there is some real news. In addition, the trustees will not want to be seen to be spending vast sums (in our experience, members generally vastly overestimate the cost of providing newsletters and the like) on design and print in order to tell members that their scheme is in financial difficulties.

## 2. Disclosure requirements

The key requirements on trustees to communicate with members are set out in the Pensions Act 1995 and the Disclosure Regulations. The Department of Work and Pensions has been consulting on simplifying these disclosure requirements, but at the time of writing has not yet published its recommendations.

The main requirements under the existing regulations that might be relevant in the context of dealing with deficits are outlined in the following table.

| Information | To whom | When |
|---|---|---|
| Scheme documents | Members, prospective members, their spouses, beneficiaries and trade unions | On request, within two months |
| Basic scheme information | Prospective members | Automatically, within two months of joining scheme |
| | Members, prospective members, their spouses, beneficiaries and trade unions | On request, within two months |
| Changes in basic scheme information | Members and beneficiaries | Automatically, within three months of the effective date of the change |
| Scheme annual report | Members, prospective members, their spouses, beneficiaries and trade unions | On request, within two months |
| Actuarial valuation, schedule of contributions, payment schedule and statement of investment principles | Members, prospective members, their spouses, beneficiaries and trade unions | On request, within two months |

Where the information must be supplied on request, trustees must make the documents available free of charge at a 'reasonable' location. If the applicant specifically requests a copy of the documents, the trustees may levy a charge for this, but only to cover the costs of copying, postage and packing. Where a copy of a document is provided, it must be accompanied by a note saying that further information is available and giving contact details.

The following aspects of the Disclosure Regulations could be seen to apply in a deficit situation:

- the requirement to provide information about scheme benefits and any proposed changes;
- the requirement to make financial information available to all members on request; and
- the requirement to make the results of actuarial valuations available to members.

In terms of scheme and benefit information, most trustees will issue this via a scheme guide. As well as outlining the benefits, this will generally:

- have information about how the scheme is funded;
- state that the assets are kept legally separate from those of the sponsoring employer; and
- give details of tax approval.

While legally, trustees can tell members about scheme changes after they have taken place as long as this is within three months, most will advise members in advance as a matter of good practice.

In terms of financial information, many trustees, especially those of larger pension schemes, go much further than the minimum required by the disclosure regulations. In such cases they will issue this information automatically every year to some or all members (this might be to active members only, to actives and pensioners/dependants or, more rarely, to all classes of member). Typically such a communication would take the form of a 'popular' or summarised version of the report and accounts. This will be issued directly to members at their home address or workplace. Information covered would include details of investments – who looks after them and how they have performed – income and expenditure, and often a comment on the outcome of the most recent actuarial valuation and where members can get more information. Where the valuation information is included, there would also be a statement of what the employer and the trustees are doing to deal with any deficit or surplus. Some schemes also produce a comparatively small quantity of 'glossy' versions of the full annual report and accounts – produced to the same standard as other pension communications material. This is then made available to members on request. Increasingly, trustees also produce versions of their summary reports in formats suitable for minority groups – large type, Braille or audio versions, or translated into one or more other languages.

Although trustees have long been required to make information available to scheme members about the scheme's valuation position, this task has been hampered by the myriad different ways of valuing the pension scheme. Pension schemes are required to test the scheme's funding position on a number of different bases, which can provide widely different results. For example, trustees could genuinely report that their scheme was fully funded on the minimum funding requirement basis (superseded by the statutory funding requirement) but be in deficit in terms of ongoing funding, Financial Reporting Standard 17 or on a buy-out basis.

## 3. Summary funding statements

Since April 2006 all funded private sector defined benefit pension schemes with 100 or more members have been required to issue a summary funding statement to their members. The deadline for the first such statement was September 21 2006. Thereafter, schemes are required to issue these statements annually.

Before schemes have completed their first actuarial valuation under the new scheme funding regime, trustees can base the summary funding statement on the most recent valuation information available. According to the DWP, the intention is that the summary funding statement "should be based simply on information required to comply with other aspects of the legislation or for another scheme purpose". Therefore, trustees are not required to undertake any additional reviews in order to establish whether the funding position has changed since the most recent valuation required under the now defunct minimum funding requirement. However, if the trustees are aware of any changes to the funding position since then – for example, if they have carried out a funding review for another purpose – this information must be included in the summary funding statement. This will then have to be updated every year until the first valuation is carried out on the new basis.

Once a scheme has completed its first valuation under the Pensions Act 2004, the trustees are required to issue the next summary funding statement "within a reasonable period" after they receive the valuation report. Although this period is not set out in the regulations, the Pensions Regulator has suggested that it should be no more than three months. From then on, the trustees are required to obtain an annual actuarial report, as at the anniversary of the valuation. This will outline any developments that have affected the scheme's funding position and these should be included in the subsequent summary funding statement.

An annual summary funding statement must be issued automatically to:

- active scheme members;
- pensioners and dependants in receipt of a pension;
- leavers with a deferred pension; and
- individuals with an entitlement to benefits under a pension sharing order (pension credit members).

For hybrid schemes which provide some members with defined benefit pensions and others with defined contribution arrangements, only those in the former section need be issued with a summary funding statement.

The exceptions are members with deferred pensions or pension credit members for whom the trustees do not have an address, if previous correspondence to the last known address has been returned.

## 4. Contents of the statement

The key contents of the summary funding statement are set out in the Disclosure Regulations, as amended by the 2005 Scheme Funding Regulations. These are as follows:

- a summary of the extent to which the assets of the scheme are adequate to cover its technical provisions (liabilities);
- an explanation of any change in the funding position of the scheme since the last summary funding statement (or the most recent valuation for the first summary funding statement);
- the actuary's estimate of the solvency position of the scheme as set out in the most recent valuation carried out under the 2004 Pensions Act;
- a summary of any recovery plan put in place to bring the funding back in line with the statutory funding requirement;

- details of any modifications to the plan made under the instructions of the Pensions Regulator;
- details of any payments made from a surplus in the scheme to the employer; and
- a statement saying where the member can obtain further information about the pension scheme.

In addition, the Pensions Regulator has published guidelines on the purpose of the statement and what should be included. According to the Pensions Regulator, "The statement will be the member's principal source of information on funding matters. Therefore trustees should make the document clear and comprehensible avoiding any undefined jargon." In the guidelines the Pensions Regulator suggests that the summary funding statement should include the following:

- an introductory paragraph stating that the purpose of the statement is to provide members with information about the scheme's funding position;
- an explanation that under defined benefit schemes, all moneys are invested in one central fund and members do not have individual 'pots' allocated to them;
- a note to suggest that any members thinking of leaving the scheme (perhaps because of its funding position) should take financial advice before doing so;
- a reminder that members should inform the trustees of any change of address;
- a summary of the scheme's investment policy;
- a reference to the Pension Protection Fund and the level of protection it offers;
- a list of relevant scheme documents which the member may request; and
- where the first summary funding statement is issued before the first valuation under the Pensions Act 2004 has taken place, a note of when the trustees expect to provide the first summary funding statement on the new basis.

## 5. Sample summary funding statements

The Pensions Regulator has posted sample summary funding statements on its website at www.thepensionsregulator.gov.uk. There are two versions – one for schemes issuing a summary funding statement before their first valuation under the Pensions Act 2004 (4b) and one for those issuing a summary funding statement after (4a).

While these are accepted as being helpful in providing a single reference point for the information that should be included, and some pension schemes have followed the format closely, there has been some criticism of them from within the pensions industry, including that:

- the example does not distinguish between what information is required under the regulations and what is suggested by the Pensions Regulator;
- the financial summary on the first page sets out the 'bad news' if a scheme is underfunded, but does not provide any context that might reassure scheme members (this is left to later); and

- the comment suggesting that members should take financial advice before leaving the scheme is alarmist, as members might interpret it as a sign to 'get out quick'.

The thinking behind the summary funding statement was to encourage openness and help members understand all the aspects of the pension scheme in order to make informed choices and plan for their retirement. The initial response from trustees, pensions managers and industry commentators has been that this is an additional exercise (and cost) to trustees which is not expected to add any immediate value for members (or make trustees' lives any easier). Schemes have reported an increase in calls to their helplines, especially from pensioners who are disturbed by the information they have received and are looking for reassurance that their pension payments will continue.

For many schemes this first summary funding statement exercise will be the first time they have communicated with members who have left with a deferred pension since they left the scheme. There are both positive and negative aspects to this – for example, the exercise will reveal the extent to which the address database for these members is out of date. Those deferreds who do receive the information might develop a new interest in the scheme and become more demanding of the trustees (eg, requesting benefit statements and transfer quotes).

There is no prescription as to how a summary funding statement should be delivered. Some schemes issue it as an addition to a regular communication (eg, a newsletter or benefit statement), while for others it is a new item in the communications calendar.

## 6. The benefits of communication

So far we have concentrated on what is legally required of trustees, rather than the potential benefits of communication. Obviously it is too late for those trustees who have not been in regular communication with their members to go back and rewrite history, but they might wish to put the new requirements into context. The main benefit of regular communication is that you can give people information in easy-to-digest chunks. You can also prepare the ground for bad news that you expect in the future. For example, most trustees will have some idea about the outcome of a valuation before the final report is available. Members can be given notice if there is likely to be a deficit for the first time or if a known deficit is expected to have increased. The trustees might wish to provide background information about why a valuation is required and what assumptions are used so that when the results are known, the members already have some background to the process. The communication setting out the valuation results can then concentrate on plans to improve the situation rather than explaining why it has arisen.

Trustees might also wish to prepare members for potential changes – to say that they expect to have to ask the employer for more money, for example – and to indicate what the compromise position might be if the employer is unable or unwilling to meet the full cost of making good the deficit. In such cases it is important to set out broad timescales so that members know what to expect and when. It is also essential to stick to those timescales, especially in terms of providing information. If things have not progressed at the expected speed, members need to be informed and told when they will hear more.

Trustees will wish to consider how much information to give to those sections to the membership who will not be affected by any changes. It is generally thought to be good practice, especially in the case of pensioners, to reassure them that they will not see any detriment to their benefits.

Where members have been primed for bad news, it may be hoped that they will be more understanding. Indeed, the evidence shows that while you would expect members to resist an increase in their scheme contributions, this is often supported where the members understand the issues – especially where they know that the employer is also bearing some of the additional cost. Trustees also reduce the risk of being accused of keeping members in the dark. Problems have arisen in the past where trustees have tried to dress up or gloss over problems in the hope that they will be resolved, only to find they have worsened and have become harder to explain.

It is important to make sure that the information is delivered in a manner that the majority of people can understand, especially as much information about scheme funding and how valuations are calculated is very technical. A successful approach is to present the key information (or that required by legislation) as succinctly as possible and accompany this with a question and answer sheet addressing the practical implications of the information. By anticipating members' questions and concerns and addressing them upfront, it is possible to save the administration team from an immediate deluge of questions. This format also allows the use of much less formal language than might be deemed necessary for the purely information part of the communication.

## 7. Issues for multi-employer schemes

The trustees of multi-employer schemes have an additional audience for any communications on deficits: the employers, which may be asked to increase their contributions or approve benefit changes. In such cases it is important, once again, to be open and to give sufficient notice of any potential change for the employers to consider the implications of any proposed change and take advice where necessary.

## 8. Communicating change

Many companies are changing the benefit structure of their pension scheme in order to manage their future financial commitment and make good an existing deficit. This could be by:

- closing the scheme to new members;
- increasing member contributions;
- reducing future benefits for existing members; or
- ceasing accrual of benefits within the scheme for all members and, say, offering to contribute towards a stakeholder pension (this list is by no means exhaustive).

In such cases the trustees will need to let the members know what is happening, and set out the timetable for change and what action they need to take and by when. The members will most likely be expecting a change, having been consulted by their employer. However, the trustees are obliged to provide information on scheme changes under the Disclosure Regulations. Most will, of course, wish to go much further than simply complying with the letter of the law.

This needs to be carefully planned, in terms of both how and when the information is to be delivered and what follow-up there will be. If it is simply a case of telling members that their future service benefits will be reduced, this is relatively straightforward, as no action is requested. It is where members have a choice that there are additional considerations, such as the following:

- What is the default position if members do not respond?
- Do you remind those members who have not replied and, if so, how often?
- What options do members have after the deadline for making a decision has passed?
- What additional guidance should be offered to members to help them make their decision (eg, road shows/presentations, independent financial advice, personal illustrations, web-based modellers, telephone help lines)?

In such circumstances, the quality of the communications and support given to members could make the difference between a workforce that values the pension their employer provides and has expectations of a reasonable retirement income and one that is disillusioned, even resentful, and loses out on a potentially valuable benefit.

# The Pensions Regulator and the Pension Protection Fund

**Andrew Powell**
**Frances Phillips Taft**
Hammonds

---

## 1. The Pensions Act 2004

The Pensions Act 2004 came into force in the United Kingdom on April 6 2005 and has precipitated the most substantial change to pensions law and practice since the Pensions Act 1995. The provisions provide a statutory framework for the government's proposals for pensions reform, originally outlined in a green paper issued in December 2002, and form part of a wider package of measures for restructuring the basis of state and private pension provision.

The act introduces many important changes to pensions regulation, including:

- new scheme-specific funding requirements;
- a new Pensions Regulator armed with wide powers to protect members' interests; and
- the introduction of a Pension Protection Fund (PPF) to meet certain benefits in the event of scheme failure.

Together with the government's tax simplification proposals contained in the Finance Act 2004, the act radically alters the conditions under which UK occupational pension schemes (and defined benefit schemes in particular) operate.

## 2. Corporate transactions

The act has changed the nature of occupational pensions risk and the way companies in the United Kingdom engage in corporate activity, and has made dramatic changes to the corporate landscape. It introduces the Pensions Regulator, providing it with wide powers to prevent the avoidance of defined benefit pension scheme liabilities by associated or connected individuals and employers.

Under the act, the Pensions Regulator is given the responsibility for protecting defined benefit pension schemes, and has the ability to impose a number of obligations on buyers and sellers alike which are triggered by common corporate actions, such as changes of control, sales of group companies, debt restructurings and special dividends or returns of capital. UK companies need clearance from the Pensions Regulator before they can proceed with a corporate transaction to ensure that they and any associated or connected person are not at risk of the consequences of the Pensions Regulator's statutory powers, outlined below. These powers are designed to ensure that the pension scheme member benefits are protected to an extent that the regulator and the scheme trustees consider reasonable in the circumstances of each transaction. This has added a new dynamic to transactions, particularly to private equity deals, and has intensified price negotiations. Consequently, potential pensions issues have been catapulted to the top of the corporate finance agenda and into the media spotlight.

Pensions have become pivotal in corporate restructuring as pension deficits have increased significantly because of declining equity markets, low interest rates and increased longevity. The Pensions Regulator, by the utilisation of the so-called 'moral hazard' provisions included in the act – known as 'financial support directions' and 'contribution notices' – has the power to hold directors, shareholders and other connected/associated companies, purchasers and lenders liable for the pensions deficit. Ultimately, if certain conditions are met, the corporate veil may be pierced and the potential risk is significant. The parties can request clearance from the Pensions Regulator which gives them comfort that a financial support direction or contribution notice will not be issued.

In light of the changes in legislation, organisations acquiring a UK company where the scheme is in deficit are determining the willingness of the seller to accept the implications on value and seeking to adjust the sale price accordingly. The market trend is developing so as to treat the deficit effectively as debt, valued on the accounting Financial Reporting Standard (FRS) 17/International Accounting Standard (IAS) 19 basis. However, this is ultimately a negotiation between a number of parties (eg, buyer, seller and the pension trustees). Given that there are a number of different valuation approaches that can be taken, there are often diametrically opposed views taken during negotiations which can ultimately make or break a corporate deal. The purchaser should be aware that its liability in relation to accrued pension rights will ultimately have to be met in full. In certain circumstances, such as a scheme wind-up, this may well prove to be the buy-out cost.

## 3. The Pensions Regulator

The Pensions Regulator is now established as the replacement authority for the Occupational Pensions Regulatory Authority (OPRA), which formerly regulated UK occupational pension schemes.

OPRA's powers were limited by the Pensions Act 1995 as it could take action in response to reported problems with pension schemes, but did not have the power to order schemes to put things right or to intervene proactively. It was decided that a more proactive, risk-based and flexible approach was required to regulate work-based pension schemes. Therefore, the government recommended the establishment of a new regulator with wider powers. Primarily to comply with the Human Rights Act 1998 and the recommendations of the Higgs Report on the role and effectiveness of non-executive directors, the structure of the Pensions Regulator differs from that of OPRA. It comprises a board, a committee to discharge the regulator's non-executive functions and a Determinations Panel. The role of the Pensions Regulator is to regulate work-based pension schemes with key objectives of protecting the interests of scheme members, promoting good administration and reducing the risk of claims on the PPF. It focuses its attention on finding and dealing with the greatest risks to members' benefits.

The Pensions Regulator has the following main objectives:

- to improve the security of members' benefits and to protect the benefits of occupational and personal pension scheme members;
- to reduce the risk of situations arising that lead to claims on the PPF, focusing its attention on finding and dealing with the greatest risks to members' benefits; and
- to work with trustees and scheme managers to raise standards of scheme administration to promote and improve understanding of the good administration of work-based pension schemes.

In order to meet its objectives, the Pensions Regulator has a number of unprecedented powers which broadly fall into three categories:

- investigative powers;
- the power to put things right; and
- the power to prevent employers avoiding their pension obligations.

In addition to the powers inherited from OPRA, the Pensions Act 2004 extends the powers available to the Pensions Regulator by enabling it to adopt a proportionate, flexible and proactive approach to regulating pension schemes.

The Pensions Regulator may:

- issue 'improvement notices' or 'third-party notices' to individuals who it believes are responsible for a plan's failure to comply with its statutory duties. These notices will set out what remedial action must be taken, and by when. Individuals may also be required to report back to the regulator on their progress. Those who fail to comply with such a notice, without a reasonable excuse, may face a civil penalty of up to £5,000;
- apply to the High Court for an injunction against any individuals whom it suspects of misusing or misappropriating plan assets. The court may order these individuals personally to make good any loss;
- intercede to recover any outstanding employer contributions, where the trustees or managers of a plan are unwilling to do so;
- 'freeze' any plan that is at risk, while conducting an investigation and deciding whether to wind it up in the interests of the members;
- impose a schedule of contributions, modify a plan's future benefit accrual or dictate how the plan should calculate the amount of its liabilities if the trustees and employer fail to agree on the relevant funding principles; and
- issue contribution notices, financial support directions and restoration orders.

The Pensions Act 2004 also imposes a statutory obligation on whistleblowers to report suspected breaches of the legislation.

In addition, the Pensions Regulator has the power to collect more detailed scheme information in order to assess any risk, to take action to reduce or remove the risk through, for example, demanding additional contributions to the plan.

Moreover, the Pensions Regulator is authorised to make claims against third parties who are 'connected' or 'associated' with the employer for funding shortfalls, in certain circumstances, in the defined benefit pension plan (the 'moral hazard' provisions). Recipients – which can, in some cases involving a contribution notice, include individuals and company directors – may ultimately be held personally liable and thus unable to hide behind the corporate veil. In certain circumstances, the regulator also has the power to require that a group of companies jointly and severally – or the parent company alone – assume responsibility for funding the scheme of a group company.

Unsurprisingly, the regulator has stated that it places particular importance on its statutory obligation to protect the PPF and shares interests in action that reduces funding deficits and the risk of employers avoiding their liability for these deficits. The regulator and the PPF also have a shared interest in schemes in the PPF assessment period and in data on the funding and solvency position of pension schemes and employers. The regulator also acts as the PPF's agent in collecting its levies from defined benefit pension schemes.

## 4. The Pensions Regulator and scheme funding

One of the more immediate challenges of the regulator is to strengthen the funding of defined benefit schemes. For various reasons (including market conditions and the increased lifespan of members) in recent years, many defined benefit schemes have developed funding shortfalls.

The act establishes statutory funding rules for defined benefit plans and establishes a PPF (similar to the Pension Benefit Guaranty Corporation in the United States) to compensate members of under-funded pension plans where the sponsoring company is deemed insolvent. A primary reason for its enactment was to ensure that occupational pension plans are sufficiently well funded to meet their liabilities.

There have been instances of employers becoming insolvent, leaving insufficient funds in their defined benefit pension scheme to meet the pensions promise. In some scenarios members received only a small fraction of the benefits due. The establishment of the PPF reduces the potential adverse consequences of under-funding for members by providing compensation for most, but not all, benefits in the event of employer insolvency. It does this, however, by spreading the risks across the whole defined benefit sector by means of a series of levies, which mean that employers in all but the best-funded defined benefit pension plans ultimately have to provide the funding to cover the risks to the PPF arising from funding shortfalls in the less well-funded schemes.

## 5. Scheme funding

Part 3 of the Pensions Act 2004 introduces a new funding framework for defined benefit pension schemes. The new framework, which replaces the minimum funding requirement, is being phased in, as scheme valuations fall due, over the period September 2005 to December 2009.

The long-term objective of the Pensions Regulator is to strengthen scheme funding through the effective implementation of the scheme-specific funding framework. The regulator expects that schemes will become progressively better funded over time. This in turn should have the effect of reducing the total risk to members' benefits and the PPF, and should also reduce the PPF's estimation of total risk used to calculate the annual levy and reduce costs to levy payers.

The regulator's approach to scheme funding is to:

- promote, through codes of practice and other forms of communication, good understanding among trustees, employers and their advisers of the matters they should consider when they agree their scheme's statutory funding objective and any recovery plan needed to raise funding to that level;
- influence key parties through a regulatory approach to scheme funding;
- ensure that the messages are widely spread through a communication programme, including workshops, speaking engagements and so on; and
- intervene in specific schemes where the funding objective or recovery plan is (or may be) agreed at an inappropriate level or duration in respect of the objective aimed for protecting members' benefits and reducing risks to the PPF.

To ensure that appropriate scheme funding arrangements are put in place, the regulator is focusing in particular on the technical provisions and recovery plans agreed by trustees and employers, together with those cases where no agreement has been reached. The regulator will challenge those arrangements where the technical provisions are not prudent or the recovery plan is inappropriate. In particular, it will review the specific circumstances of the scheme, especially the strength of the employer and its ability to pay off the shortfall, and the scheme's maturity. To achieve this, it will focus attention on those schemes that pose the greatest risk and will use a filter mechanism based on triggers to identify schemes whose funding plans seem more likely to be based on imprudent or inappropriate assumptions. These triggers relate separately to the technical provisions and the recovery plans, recognising that they are interlinked.

The criteria which will inform this assessment will be derived from some, or all, of the following:

- the likelihood that the trustees did not set prudent technical provisions or prepare an appropriate recovery plan;
- the potential impact on both members' benefits and the PPF; and
- an assessment of how likely intervention is to protect those interests.

The purpose of a further assessment of the scheme will be to identify those schemes where the trustees have made either imprudent or inappropriate funding decisions, so that the regulator can intervene, whether informally or by using its statutory powers, and achieve an improvement in the outcome.

## 6. Technical provisions

The technical provisions help the regulator identify those schemes where it may be necessary to take a closer look at how the trustees have determined their technical decisions. In setting this trigger the following may be taken into account:

- that neither the government nor the regulator requires ongoing schemes to fund to the solvency (full buy-out) level whereby all accrued liabilities could be secured immediately by the purchase of insurance policies;

- that trustees should have had regard to scheme-specific factors such as the strength of the employer's covenant and scheme maturity when determining a funding strategy for the scheme;
- the value placed on pension liabilities by employers in company accounts in accordance with FRS17 or IAS19. Research undertaken for the Pensions Regulator by PricewaterhouseCoopers shows that the equity markets have already largely factored in much of the impact of FRS17;
- the funding level that would be required to secure the level of benefits that the PPF would provide in the event of employer insolvency. The regulator has a statutory objective to reduce the risk of calls on the PPF and that risk is spread across all schemes (and ultimately employers) which pay levies to the PPF; and
- that the legislation translates into UK law the requirement of the EU Pensions Directive that schemes should be fully funded against their technical provisions.

When making an initial assessment of the adequacy of technical provisions, the regulator will compare these with a range between two liability values: the Section 179 liability and the FRS17 liability (IAS19 liability, where available), irrespective of which of the two is higher. Whether a scheme triggers concerns because of where it falls within the range will depend on its maturity and the employer's strength. The trigger point for a relatively mature scheme with a weak employer is likely to be set towards the higher of the two values. Conversely, the trigger point for a relatively immature scheme with a strong employer is likely to be towards the lower of the two values. The regulator's guidance states that it will use externally available information, including information from credit rating agencies, to assess the strength of the employer's covenant in the first instance.

As part of the filter, the regulator will also apply a sense check to the FRS17 and Section 179 figures using other available information, including buy-out valuations.

According to the regulator, defining the technical provision trigger as a range between Section 179 and FRS17/IAS19 liability values does not mean that either of these values is to be used as a funding target. Nor does it mean that schemes have to change their investment strategy. The use of a prudent discount rate for technical provisions does not necessarily require trustees to adopt the same assumptions for their investment strategy, as long as they are comfortable with the employer's covenant and have allowed for the risk that the employer may not be able to cope with any adverse experience.

The reality is that it will point trustees in the direction of precisely these considerations.

## 7. The 'moral hazard' provisions of the Pensions Act 2004

One of the Pension Regulator's main objectives is to reduce the risk of financial calls on the PPF. The purpose of the act's so-called 'moral hazard' provisions is to reduce the likelihood of pension liabilities being transferred to the PPF and to deal with scenarios in which the regulator believes that an employer is deliberately avoiding its pension obligations. To enforce this, the regulator has the power to:

- issue a contribution notice against any 'associated' or 'connected' person of any employer who has been involved in a deliberate act or failure to act, the main purpose of which was to avoid pension liabilities; and/or
- issue a financial support direction to any 'associated' or 'connected' person[1] of any employer to put in place arrangements to guarantee the pension liability of an employer which is 'insufficiently resourced' or which is a 'service company' (a company is a service company if its revenues are mainly derived from providing employees to other companies in the same group).

## 8. Notifiable events

From April 6 2005 employers and trustees are subject to a number of new requirements for reporting. Trustees and employers are required to notify the Pensions Regulator of certain events which may indicate a risk of a claim on the PPF. These events are listed at the end of this chapter. The reporting form to use can be found at www.pensionsregulator.gov.uk/pdf/reportformnotifiableevents.pdf.

Failure to comply could result in the imposition of civil penalties. The regulator intends that this will act as an early-warning system to help identify situations that might result in a call being made on the PPF. Regulations set out what constitutes a notifiable event, and a code of practice and directions set out when the trustees or employer must notify the Pensions Regulator of such an event. An event must be notified in writing as soon as reasonably practicable. What is reasonably practicable depends on the circumstances, although in all cases it implies urgency.

## 9. Financial support directions

The Pensions Regulator may issue a financial support direction if it is satisfied that an employer sponsoring or participating in a pension scheme either is a service company or is 'insufficiently resourced'. An employer is insufficiently resourced if the value of its resources is less than 50% of its estimated Section 75 liability and the value of the resources of a connected or associated person (but not individuals, except in limited specified circumstances) when added to the employer's resources would be 50% or more of the estimated Section 75 liability. No act or omission is required, but the regulator may issue a financial support direction only if it considers it reasonable to do so.

In deciding whether to issue a financial support direction, the regulator must have regard to the following:

- the relationship that the person had with the employer (including whether the person has control);
- the benefit received by the person from the employer;

1 The terms 'connected' and 'associated' are broadly defined and include directors and 'shadow directors' (ie, persons or entities that effectively exercise control of a company even though not directors) of a company and all companies in a corporate group (and shareholders holding 33 1/3% or more of the voting rights). However, a financial support direction may not be served on an individual director or shadow director.

- any involvement the person had with the pension scheme; and
- the person's financial circumstances.

The person issued with a financial support direction will, subject to the outcome of any appeal to the Pensions Regulator Tribunal, have to put in place financial support. This may include arrangements under which:

- all the companies within the employer's group are jointly and severally liable for the whole or part of the employer's pension liabilities in relation to the scheme;
- the holding company of the employer's group is liable for the whole or part of the employer's pension liabilities; and/or
- other forms of support, such as bank guarantees, may constitute financial support.

The regulator may issue a financial support detection which relates to any given point in time in the 12 months preceding the dates of the determination.

The regulator may issue a contribution notice if a financial support direction is not complied with.

## 10. Contribution notices

The Pensions Regulator can issue a contribution notice requiring a person to pay either the whole or a specified proportion of the Section 75 funding shortfall in a scheme.

The regulator may issue a contribution notice if it considers that there was an act or deliberate failure to act and the main purpose or one of the main purposes of that act or failure to act was:

- to prevent the recovery of the whole or any part of a debt under Section 75 of the Pensions Act 1995 which was due or might become due from the employer; or
- otherwise than in good faith, to prevent such a debt becoming due, to compromise or otherwise settle such a debt, or to reduce the amount of such a debt.

Broadly, a Section 75 debt occurs:

- on the cessation of an employer's participation in a pension scheme (technically, on the employer ceasing to employ employees in the category of employment to which the scheme relates);
- on the winding-up of a pension scheme;
- on the occurrence of an insolvency event in relation to the employer; and
- where the pension scheme is under-funded, on specified actuarial bases.

When determining whether it is reasonable to issue a contribution notice to a person, the regulator must have regard to such matters as it considers relevant, including the following:

- the degree of involvement of the person in the act or failure to act;
- the relationship which the person has or had with the employer (including

whether the person has control);
- the purposes of the act or failure to act (including whether a purpose of the act or failure was to prevent or limit loss of employment); and/or
- the financial circumstances of the person.

The regulator can review any act or failure to act up to six years after the act or failure to act, but may not go back before April 27 2004.

## 11. Clearance procedures

A clearance procedure is available for parties that seek comfort that they will not be the recipient of a contribution notice or financial support direction in respect of a specified transaction or series of transactions. Unlike 'notifiable events', clearance is optional. It covers a range of commercial activities, including any material changes to an employer's control structure.

Clearance is a procedure whereby a relevant party can seek a determination from the Pensions Regulator as to whether a given act, omission or set of circumstances would give rise to a contribution notice or financial support direction. Without clearance, the regulator could subsequently challenge corporate transactions and so, in order to provide employers with a degree of protection from this, the Pensions Act 2004 provides a voluntary process for seeking statutory clearance from the regulator before completion of certain corporate transactions. The relevant events are outlined at the end of the chapter. The application form to use can be found at www.pensionsregulator.gov.uk/pdf/clearanceapplicationform.doc.

The regulator has issued guidance as to when it may be appropriate to apply for clearance.[2] The guidance issued by the regulator categorises events affecting employers into three types, as follows.

### 11.1 Type A events

These are events for which, if the event is material, clearance is recommended, including:

- changes in priority (ie, the granting or extending of a fixed charge or floating charge);
- return of capital or reduction in company assets (ie, payment of dividends, share buy-backs, dividend strips, distributions in species, demergers); and
- changes in control structure (ie, a change in the parent company or ultimate holding company of an employer, or a change in connected or associated parties which could be subject to a financial support direction).

### 11.2 Type B events

These are events affecting an entity which are not financially detrimental to the ability of a pension scheme to meet its pension liabilities and will not lead to the regulator issuing a contribution notice or financial support direction. They include

2 At the time of going to press the Pensions Regulator has announced an intention to publish an updated guide to clearance.

the following, provided that none of the below involves a Type A event:

- company mergers and acquisitions, including the sale and purchase of assets, the sale of a non-employer subsidiary, privatisations and joint ventures;
- fundraising, including flotation and private placement, venture capital fundraising, rights issues and preference share issues, unsecured debt; and
- other contractual negotiations, such as operating or finance lease operations.

### 11.3 Type C events

These are events which point towards a deterioration in the employer's covenant, whether inside or outside the control of the company or its directors (eg, the loss of a major customer). Some type C events may require clearance.

When there is a significant weakening in the employer's covenant as a result of a corporate transaction – for example, where a highly leveraged transaction occurs and/or assets are being removed from the employer group – the regulator has advised (in a May 2007 press release) that clearance would be an appropriate consideration, irrespective of the funding position of a scheme.

## 12. Record keeping

On identification that an event has happened, an audit trail should be started which may include all internal correspondence. Any communication with the Pensions Regulator should be included (eg, forms), along with responses. Where reporting is voluntary, any decision not to report, along with reasons, should be recorded. In particular, a register should be maintained to keep a record of all breaches, whether reported or not, that can be considered when deciding whether a subsequent breach should be reported.

## 13. Timing

Those events for which there is a reporting requirement will generally be dealt with "as soon as reasonably practicable" – meaning days rather than weeks. Where reporting is voluntary, the timescales will be decided by the persons responsible for making the decision to notify the Pensions Regulator.

## 14. Internal reporting/review

The employer and the trustees shall share information in accordance with the information protocol. There should be a standing agenda item for all trustees' meetings of "events covered by the Pensions Regulator reporting framework" to provide an opportunity for the trustees to be briefed on particular events affecting the scheme.

## 15. Appeals

Any decision or determination made by the determinations panel or a Pensions Regulator staff member can be appealed. An aggrieved person has 28 days from the date of notification of the decision to make an appeal. An appeal is made to the Pensions Regulator Tribunal and is called a 'reference'.

## 16. The PPF

The PPF is a statutory fund run by the board of the PPF, a statutory corporation established under the provisions of the Pensions Act 2004. It has been established to pay compensation to members of eligible defined benefit and hybrid occupational pension schemes where an employer has become insolvent and where there are insufficient assets in the pension scheme to cover PPF levels of compensation.

Provided that certain conditions are met, the PPF will take over the assets of a pension scheme and pay compensation to eligible individuals. Funding will be provided through assets held and through an annual levy on defined benefit and hybrid schemes.

The PPF board is also responsible for payment of compensation to all types of pension scheme where they suffer a loss caused by dishonesty, including fraud and all types of misappropriation of assets. This compensation will be funded by a separate levy on occupational pension schemes.[3]

However, the key aim of the PPF is to protect private sector defined benefit scheme members whose scheme is stricken. As described below, compulsory annual levies are charged on all eligible schemes. The PPF will assume responsibility for a pension scheme only where a qualifying insolvency event has occurred in relation to an eligible pension scheme and;

- a pension scheme has not been rescued (eg, by a sale of the insolvent employer as a going concern with a new employer taking over the funding obligation); and
- the valuation of the pension scheme shows that the assets of the pension scheme are below the PPF fund level of protected liabilities.

Where these conditions are not met, the PPF will cease to be involved with the pension scheme once the relevant processes and procedures have been completed. Where these conditions are met, the PPF will assume responsibility for the pension scheme and compensation will then become payable to its members.

Compensation payments will be funded by:

- assets transferred from schemes for which the PPF has assumed responsibility;
- an annual levy raised from eligible pension schemes;
- cash/assets recovered from insolvent sponsoring employers; and
- returns on PPF investments.

## 17. Levies

The PPF is to be partly funded by levies that will be imposed on the trustees, managers or other prescribed persons of eligible schemes. There are various categories of levy payable under the act.

The first category is the 'initial levy', which will apply for approximately one year following the introduction of the PPF.

The second are the 'pension protection levies', which can be either risk-based or scheme-based.

---

3 Fraud upon a defined contribution plan is the one instance in which a debt may fall upon the provider of such a plan. If the employer cannot meet the debt, then the compensation scheme is involved.

The initial levy and the pension protection levies are payable to the PPF board by the trustees or managers of a scheme.[4] The PPF board or the Pensions Regulator (if the board so determines) may recover any outstanding levies. The board is also responsible for deciding which schemes the levies will apply to and the amount of the levies, and for notifying the persons who are liable to pay the levies of how much they are liable to pay and when they must pay. The board may require the regulator to carry out these functions on its behalf.

In addition to the two categories of levy referred to above, the act introduces an 'administration levy' and a 'fraud compensation levy'. The administration levy will be applied to schemes to cover the set-up and ongoing costs of the PPF and the PPF ombudsman. The fraud compensation levy will replace the Pensions Compensation Board levy and will be paid by both defined benefit and defined contribution schemes.

The PPF levy for the year to March 31 2006, referred to as the initial levy, was simply based on scheme membership. From April 2006, the PPF levy is known as the pension protection levy and has comprised both a scheme-based and a risk-based component. The PPF board has now published its estimate of the total pension protection levy that needs to be collected in the 2006 financial year; this is at £575 million and is somewhat higher than the initial estimate of £300 million. Of the total pension protection levy, 20% will be collected as a scheme-based levy and 80% collected as a risk-based levy. Both the scheme-based and risk-based components will be based on the value of PPF liabilities.

## 18. PPF liabilities

Compensation will not be as generous as the full scheme benefits, with the level of compensation depending on whether the member is under or over normal retirement age at the date of the insolvency event.

The rules are complex, so the following is a very high-level summary:

- For members over normal retirement age, the main impact will be the loss of all future increases on all pre-1997 pension (including guaranteed minimum pension), with post-1997 pension receiving future pension increases at 2.5% or RPI if less. These rules for pension increases apply to all compensation once it comes into payment.
- For members under normal retirement age, the level of compensation is 90% of the member's accrued benefit and is subject to a cap. The cap will be increased each year in line with earnings and is applied at the time the compensation comes into payment. For members retiring at age 65 between April 2007 and March 2008, the combined effect of the 90% and the cap amounts to a maximum level of compensation of £26,935.70 per annum.

However, there is also a sting in the tail in how new groups are established. Those who retired early (ie, before their normal pension age) and have not reached normal

4 The act refers to any other person prescribed being able to pay the levy, though this has not yet been brought in force.

pension age at the date their scheme enters the PPF are, for the purpose of compensation, placed in the second group.

The value of the PPF liabilities is assessed as the buy-out cost (using the basis prescribed by the PPF) of the scheme's benefits adjusted, as set out above, to reflect the level of compensation that would be paid if the scheme entered the PPF at that date.

### 19. Scheme-based levy

For 2007/2008, the scheme-based levy will be equal to the scheme's PPF liabilities multiplied by a factor which has been set as 0.00016. For the 2005/06 levy year only, schemes were required to pay an initial levy based on scheme membership numbers.

### 20. Risk-based levy

The risk-based levy is assessed using the same approach as an insurance premium.

The probability of a claim on the PPF will depend on the likelihood of an insolvency event in the coming year. To assess this risk the PPF board has retained Dun & Bradstreet to measure the one-year probability of insolvency for participating employers of each eligible scheme. It has now been decided that 100 bands should be used to match with the Dun & Bradstreet failure scores of 1 to 100.

On September 11 2006 the PPF published a consultation document setting out proposals for the 2007/2008 risk-based levy. The proposed changes focus on the practical processes behind the levy, including:

- revised standard documentation for contingent assets;
- revised Section 179 guidance; and
- revised approach to the inclusion of insured liabilities within Section 179 valuations.

The documentation also highlights that the PPF board is working with Dun & Bradstreet to consider whether aspects of the Dun & Bradstreet methodology – such as the weighting applied to county court judgments, and the application of the methodology to certain types of employer such as large employers and the not-for-profit sector – need to be adjusted for the 2007/08 levy.

### 21. Contingent assets

The PPF board recognises that a number of trustees have improved the security of the scheme by obtaining a contingent asset, which will provide additional funding and/or financial protection for the scheme in the event that the sponsoring employer fails to comply with its funding obligations or becomes insolvent. The PPF board proposes that it will take certain types of contingent asset into account in determining the level of the risk-based levy, provided that they meet certain conditions, including being established using standardised forms of documentation (available at www.pensionprotectionfund.org.uk). Contingent assets established under non-standard documentation will not be taken into account in the risk-based levy calculation. The PPF has published its own documentation and guidance as to the contingent assets that it will recognise when calculating each scheme's risk-based levy for 2006/07 and beyond. For more information on this, see the PPF's website at www.pensionprotectionfund.org.uk/index/risk-based_levy.htm.

The Pensions Regulator's guidance is generally consistent with that of the PPF. Both the regulator and the PPF note the importance of the trustees in forming a judgement about the appropriateness of a contingent asset. The following types of contingent asset, however, can be taken into account when determining the risk-based levy:

- group company guarantees, provided the guarantee is to the pension scheme and not the sponsoring employer of that scheme, subject to certain acceptability criteria. Company guarantees will be recognised provided the group company is domiciled in an Organisation for Economic Cooperation and Development country. The guarantee must remain in force until all actual or contingent liabilities of the relevant employers to the scheme have been met. When calculating the levy, the insolvency risk of the sponsoring employer is adjusted to include credit for the insolvency risk of the guarantor;
- security provided over cash, real estate or securities. Such assets must be irrevocably available to the trustees upon the insolvency of the sponsoring employer(s). To be recognised for levy purposes, the protection offered by the contingent assets must remain constant over time. These assets are effectively treated no differently from assets of the scheme and full credit is given when determining the risk-based levy. The assets are valued at market value and revalued annually. However, security over stock or work in progress and intangible assets cannot be taken into account for the purposes of the PPF levy; and
- letters of credit and bank guarantees that are structured to have a minimum 12-month maturity. Counterparties would need to satisfy certain financial strength conditions (ie, be rated at least AA3 by Moody's and/or AA- by Standard & Poor's or Fitch). The asset should be renewable annually. Credit default swaps cannot be taken into account for the purposes of the PPF levy.

Trustees will be required to certify that the contingent assets they wish to be taken into account are in the standard form and are legally valid, binding and enforceable. The trustees will also be required to obtain a legal opinion to satisfy themselves that this is the case, and to provide a copy of that opinion to the PPF board.

## 22. Assessment period

If a qualifying insolvency event occurs in relation to an employer of an eligible scheme, this will trigger the beginning of an assessment period. During this period the PPF will assess whether it must assume responsibility for the scheme.

The assessment period will allow the PPF to determine whether a scheme is eligible for entry. During this period the scheme continues to be administered by its trustees, subject to various restrictions and controls.

During the assessment period the PPF will look to establish the answer to two main questions:

- Can the scheme be rescued? (For example, can the original employer continue as a going concern, or is another employer going to take the original employer over and assume responsibility for the scheme?)

- Can the scheme afford to secure benefits which are at least equal to the compensation that the PPF would pay if it assumed responsibility for the scheme?

If the answer to either of these questions is 'yes', then the PPF will cease to be involved with the scheme once the relevant processes and procedures have been completed.

However, if the answer to both the questions is 'no', and the relevant processes and procedures have been completed, then the PPF will assume responsibility for the scheme and compensation will then become payable.

A PPF assessment period must last a minimum of one year and could well last longer in many cases, depending on the complexity of the financial situation of both the employer and the scheme, and the possibility of a scheme rescue.

During an assessment period, the PPF will undertake a monitoring role in relation to the trustees of the scheme. This is to ensure that the trustees maintain the scheme in an appropriate manner for potential entry into the PPF. In certain circumstances, the PPF can issue directions to trustees in relation to areas such as the investment of the scheme's assets, the incurring of expenditure and the bringing or conduct of legal proceedings.

The PPF will also monitor the progress of the insolvency proceedings, liaising closely with the insolvency practitioner. Where the PPF ultimately assumes responsibility for a scheme, arrangements will then be made to pay compensation to the scheme members.

The following schemes have gone through a PPF assessment.

### 22.1 Heath Lambert Group pension scheme

The Heath Lambert Group pension scheme was the first application that the Pensions Regulator considered. In June 2005 the regulator agreed a deal whereby insurance brokerage group Heath Lambert effectively restructured itself out of insolvency, placing its defined benefits pension arrangements into the PPF, and the PPF took an equity stake in the new Heath Lambert Company formed from the ashes of the former group. At the time the regulator 'cleared' the Heath Lambert deal from a pensions perspective, stating that one of the regulator's main tasks is to try to save jobs in sponsor companies. The regulator said it may in appropriate circumstances allow companies which would be able to trade were it not for their pension debts to go into administration with a view to transferring their liabilities to the PPF. However, the circumstances in the case were unusual. The decision also elicited a great deal of criticism in the financial press (although much of it may be seen as improperly informed). Whether the same approach would be taken now is a moot point.

### 22.2 Swissport

Candover's sale of Swissport to Ferrovial for €664 million required a deal with trustees of Swissport's Heathrow pension scheme to be agreed. There was a reported £20 million deficit in Swissport's Heathrow pension scheme and Swissport's Heathrow business had already gone into administration. Candover injected £6 million into the pension scheme and allowed scheme members to choose between moving their benefits to another Swissport scheme or to a personal pension scheme and accepting that their benefits would be transferred to the PPF.

## 23. Conclusion

If a company is planning to merge with or acquire a UK company that sponsors a defined benefit scheme, it would be prudent for the company to put in place strategies to minimise the risk of the Pensions Regulator requiring cash injections, cross-company guarantees, the appointment of independent trustees or the ultimate wind-up of the scheme. These strategies would include:

- pricing the pensions risk properly;
- tackling the pensions issues in a deal early on (where appropriate);
- negotiating with the trustees and/or the regulator (although this will not necessarily always be appropriate);
- laying an 'audit trail' of the commercial rationale for the deal (this could help to ground an argument later that moral hazard intervention by the regulator would be unreasonable); and
- taking specialist advice.

Given the potential exposure, the implications are clear that sellers (and in some circumstances acquirers) of companies in the United Kingdom with defined benefit schemes should consider whether clearance is needed. Early identification of all relevant issues and communication with the regulator will be crucial to a successful outcome.

## 24. Appendix

### 24.1 Notifiable events – no conditions

| Event | Body responsible for making decision on action to take | Action |
|---|---|---|
| Decision by trustees to take action which will, or is intended to, result in any debt of 0.5% or more of the scheme's assets not being repaid in full to the scheme | Trustees | Notify the Pensions Regulator<br>Note: the Pensions Regulator needs to be notified prior to the final decision to compromise the debt |

| Event | Body responsible for making decision on action to take | Action |
|---|---|---|
| Decision by trustees to grant benefits or a right to benefits on more favourable terms than those provided for by the scheme's rules | Trustees | Seek advice from actuary and secure any additional funding he advises from employer OR notify the Pensions Regulator |
| Decision by employer to take action which will, or is intended to, result in a debt which is or which may become due not being repaid in full | Employer | Notify the Pensions Regulator |
| Change in employer's credit rating from investment grade to sub-investment grade | Employer | Notify the Pensions Regulator |
| Employer ceases to carry on business in the United Kingdom | Employer | Notify the Pensions Regulator |
| Receipt by employer of advice that it is trading wrongfully, or knowledge on the part of any director or former director of employer that there is no reasonable prospect of avoiding insolvent liquidation | Employer | Notify the Pensions Regulator |
| Dishonesty conviction of any director of employer where the offence was committed while the individual was a director of the employer | Employer | Notify the Pensions Regulator |

## 24.2 Notifiable events – conditions

| Event | Body responsible for making decision on action to take | Action |
|---|---|---|
| Decision by trustees to take action which will, or is intended to, result in any debt of less than 0.5% of the scheme's assets not being repaid in full to the scheme | Trustees (if applicable) | If conditions are not met, notify the Pensions Regulator |
| Two or more changes in the scheme's actuary or auditor within 12 months (or one of each) | Trustees (if applicable) | If conditions are not met, notify the Pensions Regulator |
| Decision by trustees to make a transfer out or accept a transfer in which exceeds the lower of 5% of the scheme's assets and £1.5 million | Trustees | Seek advice from actuary and/or scheme administrator as appropriate on any event that could potentially trigger this report. If conditions are not met, notify the Pensions Regulator |
| Decision by trustees to grant benefits or a right to benefits to a member, the cost of which exceeds the lower of 5% of the scheme's assets and £1.5 million | Trustees | Seek advice from actuary and/or scheme administrator as appropriate on any event that could potentially trigger this report. If conditions are not met, notify the Pensions Regulator |

| Event | Body responsible for making decision on action to take | Action |
|---|---|---|
| A breach of a banking covenant by the employer (except where the bank agrees not to enforce the covenant) | Employer | If conditions are not met, notify the Pensions Regulator |
| A change in employer's credit rating (apart from investment to sub-investment grade) | Employer | If conditions are not met, notify the Pensions Regulator |
| A decision by a controlling company to relinquish control of an employer | Employer | If conditions are not met, notify the Pensions Regulator |
| Two or more changes of the chief executive or of any director wholly or partly responsible for the financial affairs of the employer in a 12-month period (or one change in each category) | Employer | If conditions are not met, notify the Pensions Regulator |

## 24.3 Clearance

| Event | Body responsible for making decision on action to take | Action |
|---|---|---|
| Proposed action which would change the priority of employer creditors (eg, a new loan secured by a fixed or floating charge over existing employer assets) | Employer | Employer should consider requesting clearance from the Pensions Regulator if the fixed or floating charge will affect:<br>• more than 25% of the total assets of employer's group; or<br>• more than 25% of the total assets of employer.<br>It is recommended that the trustees be consulted first and their support obtained |

| Event | Body responsible for making decision on action to take | Action |
|---|---|---|
| Employer is considering returning capital (eg, through dividends, share buy-backs or as part of a demerger | Employer | Employer should consider requesting clearance from the Pensions Regulator if:<br>• the return of capital would reduce dividend cover to less than 1.25 times;<br>• the return is more than twice the average of the last three years return of capital;<br>• the return is outside the group or European Union or to an entity not subject to financial support directions; or<br>• the employer will have negative reserves after reflecting the deficit or making the return.<br>It is recommended that the trustees be consulted first and their support obtained |

| Event | Body responsible for making decision on action to take | Action |
|---|---|---|
| Employer is considering a change of ownership or some other change in structure | Employer | If the event is material (eg, if it is likely to affect negatively the employer's credit rating), employer should consider requesting clearance from the employer should consider requesting clearance from the Pensions Regulator. It is recommended that the trustees be consulted first and their support obtained |

# Moving a scheme into the Pension Protection Fund

**Kulin Patel**
Higham Dunnett Shaw

This chapter examines the way in which trustees typically transition insolvent employer pension schemes into the Pension Protection Fund (PPF). This transition is covered by Sections 120 to 171 of the Pensions Act 2004, together with the various associated regulations.

A useful start is to consider the process whereby entry to the PPF is gained for a simple, single employer pension scheme. This approach can then be developed through discussion of the various complexities that can arise.

**Illustration of the process for transition into the PPF (simplified)**

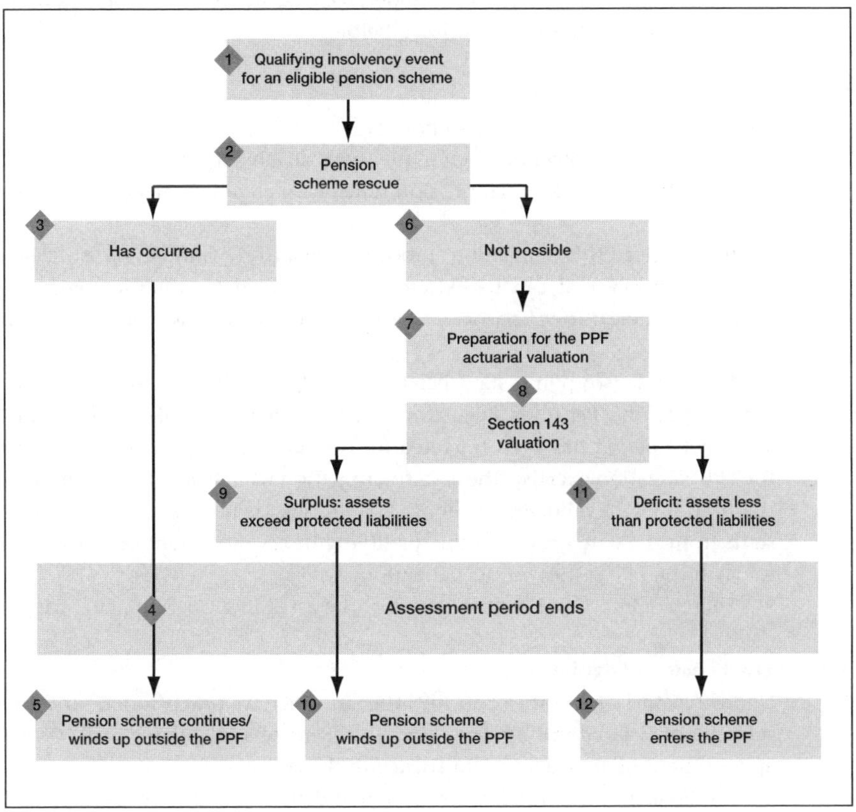

In practice, events may not take place in the sequence shown in the diagram. Instead, some may occur simultaneously, depending on the situation you are presented with.

In the explanation below, we discuss each stage of the process illustrated in the diagram above.

## 1. Occurrence of a qualifying insolvency event for an eligible scheme

The process begins when an employer that operates an occupational pension scheme enters some form of insolvency event as defined within the Pensions Act 2004 and corresponding regulations. The insolvency event must take place on or after April 6 2005.

The insolvency practitioner appointed to the employer is obliged to submit notification of the insolvency event to three parties:

- the PPF;
- the Pensions Regulator; and
- the scheme trustees.

This notification is called a 'Section 120' notice and must usually be submitted within 14 days of the insolvency practitioner becoming aware of the existence of the pension scheme.

Each of the three parties must undertake a particular course of action on receipt of the Section 120 notice, as outlined below.

### 1.1 The PPF

The PPF will seek to validate two points:

- Was the insolvency event a qualifying insolvency event?
- Was the occupational pension scheme an eligible scheme for PPF purposes?

In practice, this validation process is relatively simple for single-employer schemes. However, it can be extremely complicated for multi-employer schemes, especially where former participating employers withdrew from the scheme over time.

Once these two points have been validated, the PPF will write to the insolvency practitioner, the Pensions Regulator and the scheme trustees to confirm that an assessment period has been triggered for the scheme in question. Notwithstanding the PPF validation exercise, the assessment period will already have been triggered by the time the PPF validates the above points. This is because the assessment period starts from the date on which the qualifying insolvency event occurred, as opposed to when the PPF carries out its validations.

There are important consequences of the assessment period being triggered.

### 1.2 The Pensions Regulator

Upon receipt of notification by the insolvency practitioner, and following subsequent validation by the PPF, the Pensions Regulator will consider the appointment of an independent trustee to the scheme.

While such appointments are not mandatory, experience shows they are the norm, unless the scheme already has an appropriate independent trustee in place or the Pensions Regulator expects it to be able to pass through an assessment period using lay trustees alone.

From April 6 2005, the Pensions Regulator became the sole source of independent trustee appointments on employer insolvency. Moreover, these appointments must now draw upon one of the independent trustees listed on the Pensions Regulator's specialist panel of independent trustees.

### 1.3 The scheme trustees

The trustees will be keen to ensure they have the most appropriate team in place to help them transition the scheme through the assessment period and into the PPF in an efficient and cost-effective manner.

Upon receipt of the insolvency practitioner Section 120 notification and PPF validations, the scheme trustees review the appropriateness of their scheme advisers. Advisers reviewed typically include the scheme administrator, scheme actuary, pension consultant and legal adviser.

It is important to recognise that on entry to, as well as in preparation for, the PPF assessment period, the scheme takes on a new stage in its lifecycle. Specialist skills, as well as a different mindset from that used for ongoing schemes, are usually required within the assessment phase.

### 1.4 Consequences of a PPF assessment

Various consequences follow the trigger of a PPF assessment period. Three of the most significant are as follows.

#### *(a) PPF benefit levels*

Once in assessment, pensions must be paid at not more than PPF levels. This requirement applies from the very start of the assessment period (known as the 'assessment date'), despite the PPF validation exercise taking place at a later date.

In practice, this means:

- undertaking an early comparison of the current scheme benefit levels;
- comparing scheme benefit levels against PPF compensation levels; and
- making the appropriate adjustments to pay the lower of the two amounts.

Pensioners who retired early and who are still below their normal pension age at the assessment date are normally the first to be affected. They typically suffer an immediate restriction of their benefits up to the level of the PPF compensation cap (currently £29,928.56 per annum at age 65), followed by a further 10% scale-back. This results in a maximum pension of £26,935.70 per annum for those aged 65, a maximum of £24,394.51 per annum for those aged 60 and lower figures for earlier ages (for the 2007/08 financial year).

In practice, this benefit comparison and conversion to correct levels may take several months to perform and implement. Consequently, overpayments can emerge at the start of the assessment period which may need to be recovered during the assessment process.

*(b)* ***Creditor of the employer***

During the assessment period, the trustees remain responsible for the scheme in all aspects except one: the PPF takes over the responsibility as creditor of the employer for the purpose of the pension scheme. In practice, this means the PPF will:

- decide whether to commission a Section 75 'debt on employer' claim from the scheme actuary;
- arrange for the calculation to be performed;
- serve the Section 75 debt on the employer; and
- negotiate terms for the recovery of the debt.

In practice, the PPF may arrange for the trustees to take on some of these actions on its behalf, although the PPF retains overall responsibility for this area.

*(c)* ***PPF guidance to/feedback on trustees***

The PPF's assessment period teams help to guide the trustees through the assessment period. In particular, they will ensure trustees are aware of their responsibilities during PPF assessment and be keen that trustees have workable, realistic management plans in place.

The PPF also delivers feedback to the Pensions Regulator's trustee appointment teams on the performance of those trustees appointed from the Pensions Regulator's independent panel. This in turn enables the Pensions Regulator to gain intelligence and refine their appointment processes over time.

**2. Pension scheme rescue**

Following the notification that an insolvency event has occurred, the insolvency practitioner is now required to provide notification of the rescue position of the scheme. This notification is called a 'Section 122' notice and the same parties are notified as for the Section 120 notice.

In some cases, this notification may take place alongside the insolvency event notification. In other cases, it may take many months to provide confirmation of the rescue position, especially where negotiations may be taking place on the sale of the company involved. Unlike the Section 120 notice, there is no time limit imposed by the Pensions Act 2004 for receiving this notification.

The insolvency practitioner's notification will confirm one of three things:

- Scheme rescue has occurred;
- Scheme rescue is not possible; or
- Scheme rescue position is uncertain.

For PPF purposes, a 'scheme rescue' takes place when a sponsor retains responsibility for meeting the pension liabilities under the scheme. In this regard, pension liabilities relate to the entire scheme liabilities, as opposed to, for example, just the PPF levels. Because this is unlikely to happen regularly in practice, the majority of cases will result in a scheme rescue not being possible, which is also referred to as 'scheme failure'.

It is rare for the notification of the rescue position to be uncertain. This is because it is limited to those circumstances explicit within the PPF Entry Rules Regulations.

3. **Scheme rescue has occurred**

Notification of a scheme rescue occurring takes place when the insolvency practitioner issues a withdrawal notice to the PPF. Provided everything is in order, the PPF will then approve the withdrawal notice and issue a determination notice.

4. **Assessment period ends**

The PPF's determination notice becomes legally binding once any appeals in relation to it have been resolved. At that point, the PPF ceases to be involved with the scheme and the assessment period ends.

5. **Scheme continues outside PPF/winds up**

Once out of assessment, the scheme's future is back in the full control of the sponsoring employer and the scheme's trustees.

At this point, pension accrual may recommence, the scheme could continue in a paid-up state or a scheme wind-up could be triggered (the latter being unlikely as it would trigger a full buy-out Section 75 debt payable by the scheme's employers).

This route out of PPF assessment is usually positive news for the members concerned, as the sponsor has shown it is prepared to support the scheme going forward. Similarly, it is a favourable outcome for the PPF, since no compensation payments are necessary.

6. **Scheme rescue not possible**

As discussed under section 2 above, the insolvency practitioner issues a 'scheme failure' notice when scheme rescue is not possible. Provided everything is in order, the PPF will approve the scheme failure notice and issue a determination notice.

As before, the PPF's determination notice becomes legally binding once any appeals in relation to it have been exhausted. At this point, the scheme will ultimately need to be wound up or will enter the PPF in due course. The eventual outcome will depend on the results of the PPF actuarial valuation.

7. **Preparation for the PPF actuarial valuation**

The trustees are required to prepare the scheme for the PPF's actuarial valuation.

In practice, most of the preparation tasks can commence at an early stage in the assessment period. Normally, these will start prior to the PPF's determination notice in response to the insolvency practitioner's scheme failure notice becoming legally binding.

The preparation tasks will vary from scheme to scheme and will usually include some of the following:

- member tracing;
- pensioner existence checks;
- data cleaning; and
- reconciliation of guaranteed minimum pensions (where applicable).

The last two tasks often determine the length of the assessment period, which must last for a minimum of one year. There is no maximum length for an assessment period and, in particular, the reconciliation of a scheme's guaranteed minimum pensions with those held by Her Majesty's Revenue & Customs (HMRC) has traditionally been a time-consuming task. This stems from the labour-intensive nature of the work involved.

The introduction of the HMRC "Shared Workspace" initiative to facilitate more efficient guaranteed minimum pension reconciliation should help bring down average timescales in this area. Also, at least in theory, there is the power for the PPF to take on aspects of a scheme's guaranteed minimum pension reconciliation process – for example, towards the end of the reconciliation process when schemes may struggle to resolve the remaining queries needed to complete the reconciliation.

### 8. PPF obtains actuarial valuation (Section 143 valuation)

Once the preparation tasks described above are complete, the PPF is required to obtain its own valuation of the scheme. This valuation is commonly referred to as the 'Section 143' valuation, pursuant to that section of the Pensions Act 2004.

The valuation methodology is largely prescribed and full details can be obtained from the PPF's website. The valuation compares a scheme's assets with its protected liabilities.

For the purpose of the Section 143 valuation, a scheme's assets comprise the assets held at the assessment date, together with recoverable Section 75 debts. Any debts due from contribution notices, as well as obligations arising under financial support directions and from restoration orders, should also be taken into account.

The term 'protected liabilities' is taken to include three items:

- the cost of securing PPF levels of compensation for scheme members;
- those liabilities of the scheme which are not member-related liabilities; and
- the estimated cost of winding up the scheme.

Importantly, the effective date for the valuation is the assessment date, at the outset of the assessment period, as opposed to the date when the valuation is actually performed. In practice, this means that the Section 143 valuation results are likely to be a few years out of date.

The historical nature of the Section 143 valuation calculations means that a deficit emerging from the Section 143 valuation will lead to the scheme entering the PPF, regardless of the investment performance achieved by the trustees during the assessment period. However, the converse does not apply: a Section 143 valuation surplus does not necessarily mean the scheme will not enter the PPF. This is because the trustees have the ability to apply for reconsideration of their scheme at a later date, as discussed below.

Once the Section 143 valuation is produced, the PPF will consider the details. If it is satisfied with the Section 143 valuation, the PPF will approve it. The Section 143 valuation becomes legally binding once any appeals in relation to it have been settled.

Notably, legislation does not require the scheme actuary to perform the Section 143 valuation, although in practice he is involved in most cases.

## 9. Surplus displayed by the Section 143 valuation

The results of the Section 143 valuation will show that the scheme is in deficit, equilibrium or surplus on the prescribed valuation basis (following confirmation of scheme failure).

If the equilibrium position or a surplus emerges – in other words, if the scheme's assets are sufficient to support its protected liabilities – then the trustees are required to wind up the scheme. There is usually no option for the trustees to run the scheme on, unlike when scheme rescue takes place (although see below for two exceptions to this rule).

Winding-up secures members higher benefits than would otherwise have been possible through entry into the PPF. Moreover, the PPF can be absolved from underwriting the scheme should a deficiency emerge in the future.

There are two exceptions to the trustees having to wind up the scheme in this situation.

The first arises in the event that the scheme is too large to obtain a full buy-out quotation. If this is the case, the trustees must apply to the PPF for authority to continue as a 'closed scheme'.

Once PPF authorisation is granted, and despite the PPF assessment period having ceased, certain provisions that applied to the scheme during the assessment period will continue to apply (eg, no new members may join the scheme and no benefits may accrue). However, as assessment has formally ceased, there will be differences to observe (eg, the trustees are no longer to restrict scheme benefits to PPF levels).

Closed schemes are required to prepare regular valuations to monitor their funding position over time. Perhaps most importantly, closed schemes become eligible for possible PPF entry through 'reconsideration' (a term explained below). However, this is coupled with recommencement of the PPF levy.

The second exception to wind up arises in relation to the trustees applying to the PPF for 'reconsideration'. As discussed earlier, the effective date for the Section 143 valuation is at the outset of the assessment period, so the Section 143 valuation results are likely to be a few years out of date.

As a result of the historic nature of the Section 143 valuation, it is possible that during the assessment period, a scheme's assets may not keep pace with its liabilities. This could happen, for example, where buy-out rates have hardened during the assessment period. The practical effect of this is that situations might arise where a surplus on the (historic) Section 143 valuation compares with a deficit using insurers' buy-out costs of the same liabilities, measured at a current date. In this situation, the trustees may make an application to the PPF for it to resume responsibility for the scheme. As long as the application process is satisfied, the PPF has a duty to assume responsibility for the scheme following reconsideration.

## 10. Deficit displayed by the Section 143 valuation

If the binding Section 143 valuation displays a deficit – in other words, if the scheme's assets are insufficient to support its protected liabilities – the PPF will issue a transfer notice to the trustees.

The effect of the transfer notice is that the PPF will take over responsibility for the scheme and, in particular, for securing compensation to members in line with PPF levels.

**11. Assessment period ends**

As a result of the PPF's transfer notice, the scheme is treated as having been wound up at that time and the trustees are discharged from their pension obligations.

**12. Potential complexities**

Set out below are examples of complexities that may arise during the transition into the PPF.

12.1 **Multi-employer schemes**

*(a)* ***Last man standing***

For multi-employer schemes, triggering an assessment period can become complicated where the scheme operates on a last man standing basis.

Broadly speaking, in this context the term 'last man standing' for multi-employer schemes means that if a participating employer becomes insolvent, its pension liabilities are picked up by the remaining solvent employers within the scheme.

Multi-employer schemes operating on a last man standing basis normally require all current participating employers to become insolvent before the scheme can enter a (single) PPF assessment period.

However, this requirement implicitly assumes that all former participating employers that previously withdrew from the scheme have indeed settled any debts due on withdrawal. Otherwise, former participating employers may still be classified as current participating employers of the scheme. Understandably, the settlement of such withdrawal debts is of particular interest to the PPF.

The difficulty that some trustees face in this situation is that they cannot always provide the PPF with documentary evidence that historic withdrawal debts were actually settled by former participating employers. In some cases it can be difficult to determine whether such withdrawal debts were even calculated.

An amendment to the regulations issued by the Department of Work and Pensions in July 2005 went part of the way towards assisting the trustees with these issues. However, the need to understand the (historic) corporate framework, especially where restructuring and company name changes have taken place, can make the process of triggering a PPF assessment period particularly complex for pension schemes operating on a last man standing basis.

*(b)* ***Multiple assessment periods***

Multi-employer schemes operating on a segregated basis have their own unique complexities.

In this context, the term 'segregated' is, again broadly speaking, taken to mean that upon insolvency, the assets and liabilities of the insolvent employer are identified and then ringfenced within a new section of the scheme. This new section operates separately from the remaining solvent employers participating in the scheme and begins the transition into the PPF.

Since each segregated section is treated separately in terms of its transition into the PPF, it is possible that multiple assessment periods can be triggered for a given scheme. To illustrate this, there are already several separate sections of schemes which have triggered different PPF assessment periods, details of which are available from the PPF's website.

From a practical perspective, multiple assessment periods for closely related employers of a scheme operating on a segregated basis can require very careful communication with scheme members. This is because the PPF compensation calculations will be different for each employer. At one extreme, this could result in employees of different employers, with the same age and identical pension entitlements and possibly in close geographical proximity, receiving significantly different levels of PPF compensation.

### 12.2 Second insolvency events and triggering scheme wind-up: benefits payable?

It is still possible for pension schemes to gain entry to PPF assessment periods if the sponsoring employer became insolvent prior to April 6 2005. However, this requires the employer to enter a subsequent insolvency event on or after April 6 2005. This could happen in practice where a pre-April 2005 administration converts to a liquidation after April 5 2005.

Interesting issues can arise in these situations if the wind-up of the scheme is triggered after April 5 2005. A natural question to ask is why wind-up might be triggered while waiting for the second insolvency event to take place.

One reason is that the insolvency practitioner handling the pre-April 2005 proceedings may request that the trustees present the pension scheme debt for consideration. However, this debt can be certified by the scheme actuary only once scheme wind-up is triggered.

In the event that a scheme wind-up is triggered after April 5 2005, it is important for the trustees to determine the level at which benefits are to be paid to the scheme members from the date the wind-up is triggered.

For multi-employer schemes operating on a last man standing basis, the trustees may be able to invoke the PPF Modification Regulations. The benefit of using these regulations is that trustees may be able to pay benefits at PPF assessment period levels in advance of the official start of an assessment period.

To invoke these regulations, the trustees will need to demonstrate that at least one of the participating employers had experienced an insolvency event on or after April 6 2005. They will also need to be of the view that a true assessment period will commence within one year, checking that this is still the case every three months.

By contrast, multi-employer schemes operating on a last man standing basis without a post-April 5 2005 employer insolvency event will not be able to invoke the Modification Regulations. In these cases, benefit payments will normally have to be scaled back from the date of wind-up, in line with the scheme's asset coverage on the Section 73 statutory priority order. Put simply, pensioners may experience sudden reductions to their pensions, consistent with the scheme's ability to meet PPF benefit levels under Section 73. A mitigating factor in these circumstances is that this reduction to pensioners' benefits should only be temporary, between the date that wind-up is triggered and the assessment date. However, the temporary reduction is a true one, in that it is not made good retrospectively once the assessment period starts.

## 13. Appeals procedure

Interested parties (eg, trustees, employers, members and insolvency practitioners) can request reviews of certain decisions taken by the PPF, otherwise known as 'reviewable matters'. PPF guidance sets out which parties have the right to request a review of each reviewable matter, as well as the time limits that apply for seeking a review. Broadly speaking, the review process can extend to the following three stages:

- stage 1 – investigation by a team leader that was not involved in the original decision;
- stage 2 – investigation by the PPF Reconsideration Committee; and
- Stage 3 – referral to the PPF ombudsman

In addition, members of the public can always contact the Pensions Advisory Service to help them resolve any difficulties they may face.

## 14. Conclusion

The introduction of the PPF is no doubt a major benefit to most pension scheme members that find themselves faced with employer insolvency. However, as described above, the process of navigating a pension scheme through the assessment period into the PPF can be far from straightforward.

# The effect of the Pensions Regulator on M&A activity

**Paul Jagger**
Hewitt Associates

## 1. Introduction

There can be no doubt that the introduction of the Pensions Regulator has had a significant impact on the world of UK defined benefit pension schemes. Perhaps the biggest effect of the regulator has been to transform pensions from a comfortable, insular afterthought to a major issue that can influence major corporate decisions. This is never felt more than when sponsoring companies are bought and sold, causing pension deficits to crystallise into pension debts. Here the regulator has the power to make or break a deal.

How can the regulator wield such influence? It has sweeping powers to require substantial contributions from companies if, by actions relating to a corporate transaction, they are perceived to have acted to weaken the security of a pension scheme. Companies wishing to avoid the risk of substantial additional contributions or other forms of financial support must instead make applications to the regulator for clearance or for approval of a withdrawal arrangement. Often, but not always, the price for the regulator's approval is to pay additional contributions to the pension scheme as part of the deal.

Perhaps more profoundly, the regulator's indirect influence can be felt in a much wider field. Trustees can feel empowered by the supporting presence of the regulator and will more readily take a stance against the company. This could involve demanding money in return for 'going quietly' and in some cases poisoning transactions where they feel these would damage the security of their pension schemes. Companies, too, can be put off by what they see as the potential risk of unwanted regulator action and seek ever more elaborate ways to divest themselves of defined benefit pension liabilities.

## 2. Clearance and the employer covenant

Not so much a new concept as a fresh imperative placed by the regulator on an old idea, the employer covenant now haunts every trustee's nightmares. The extent to which there is a shortfall compared to the cost of securing liabilities in full is the extent to which a scheme is reliant on the employer covenant. The covenant could be re-phrased as "the ability and willingness of an employer to make future contributions". Under the regulator's codes, it is now imperative that trustees monitor this covenant and react to any changes.

In transaction terms, every time there is a change in ownership involving some or all of a sponsoring employer's business, there is a change in the employer covenant. In the crudest terms, if the sponsor (commonly referred to as the 'principal employer') of an under-funded pension scheme is sold by a strong owner to a weaker owner, or if the strength of the sponsor itself is reduced (eg, by the sale of some or all of its business/undertakings), then the covenant has declined. Only one course of action is available to the trustees at this stage: that is, to demand extra security, in the form of either extra cash contributions or some form of contingent asset (ie, guarantee). For both buyer and seller, this may well tie up resources they feel could be better used elsewhere.

A recent high-profile example in the press relates to Sainsbury's. With their sponsoring employer the target of a private equity buy-out, the trustees of the Sainsbury's pension scheme had grave concerns about the employer covenant. Would a move from a 'nice, stable' family-owned business to a geared private equity captive mean that there was a higher risk that the company might default on its pension liabilities at some point in the future? The trustees then suggested that the current funding requirement of around £400 million might increase to £1 billion or even £3 billion to reflect the change in the employer covenant. For a company valued at around £9.5 billion, cash requirements of this size are not to be ignored. At the time of writing, it is unclear what an eventual deal might look like.

In a similar headline-grabbing example, the trustees of Alliance Boots recently struck a deal with their private equity buyers to protect the members of the pension scheme. The trustees had been battling to secure £1 billion in cash and security, which they claimed was required to guarantee members' benefits should the buyer (led by Kohlberg Kravis Roberts and Stefano Pessina) become insolvent. This amount contrasts with the declared funding deficit of £305 million and reflects the impact of a geared acquisition on the employer's covenant. Reports suggest the deal struck means the trustees will receive £418 million in cash over 10 years, secured by a bank guarantee. In addition, a 'security package' of £600 million will be made available, with the fund having first call on £200 million and then ranking alongside the banks for the additional £400 million. This is one of the first times a pension fund has ranked equally with the banks in the event of insolvency.

Yet there are repercussions beyond the schemes directly affected by the change of ownership of a sponsoring employer. If the seller of part or all of its cash-generating business is itself a sponsor of a defined benefit scheme, the act of selling a chunk of its business could damage the covenant. The buyer may similarly sponsor a scheme – in which case, by using cash to buy its target, it too has altered its own covenant. Yet in both cases the issue is largely academic at the transaction stage. The seller has gained cash of theoretically the same value as the business it has sold and the buyer has purchased a business at least as valuable as the price it paid (again, in theory). Trustees are not yet in the habit of questioning whether their sponsor's deals are transacted at the right price.

Far more important for the seller and the trustees of its defined benefit pension plan is the destination of the sale proceeds. A return to shareholders, for example, would remove cash from the seller's remaining business irrevocably and in so doing reduce the covenant.

## 3. Pensions Regulator's power

In most cases trustees lack the legal power to force the sponsor to contribute more money immediately. Yet this is exactly where the Pensions Regulator's powers come into play. The regulator can determine that a company or individual has taken action (or refrained from taking action) with the main purpose of avoiding an obligation to meet a debt on the employer under Section 75 of the Pensions Act 1995. That person can then be required to pay a 'contribution' to the scheme (or the board of the Pension Protection Fund), essentially with the aim of recovering the money that would otherwise have come from the Section 75 debt. A contribution notice can also be served in a situation where an action has been taken to compromise or reduce a known debt. In either case the regulator is obliged to ensure that the imposition of the contribution notice is reasonable by considering the degree of involvement of the party and the relationships between the parties. The types of action that it is envisaged could come under this power are corporate restructuring, asset stripping and artificially increasing the scheme asset value at the 'applicable time' for a debt calculation.

Even if there has not been a deliberate act to avoid or reduce a debt, the regulator can in certain situations still issue financial support directions. These powers are intended to apply in cases where corporate structures exist for legitimate business reasons, but where the effect is that the 'employer' in relation to the scheme is insufficiently resourced to deal with a potential Section 75 obligation (or is a 'service company'). Here, the regulator can require the company group to put in place financial support arrangements. Permissible arrangements include:

- an agreement from the parent company to assume responsibility;
- a joint and several liability arrangement across a group; or
- an appropriate bank guarantee.

But what does that mean? If the buying entity runs into trouble three years down the line and becomes insolvent, lacking assets to pay its pension liabilities pursuant to the debt on employer regulations, then could the Pensions Regulator demand that the original selling party make good the shortfall? The fact that it had nothing to do with the scheme for the intervening three will very likely defeat any regulator action, but the legislation does allow the regulator to "look back" up to six years to April 27 2004 in deciding whether to issue a contribution notice.

To remove the risk and uncertainty, each party involved in the transaction may wish to apply to the regulator for clearance. Once granted, clearance is a guarantee that no contribution notice will be served on any individual or entity named in the clearance application for its actions or omissions in this particular transaction. However, there can often be a price to pay at the time of the clearance application: the regulator may require remedial action to be taken at this point to benefit the scheme in order for clearance to be granted. Usually (but not always), the regulator requires the trustee's agreement to any clearance application – often in the form of an agreed recovery plan or package of measures designed to improve the circumstances of the scheme where the value of the employer covenant is being reduced materially – and so the ball can often fall back into the trustees' court.

The above covers the situation where the scheme transfers in its entirety with the sale of its sponsoring employer. Similar, yet different, is the situation where the transferring entity is only one of two or more employers participating in a single pension scheme. We consider that situation next.

## 4. Employer debt and approved withdrawal

Since 2005, an employer ceasing participation in an under-funded defined benefit pension scheme triggers a debt payable by that employer to the scheme. The amount of debt is equal to its share of any scheme shortfall relative to the cost of securing pension benefits with an insurer. For many schemes this shortfall and hence any resultant debt is substantial and one that employers would rather not pay.

A number of ways for avoiding this debt have been hypothesised. Some are tried and tested; others are not. An example of such a mechanism is the demerger of WH Smith and Smiths News in 2006, when it was decided that both entities would continue to participate in the single scheme after the demerger. The administrative complexities of this were considered preferable to payment of the (substantial) debt that would have otherwise arisen on the withdrawal of Smiths News from the scheme.

The only way of mitigating the debt without the risk of a future Pensions Regulator investigation is to apply to the regulator for an approved withdrawal arrangement. Depending on the circumstances, the regulator might require a lower amount to be paid (possibly zero) in return for any unpaid debt to be guaranteed by another group company. Once again, the terms of an approved withdrawal arrangement must often (but not always) be agreed with the trustees. The negotiations around the exact terms of the approved withdrawal arrangement then get caught up in the negotiations around changes to the employer covenant and the destination of sale proceeds.

However, there is an overriding requirement that the withdrawal debt should be more likely to be met if the arrangement is agreed. This requirement can often prove problematic in the context of a deal.

Even if a company is prepared to pay the debt in full, that may not be the end of the seller's problems, as clearance and employer covenant issues may still apply. For example, consider a company selling one of its subsidiaries based in the United Kingdom. A modest debt might be triggered based on the subsidiary's share of the scheme's Section 75 deficit (say, 5% of the relevant deficit). However, of all the entities participating in the seller's scheme, let us assume this was the only one that had a positive balance sheet and a positive income stream. In order to receive the trustees' support to the seller's clearance application, the seller might have to agree to pay the scheme a lot more than the calculated debt due from the departing sold subsidiary.

So whether directly or indirectly (through newly empowered trustees), the Pensions Regulator has the power to influence significantly corporate M&A activity. But have these powers been used, abused or just misunderstood, and what has this changed in the world of pensions and mergers and acquisitions?

## 5. Secure pensions

About a year ago, on my way to visit a client, I happened to let slip to my taxi driver that I was a pension consultant. What followed was his own personal tale of the utmost pension woe, featuring a cast of mis-selling scandals, scheme wind-ups and reduced transfers. Chief among his misfortunes occurred when the pension scheme in which he had completed 20 years of service transferred to a new owner as part of a sale to an indebted foreign buyer. Within two years, the company had been largely asset stripped and was wound up. The pension scheme, now also severely short on assets, was also wound up, leaving him with a benefit worth a fraction of the pension he had earned through his years of long service.

Of course, I was very sympathetic and quick to distance myself from such associations. It is of little reassurance to him to realise that his story is one that ought never to be repeated now that the Pensions Regulator exists. The powers of the regulator to act in the interests of scheme members during M&A situations are key to avoiding such problems (especially as a key objective of the Regulator is to avoid inordinate strains on the Pension Protection Fund). It is certainly true that many transactions now lead to extra funding or guarantees being put in place for affected pension schemes. Few would deny that this can only be a good thing for the security of member's accrued benefits, but what has been the experience of companies?

## 6. Happy companies?

If schemes are receiving more funding than before, then companies must be paying more by definition. Almost invariably, company directors would prefer to have the flexibility of not committing cash to the pension scheme – the reason often given being that such resources are often better employed in developing the company's business. However, in the M&A context, a substantial increase in risk in any given company might trigger all manner of banking covenants. The question therefore arises: should a debt to a pension scheme be given equal standing to a debt to a banking institution?

We must remember that trustees are not bankers. Trustees are still nervous and uncertain about their new responsibilities arising from the existence of the Pensions Regulator, its statutory powers and its guidance to trustees. Inevitably, the amount of security requested for any given transaction is not always proportionate or fair in all cases. The Pensions Regulator has taught trustees to ask for financial reassurance whenever the employer covenant comes under threat, but has given no guidance as to how much to ask for. Faced with the risk of litigation from disgruntled members, trustees tend to err on the side of caution, with some trustee bodies asking for the most cast iron of guarantees. This can mean opening their bargaining position based on full and immediate funding of the scheme's shortfall relative to securing annuities with an insurer.

This leads to some substantial figures being bandied around (eg, the £3 billion mentioned in connection with Sainsbury's and the £1 billion in connection with Boots). Companies can also get nervous. In one recent survey, one-fifth of private equity companies reported pulling out of deals because of concerns over pension deficits. Still more run the risk of compromising too early and settle a deal by paying far more than need necessarily be paid.

Perhaps paradoxically, the Pensions Regulator often appears to have been reasonably commercial when making rulings. I know of only a few cases of trustee-supported applications from a company where the regulator has requested a higher payment than the amount already agreed. Perhaps more interestingly, I am aware of cases where the trustees and company have disagreed and the regulator has found in the company's favour. The regulator is not as terrifyingly pro-trustee as companies might have first feared, and trustees, too, need ultimately to take a balanced view.

## 7. Wider implications

There are other repercussions, though. The traditional trustee world of quarterly meetings and part-time semi-professionalism is not one that fits easily with the pressures of a corporate transaction. It is still rare for companies to start talking to trustees early enough in the transaction for the trustees to have the time to form a robust and considered view of the situation. Companies can sometimes see trustee bodies as stubborn and as deliberately using transactions as opportunities to benefit their scheme. Trustees, conversely, can feel antagonised and victims of brinksmanship.

Worse still is the impact of conflicts of interest. Key deal drivers who also sit on a trustee board may feel unable to be objective about the process. Additionally, should the seller's trustees also have separate advisers to the selling company? And the buyer? And the buyer's trustees? What about other bidders? The answer is often a resounding 'yes'.

What is clear is that the Pensions Regulator expects trustees to be involved. It is often of greatest benefit to trustees to be informed of deals at a very early stage, which can bring its own complications. Often deals are highly confidential and the circle of people who now need to be informed has grown wider – and may include member-nominated trustees or union representatives who are trustees.

The increased focus on pensions has led companies to reconsider pricing. An increasing number of buyers are pricing a pension deficit closer to the annuity buy-out shortfall, worried about the risk of understating their maximum exposure should the trustees or the Pensions Regulator turn against them in the future. This can rule them out of the bidding process.

The combinations of these effects (increased complexities and hidden pitfalls of negotiations, added to the increased pricing implications of a pension deficit) add up to yet another good reason for companies not to sponsor a defined benefit plan. WH Smith saw a potential sale to a private equity bidder fall through because of negotiations between the buyer and its own trustees in relation to the deficit. In 2007, WH Smith closed its scheme to all employees. I'm sure there were many aspects to this decision, but did a glimpse of the power wielded by its trustees play a part in the decision to move away from final salary, I wonder?

## 8. Closing thoughts

Certainly, the Pensions Regulator has made a splash in the world of corporate transactions. There have been numerous sensational headlines over the last few months to demonstrate that. The result has been to create a process that is increasingly complex and often costly to companies.

Yet key to the regulator's role is to offer a fairer deal for pension schemes. Financial backers are allowed to make or break deals, but pension schemes are not yet able to do the same if companies really do intend to honour their pension promises and can demonstrate an ability to do so. It seems right that the regulator should require that the pension debt be treated with some respect in M&A situations.

The headline-grabbing actions of some trustees are not indicative of the wider trend. Trustees may ask for the most they think they can get away with, but it isn't always reasonable for them to get it. In the recent volatile period of change, there will certainly be cases of schemes getting far more than they deserve, but also of companies unwilling to pay what, by rights, they ought to.

Over the next few months and years, the Pensions Regulator's influence will hopefully be a calming one. The regulator has restored to companies a sense of responsibility for pension deficits, but it now needs to promote a sense of commercialism among trustees. With any luck, we will settle down into an environment where pension schemes continue to play a key role in M&A pricing and where trustees on all sides of a deal are engaged in discussion with their sponsors as early as possible.

The storm is abating. Welcome to the bright new world.

# The emergence of an alternative buy-out market

**Kenneth Donaldson**
Higham Dunnett Shaw plc

## 1. Traditional buy-out market – overview

Before discussing the emergence of an alternative buy-out market, it is useful to look first at the traditional buy-out market.

As with any market, there are buyers and sellers, as well as a range of other interested parties. A brief look at their objectives and perspectives will inform a discussion of the alternatives that are becoming available.

### 1.1 The 'buyers' – pension funds in wind-up

The demand in the traditional buy-out market is largely created by pension funds that have come to the end of their lifecycle, are in the process of being wound up and are shortly to be dissolved. Historically, the main reason that a pension fund is wound up is usually because the employer has become insolvent and is itself being wound up or is otherwise unable to meet its obligations under the terms of the trust.

The trustees of the scheme will conduct the wind-up of the trust in accordance with the terms of the governing trust deed and overriding legislation. The process of winding up a pension fund is extremely complex and is fraught with logistical, actuarial and legal difficulty. A description of the wind-up process is outside the scope of this chapter. However, it is relevant to note that the trust deed will usually tell the trustees explicitly that in order to conclude the wind-up, they may invest in an insurance policy, known as a 'bulk buy-out policy' or a 'bulk annuity policy'.

The bulk buy-out policy is a contract between the issuing insurance company and the trustees. Broadly, the insurance policy obliges the insurance company to pay benefits to the trustees in return for a one-off premium. Assuming that the trustees can afford to pay the required premium in full, the benefits will be the same as (or a very close approximation to) those promised to the members under the terms of the trust. The premium will be whatever amount the insurance company wishes to charge the trustees in return for promising to pay the benefits.

In a perfect world, the benefits that the insurer contracts to pay to the trustees will exactly match the full accrued pension promised to every member (and their beneficiaries) under the trust. In this perfect world, the premium demanded will exactly match the assets in the trust.

Having bought the bulk annuity policy, each month the trustees receive a payment from the insurance company that is exactly equal to the total payments that the trustees must in turn make to each of their members. The trustees' sole asset is the insurance policy, all moneys having been transferred to the insurer by way of the premium that was quoted.

Having so arranged the affairs of the trust, all other matters and formalities of the wind-up being concluded, in a perfect world the trust is then dissolved and the bulk annuity policy is split up into lots of separate, individual annuity policies – one for each member – and ownership of these individual policies is transferred from the trustees and assigned to the members.

The trustees are now no longer a part of the picture, having done their duty. The insurance company's obligation is now directly with each individual member of the scheme, so when, for example, a deferred member retires or dies, he or she will turn to the insurance company in order to receive his or her pension entitlement.

Of course, the world is far from perfect, and the assets that the trustees hold never match the premium that the insurance companies require. As is well known, in the current market, most pension funds in the United Kingdom have insufficient assets to meet the bulk buy-out premium. As a very rough rule of thumb, a pension scheme that is fully funded on a Financial Reporting Statement (FRS) 17 accounting basis might currently be able to afford only 70% of the bulk buy-out premium in order fully to secure members' benefits with an insurer.

In this case, at the end of the wind-up, the trustees will again turn to the trust deed to establish what must happen if there is a deficit (or surplus) with respect to the bulk annuity premium. This usually involves trying to collect the shortfall from the (probably insolvent) employer, scaling back benefits or, since the Pensions Act of 2004, seeking admission to entry to the Pension Protection Fund (PPF).

## 1.2 The 'sellers' – the insurance companies

The trustees usually have the power under the trust deed to buy a bulk buy-out policy from a UK-registered insurance company. Any such insurer must be authorised to sell such a policy by the Financial Services Authority (FSA).

The selling of such a policy is a natural extension to the market activities of most life and pension insurance companies. Many insurance firms have for years sold individual annuities to people at retirement. A bulk buy-out policy is really just a collection of such individual policies, although the policy will cover not only people at the point of retirement, but also members who have been retired and in receipt of a pension for many years, as well as deferred members who have yet to reach retirement age.

Similarly, many insurance companies have for years run insured schemes. The term 'insured' often causes confusion. An 'insured scheme' is simply a pension scheme set up under trust in the conventional manner, save that all services are provided by an insurance company, from investment to actuarial to administration to documentation. A better term might be 'bundled schemes', as there is usually no underlying 'insurance-like' obligation on the part of the insurance company to underwrite any funding shortfall that may from time to time arise.

This is a key point to note. An insurance company that offers an insured scheme enters into a contract to administer the assets and liabilities of the scheme, but the obligation to fund the scheme is between the employer and the trustees, and is made under trust. An insurance company that offers a conventional bulk buy-out policy enters into a contract with the trustees to pay specified benefits, and thus in essence takes on the funding liability in exchange for a 'once and for all' premium payment. Having entered into that contract and having received the required premium (the scheme's assets), the insurance company cannot demand additional future payments from the trustees (or the sponsoring employer) should the premium prove in time to have been insufficient. Any such shortfall must be met by the insurance company's shareholders.[1]

Largely for this reason, the bulk buy-out contract has always, rightly or wrongly, been considered a stronger quality of obligation than the promise made by an employer to pay pension benefits under a trust. For example, until June 2003, a sponsor usually had the right under the trust deed unilaterally to terminate its financial obligation under the trust, putting it into wind-up. A sponsor could thus walk away from the scheme even though it had insufficient assets to pay for a bulk buy-out policy. However, the tide seems to be turning. Since June 2003 an employer that terminates its financial obligation is faced with overriding legislation that requires it to fund the scheme up to full buy-out level – that is, so that the assets are sufficient to pay for an insurance company bulk buy-out policy for 100% of members' entitlements under the trust.

## 1.3 The regulators

In discussing the conventional bulk buy-out market, it is worth also mentioning the various regulators and their role in this market.

Occupational pension schemes, their trustees and the sponsoring employer are now regulated by the Pensions Regulator, in conjunction with a number of other relevant authorities (notably Her Majesty's Revenue and Customs and the pension ombudsman/PPF ombudsman). Bulk annuity contracts and the issuing insurance companies are regulated by the FSA.

The Pensions Regulator and the FSA have very different approaches to regulating solvency. A detailed examination of solvency regulation is well outside the scope of this chapter. However, the following points are probably helpful in understanding the difference and its impact.

The reason for the historic difference probably goes back to the quality of the obligation. As noted above, the quality of the pension promise in a trust was historically considered of a lower order than the strength of promise inherent in an insurance company's contract. This may be because 100 years ago, paying a pension to a long-serving and faithful employee was an act of enlightened, *ad hoc* discretion on the part of the employer. Eventually, the practice became more formalised and separate trusts were set up. The funding of these trusts was for decades a matter of a very long-term view of the size of the obligation, particularly as schemes were

---

1 There are two ways in which an insurance company can be constituted. The first of these is as a 'mutual' company. Each customer who holds a (qualifying) insurance policy issued by the mutual is treated as a part-owner (in proportion to the deemed value of the policy). Distributable profits are shared between the policyholders as bonus. The other type of insurance company is known as 'proprietary'. It will have shareholders who have legal ownership. In the rest of this chapter, for 'insurance company shareholder' read 'owner', whether shareholder or policyholder, as appropriate.

'immature', meaning they had far more active members than they did current pensioners. This being the case, inward monthly contributions far exceeded monthly pensions out. Without a pressing need to draw money from the fund, the risks posed by investment volatility were considered negligible. Trustees and employers felt able to ride out downturns ('temporary' shortfalls in funding) over the longer term without the need for cash injections. Pensions within trusts have subsequently come to be viewed as deferred pay and slowly more stringent requirements have been made of the trusts, which came under particular scrutiny at the time of the Maxwell scandal. Eventually, in 1997, for the first time, a statutory measure of minimum funding was imposed on trusts. However, the mechanism was flawed and set at a far lower level than that which the FSA requires of insurers. Eventually this initial 'minimum funding requirement' was replaced by a 'scheme-specific funding' standard. A scheme-specific funding target is set by the trustees in conjunction with the employer. The Pensions Regulator has oversight of this process. If the Pensions Regulator believes the funding agreement is insufficiently robust, it can intervene. The Pensions Regulator has broadly indicated it would like to see all schemes targeting funding levels of at least 100% within the next 10 years at most, and sooner if possible. The measure of the funding should be at least as strong as that required under the UK accounting standard known as Financial Reporting Standard (FRS) 17.

On the other hand, an insurance company contract was always that – a contract. In terms of solvency, the FSA (which authorises and regulates insurance companies) has sought to ensure that insurers will at all times be able to meet their obligations. The phrase 'at all times' is key here. Downturns leading to 'temporary' shortfalls in funding were considered an unacceptable risk. In other words, the risks posed by investment volatility were regarded as considerable – indeed, unacceptable. This led to the imposition of a far more stringent solvency test and a correspondingly far more conservative investment strategy.

This difference in solvency regulation has some immediately obvious consequences. The tough FSA requirement means an insurer (except in unusual market conditions) must hold substantially more assets to back £1 per annum (pa) of pension than a trust – even a trust that is fully funded on a scheme-specific funding basis acceptable to the Pensions Regulator.

In other words, the reserves required to back £1pa pension to an insurer are much higher than the reserves required to back £1pa of pension to a trust, in most market conditions. This gap can widen and narrow as equity and bond markets fluctuate from time to time. As a very approximate rule of thumb, you might expect an insurer to hold 30% more assets to back a pension promise than a trust that was fully funded on the FRS17 accounting basis.

This difference is not solely attributable to a highly conservative view on investment risk. Insurers (regulated by the FSA) also take a more conservative view on likely longevity improvements than many trusts, and will also factor in expenses and the requirement to earn dividends for their shareholders.

A trust that wishes to transfer the obligation to pay pensions to an insurer will ordinarily find itself paying up to 30% more than the amount of money it would have held, assessed by reference to FRS17.

Bulk annuities policies have therefore tended to be a 'distress' purchase, rather than one made of choice. That is, trustees at the end of the process of winding up a trust (an event normally triggered by insolvency of a 'distressed' employer) have little choice other than to buy out the remaining liabilities and dissolve the trust. Other than that, there has been little demand from trusts for bulk buy-out contracts. It is against this backdrop that the emerging market for bulk annuities is developing.

### 1.4 Other key stakeholders

We have so far mentioned trustees, sponsors and insurance companies and regulators. To complete the picture of the existing market, it is necessary to mention the part that scheme members play.

In the traditional setting of a pension scheme wind-up, members will usually be offered some degree of choice. The exact choices will depend on the trust deed and rules, and also on the decisions the trustees make as to the exact winding-up process.

Deferred pensioners can usually opt to take a transfer to an alternative arrangement (eg, a new employer's scheme or a personal pension). They may also be able to take early retirement or to commute the whole of their pension under the so-called 'trivial commutation rules', depending on the circumstances. If they choose none of the above, the default position is that the trustees will have the power to buy out their pension under a bulk buy-out policy which will eventually be assigned to each individual member as described above.

Pensioners, by contrast, generally have little choice. The trustees will enter a bulk buy-out policy which at the end of the wind-up will be broken up and assigned to each individual pensioner (and their beneficiaries). Although pensioners have little or no choice in the matter, they have historically been the best-protected category of member if the scheme is underfunded at the point of wind-up and cannot afford the full buy-out premium.[2]

## 2. Existing alternatives to buy-out

Before discussing the emergence of an alternative buy-out market, it is also worth first looking at existing variations on the standard bulk buy-out policy.

### 2.1 Closed scheme

It is not necessarily the case that a scheme that has ceased to have active members who are accruing benefits must always wind up. Depending on the trust deed, it may be possible to run the scheme on rather than wind it up. No further benefits will accrue to members, but apart from that the trust will continue to run its affairs as before.

If the sponsoring employer is still a going concern, it will be obliged to agree a scheme-specific funding plan with the trustees and may, for example, set a target of reaching or maintaining a 100% level of funding assessed by reference to FRS17.

---

2 Technically, since April 2006, pensioners can exercise a theoretical right to a transfer value, just as a deferred pensioner can, and therefore could exercise a similar choice as a deferred pension in a scheme wind-up. However, there is very little, if any, sign of activity in the pension transfer market to date.

Specifically, if the trustees and the employer agree to run on the scheme as a closed fund, the employer may avoid, for the time being, triggering a formal 'debt' requirement. As noted above, since June 2003 an employer that terminates its financial obligation is faced with overriding legislation that requires it to fund the scheme up to full buy-out level – that is, so that the assets are sufficient to pay for an insurance company bulk buy-out policy for 100% of members' entitlements under the trust. The difference between the bulk buy-out premium and the assets in the scheme is treated as an unsecured debt, once notice is served on the employer by the trustees.

Running on as a closed scheme means the full debt is not triggered. If matters change in the future (eg, if the employer fails to meet its obligations under the scheme-specific funding agreement and terminates future obligation to pay contributions), the trustees will still have recourse to serving a debt notice.

There are very complex and delicate 'balance of power' considerations around a solvent employer's decision to close a scheme. Yet many schemes have gone down this route in order to fund a shortfall in the assets over time.

In addition, for many years it was conventional wisdom that very large pension schemes would be unable to wind up, as they were too big to find an insurer or insurers prepared to take on such large liabilities by way of bulk annuity contracts. If this were true, then the trustees would have had no choice but to run the trust on as a closed scheme, whether or not the employer was solvent.

Finally, for completeness, once an employer has become insolvent, it will be entirely a matter for the trustees to decide whether to wind up the scheme or to run it on as a closed scheme – assuming that the trust deed gives them the power to make this decision. If they do not have this power (to elect to continue as a closed scheme) at the point of insolvency, then usually the wind-up will become automatically triggered.

There is no reason why a closed scheme (with or without solvent employer) could not continue in this manner for decades, paying out benefits as and when they fall due. In this scenario, liabilities and assets will tend to grow at first, with investment returns and as people age. But eventually the size of the scheme will gradually dwindle as people retire, draw their benefits and eventually die.

### 2.2 Transfer exercises

As noted above, non-pensioners have an option to take a transfer from an occupational pension scheme to another vehicle, such as a personal pension plan or a 'stakeholder' plan.

As part of a winding-up exercise, it is usual for the trustees to offer members the opportunity to take a transfer prior to buying a bulk annuity policy.

### 2.3 Section 32 buy-outs

This is a legally complex area. It applies to non-pensioner (deferred) members.

At the end of a wind-up process, it may be possible for the trustees to buy not a traditional bulk buy-out policy (a contract to pay a defined level of benefits, based on the members' scheme entitlements), but a so-called 'Section 32' policy. This is essentially a defined-contribution type of policy. The trustees transfer over the assets as a premium to the chosen insurer in order to buy the policy. The assets are split into separate 'pots' of money, member by member, and invested by the insurer on each member's behalf. The contract terms do not guarantee a defined level of pension – simply the proceeds of the 'pot' at retirement, plus or minus investment returns. These Section 32 policies therefore transform the defined benefit promise under the scheme into a defined contribution contract. This is, as noted, legally complex, unless member consent is obtained. A bulk Section 32 buy-out policy purchased by trustees in a wind-up situation is usually, by definition, absent member consent, and it is this alteration to the nature of the benefit that causes the legal argument, when member consent has not been explicitly obtained beforehand. Nonetheless, it is an existing alternative and has been used in the past by trustees as a means of discharging the trust's liabilities and completing the wind-up.

Most Section 32 policies do have a defined benefit 'underpin' element in order to cater for contracted-out guaranteed minimum pensions.

### 2.4 The government

Until April 1997, the government effectively acted as 'insurer of last resort' for contracted-out liabilities. If a scheme had insufficient funds to secure even the GMP liabilities under a bulk buy-out contract, the trustees could transfer the remaining assets to the state by way of premium and the member would be reinstated into the State Earnings Related Pension Scheme, as if they had not been contracted out in the first place.

Since 1997 this process has been replaced by a complex process known as 'deemed buyback', which is similar although restricted in scope. A detailed explanation is outside the scope of this chapter. However, trustees winding up badly funded schemes should be aware of this possibility as an alternative to buy-out with an insurance company.

### 2.5 The PPF

The PPF was set up by the government, although it is not a government department. It sets a minimum level of pension 'safety net' when sponsoring employers of an underfunded pension scheme become insolvent. The PPF is fully described elsewhere in this book and is not merely an alternative to buy-out for eligible schemes, but instead becomes a mandatory process. The PPF is not an insurer (it is a compensation arrangement).

## 3. New entrants and established players

Until 2005 and for the previous decade two companies dominated the buy-out market. These were the Prudential and Legal & General. In 2005 the Prudential took in premiums totalling £562 million, while Legal & General took in £886 million.

However, this was not always the case. At various times, other insurers were also active in this market, such as Standard Life.

Nonetheless, only the Prudential and Legal & General were consistently willing to quote a premium and take on pension scheme risks from trustees.

Now a number of new players are emerging. These can be broken down into several different categories as follows.

### 3.1 Existing 'diversified' insurance companies

These are insurance companies that sell many different types of policy, such as life assurance policies, sickness cover policies or individual defined contribution pension policies.

Examples of existing diversified insurance companies that have recently started to compete in this market include AIG, Ageon, Aviva and, briefly, Wesleyan (which has now withdrawn having secured one major mandate).

### 3.2 New 'monoline' insurers

These are new insurance companies, authorised and regulated by the FSA just as any other existing insurer. The adjective 'monoline' means that they (currently) sell only one type of policy – bulk buy-out policies.

Examples of new, FSA-authorised insurers include Paternoster, Pension Insurance Corporation and Synesis Life (although at time of writing Synesis Life is not yet technically authorised; instead it holds a letter from the FSA indicating that the FSA is "minded" to authorise the new company to write insurance policies once Synesis Life's executives make the final, formal application).

### 3.3 New 'non-insurance' consolidator companies

These are companies that are interested in taking on the risks of a pension scheme, but are not set up as insurance companies, and are therefore not subject to FSA authorisation and regulation. If such a company did take on the pension scheme risks, the trust would continue as before (perhaps with different trustees) and the pension scheme would continue under the Pensions Regulator's jurisdiction, as any other trust. In essence, the new company replaces or takes over the obligations of the old sponsoring employer. This is a commercial transaction and would typically require clearance from the Pensions Regulator. ('Clearance' is a formal procedure for, essentially, obtaining the Pensions Regulator's agreement to a corporate transaction in which a pension scheme is or could be affected.)

One such new company that is actively exploring this market is Aleva Advisors.

At core, the new insurers in this market (whether existing, diversified or new, monoline insurers) simply offer trustees a wider market with greater price competitiveness. However, they are also beginning to introduce 'product variation' into the market, being variations on the traditional bulk buy-out policy. By contrast, the new 'non-insurer' model is more like the closed-fund approach – running the scheme off within the existing Pensions Regulator regime.

### 3.4 Special purpose vehicles

Special purpose vehicles (SPVs) are rather like an intermediate point between insurance companies and the consolidator companies mentioned above. SPVs are traditionally used to isolate financial risks from a parent company, so the parent company can finance a large project without the risk that if the project fails, the financial knock-on will bring the parent company down. SPVs are sometimes referred to as 'off-balance sheet' companies.

In 2006 the FSA introduced insurance SPVs, which can be set up by an insurer as a reinsurance vehicle, in order to help the insurer manage its balance sheet. Put simply, the insurer transfers liabilities under a reinsurance treaty to the insurance SPV, which issues debt securities to the financial markets sufficient to cover these obligations. This is more likely to be a matter of internal financing for the parent insurer, regulated by the FSA, and may not therefore involve the trustees directly.

In general, a transaction involving SPVs is almost by definition complex, as it will involve the SPV, a parent company, refinancing via the issuance of debt securities to the financial markets, possibly credit insurance (insuring against bankruptcy of the parent) and potentially a number of different regulatory jurisdictions, not necessarily in the United Kingdom. Any trustee contemplating entering such a transaction directly with an SPV (assuming that this were possible, and that the trustees had the power to make such an investment under their trust deed) will need to take highly specialised advice.

### 3.5 Overseas insurers

In section 3.4, the possibility was raised that non-UK registered or authorised insurance companies could enter the bulk buy-out market. Such companies may be at an advantage to insurers authorised by the FSA. This is because the FSA sets particularly stringent requirements for the amount of money an insurer must hold to back a bulk buy-out contract and in relation to how this money is invested. Overseas authorities may not set such stringent standards, enabling the insurer to quote a lower premium.

Again, trustees contemplating entering such an arrangement will need to take highly specialised advice. They should be aware that there is a compensation scheme in place for customers of FSA-authorised insurers, should that insurer become bankrupt. In comparing the premium quotations, they should at a minimum take care to compare like with like, placing a value on the whole package including the contingent value of the compensation arrangements, rather than simply comparing the face value of the premium demanded.

## 4. Emerging variations

### 4.1 Ongoing buy-out

The key obvious variation (and not so much a new one) is that buy-out need not be at the end of a wind-up. It may simply be an investment in the form of an insurance policy held by the trustee. In this case it may or may not be broken up and assigned to individual members, as it would be at the end of a wind-up. Whether this step is taken is a decision of the trustees and their power to make it will depend on the trust deed. Regardless of whether the policies are transferred to individual members or there is a master policy retained by the trustees, risk will have been transferred to the insurer.

This variation offers closed, and indeed open, schemes an opportunity to manage risk. The key risks that are transferred to the insurer via the buy-out policy are investment risk (including inflation risk, credit default risk in relation to corporate bonds and manager risk) and mortality risk.

Ongoing buy-out might relate to a given tranche of members. For example, the trustees may choose to buy a bulk annuity policy for pensioners in payment currently aged over 75, or for deferred pensioners currently aged between 50 and 60.

In doing so, the trustees are in effect taking advantage of the insurers' appetite for the type of business and correspondingly the perceived 'competitiveness' of the policy versus the reserves the trustees/sponsor would hold for those members anyway (assessed by reference to scheme-specific funding or FRS17, perhaps). If that gap is sufficiently small, trustees (in consultation with the sponsoring employer) may feel that the policy and the risk transfer it offers represents good value for money without jeopardising the financial security of the remaining members.

### 4.2 Spread premiums or 'phased buy-out'

The second rather obvious variation is that instead of being paid upfront (which is traditionally the case), the premium could be spread to suit the trustees' and sponsor's needs. Again, this is not really novel and both the Prudential and Legal & General would have been prepared to quote on this basis in the past. However, it has not been a common approach until now (and indeed we are yet to see any substantial business written on this basis).

Under this approach the trustees typically would agree with the insurer that the premium will be paid over a period of, say, five or 10 years. The terms on which the future payments are to be made and the benefits the policy will secure will be agreed upfront. Future payments could be absolute (fixed in pound terms) or more likely linked to the price of a specific bundle of investments (probably fixed and index-linked bonds).

As long as future premiums are paid on time in full, the trustees again achieve risk transfer to the insurer.

### 4.3 Risk or profit sharing

Next is the possible emergence of risk-sharing solutions. This would more typically apply to a closed scheme than at the end of a wind-up. However, it could apply in wind-up situations where the duration of the wind-up was expected to be several years, perhaps because of a court-approved compromise agreement to obtain 'debt payments' over a period of years (colloquially known as 'Bradstock arrangements').

In the profit-sharing type of contract variation, the insurer says, "I quote you a premium of £X, but if as the experience unwinds over the coming years I find this was too much money, I will pay you some back."

In the risk-sharing type of contract variation, the insurer says, "I quote you a premium of £Y, but if as the experience unwinds over the coming years I find this was too much money, I will pay you some back. In addition, if future experience was underestimated, either I will cease to pay benefits or you will pay me an additional premium."

In both cases, the experience referred to will usually be mortality experience. The policy will be priced by reference to a particular mortality projection. Actual future mortality experience will be tracked. If this lies outside a specified corridor (eg, based on the underlying pricing assumption plus or minus 10%), then the refund or additional payment will be triggered.

Risk sharing by reference to emerging mortality experience is not a new concept. This was essentially the basis of the original 'with-profits' concept conceived over 150 years ago by Equitable Life.

### 4.4 Partial buy-out

Another (easier to measure) way of risk sharing would be to insure pensions in payment up to a certain age. After that age, the trustees/sponsor would be obliged once again to fund the pension. The higher the age, the closer one approaches to full buy-out. If the age limit were 120 years old, the risk would be almost entirely transferred to the insurer and the premium might be expected to be very close to the full buy-out premium. But if the age limit were 80, then many members and their dependants might be expected to live beyond this and so the sponsor/trustee would retain a larger element of risk and would expect to bear the cost for all these people as time went by. The premium ought to be correspondingly reduced.

### 4.5 'Do-it-yourself' buy-out

Recently there has been much talk of 'liability-driven investment' in the pension trade press and on the conference circuit. This is essentially an investment strategy that seeks to match cash flows: the expected payments out to pensioners are matched to expected interest, dividend, rent and coupon payments due from the assets held. Liability-driven investment tends to go one step further and invest in derivatives in order to achieve the same effect. Hedging strategies are also used to try to protect against the possible adverse effect on the solvency position of the scheme caused by, for example, interest rate changes or default on bond payments.

As noted, insurance companies regulated by the FSA have generally adopted highly conservative investment strategies as they are obliged to hold sufficient assets at all times to honour their contracts. Although a liability-driven investment strategy is rather novel in the context of pension schemes, it is essentially the approach that has been adopted by insurance companies for many years.

'Do-it-yourself' buy-out refers to the concept of running a closed scheme along the lines of an insurance company – following a liability-driven investment strategy such as those which have been followed by an insurer to which the trustees have executed a bulk buy-out and, in addition, 'hedging' the longevity risk. However, at present, there is no established market for hedging longevity risk. 'Hedging' in this sense means buying a financial instrument that transfers an unwanted risk (longevity risk) to a willing buyer. Thus the trustees would (theoretically) buy a bond which pays coupons linked to a mortality index. If people live longer than expected, the trustees receive higher coupon payments from the bond issuer (and vice versa). The risk of longevity causing a financial strain has thus been transferred to the bond issuer. Such a hedge is therefore rather like an insurance policy in some senses.

Leaving aside for one moment the absence of a market in longevity bonds, if the trustees have implemented and maintained a liability-driven investment strategy and a longevity hedge, then in theory they have transferred investment risk and longevity risk to the financial markets (although ultimately the buck still stops with the trustees). The risks that remain in the trust are generally considered to be of much smaller order:

- operational risk (the risk that the administration goes awry);
- regulatory risk (the risk that the government 'moves the goalposts' and imposes further financial burden on the trust); and
- legal risk (similar to regulatory risk, this is the risk that the courts effectively impose further burden on the trust).

The DIY buy-out can be considered as trying to mimic the behaviour of an insurance company in order to obtain some of the benefits that an insurance contract for a bulk buy-out policy might bring.

## 4.6 Liability management

Another theme which has been emerging of late is the idea of actively managing the liabilities. Rather than move to closed-scheme status and then simply wait for the assets and liabilities to run off over time, the rationale behind liability management is to reshape the pension scheme in order to hasten the time when the gap between the accounting value of the liabilities (FRS17) and the cost of a buy-out policy shrinks to an 'affordable' level in absolute terms.

The principal method of liability management is the 'enhanced transfer value' exercise. The usual form of this exercise is that the sponsoring employer will write to deferred members of the scheme with an offer that if any member exercises the right to take a transfer value to another approved pension vehicle, the sponsor will enhance that transfer value.

Such exercises have drawn criticism from the Pension Advisory Service and from the Department for Work and Pensions, as well as from the press. However, a well-run exercise carried out jointly by the trustees and the sponsor, with legal advice on both sides, clear and complete communication material and preferably access to independent financial advice for any interested members, could benefit all parties – both the transferring and the remaining members. The devil lies in the detail and no such exercise should be entered into without excellent advice and thorough preparation.

There are other forms of liability management, such as reshaping awkward benefits in a manner that is cost neutral to the trust, but which will facilitate ultimate buy-out. The most common, simplest example of this is that some schemes grant annual increases to pensions on the anniversary of the date on which the pension came into payment – giving rise to a spread of increases during the year. Few insurers are happy to take on such administrative burden, so harmonising the increase date is a sensible precursor to buy-out.

## 5. Conclusion

Despite a good number of new players entering the bulk buy-out market, anecdotal evidence suggests that very few transactions have taken place to date, despite a high volume of enquiries. It is probably too early to tell whether real innovation will come through in time, but certainly the widening of the market has to be good news for trustees, sponsoring employers and scheme members.

# Directors' duties and conflicts of interest

**Däna Burstow**
Allen & Overy LLP

## 1. Introduction

Conflict is endemic to a board of an occupational pension scheme. The individuals serving on the trustee board are likely to come from a variety of backgrounds: the employer board, the employer finance or HR department, ordinary scheme members (often active), former employees or trade union-linked individuals. Each will have real potential, or at least perceived, conflicts to address. Where someone is a 'Companies Act director' of both the employer and the corporate trustee, he will have additional concerns that his fiduciary duties in relation to each board may compete.

A common description for this dual role is one of wearing 'two hats'. Numerous corporate governance codes aim to provide guidance on the traditional duties of directors in England and Wales that derive from a mix of common law, equitable principles and statutory provisions. This chapter highlights the key issues of directors' duties generally and where they fit in a pension scheme context, and suggests ways to minimise the impact of conflicts.

## 2. Fiduciary duties

A director, like a trustee, is subject to common law fiduciary duties by reason of his relationship to the company and its stakeholders. There are many definitions of the fiduciary relationship, but the idea that "a fiduciary is someone who has undertaken to act for or on behalf of another in a particular matter in circumstances which give rise to a relationship of trust and confidence" suffices.

Fundamental to this concept is the role of loyalty: "The principal is entitled to the single-minded loyalty of his fiduciary… A fiduciary must act in good faith; he must not make a profit out of his trust; he must not place himself in a position where his duty and his interest may conflict; he may not act for his own benefit or the benefit of a third person without the informed consent of his principal."

In a pensions context, a director who is an individual trustee but who also sits on the board of the sponsoring company will owe direct fiduciary duties to both the company and the pension scheme members. If he is a director of a trust company, then he owes a direct fiduciary duty to it and not the members. The trust company then owes a fiduciary duty to the members.

Before considering where conflicts chiefly arise, the following is a summary of the fiduciary duties of a director:

- Duty to act in good faith – a director must act at all times in good faith in what he considers to be on the best interests of the company.

- Duty to act within the powers conferred – a director must act in accordance with the company's constitution and must exercise his powers only for the purposes allowed by law.
- Duty not to make a secret profit – a director must account to the company for any personal profit he makes by virtue of his directorship, unless such profit was authorised.
- Duty not to fetter discretion – a director may not agree to restrict his power to exercise independent judgement.
- Duty to act fairly – a director must act fairly as between different shareholders; this duty does not require equal treatment to all shareholders, but only that the treatment should be fair.
- Duty to avoid conflicting interests and conflicting duties – if a transaction or situation gives rise to a conflict between an interest of the company and another interest (or duty) of the directors, the director must account to the company for any benefit he receives from the transaction and must indemnify the company for any loss it suffers.

### 3. Statutory duties

In addition, directors are subject to a variety of other statutory duties. These duties – such as an obligation to disclose interests in contracts, a prohibition on loans and an obligation to disclose any shareholdings in the company – are contained in the Companies Acts and other legislation, but rarely impinge on directors of trustee companies for the purposes of an occupational pension scheme.

### 4. Skill and care

A director must exercise due care and skill in fulfilling his functions. The standard of care that a director must satisfy is judged according to both an objective and a subjective test. A director must conduct himself in the manner of a reasonably diligent person having both:

- the general knowledge, skill and experience that may reasonably be expected of a person carrying out the same functions as are carried out by that director in relation to the company; and
- the general knowledge, skill and experience which that director has.

Traditionally, the standard required under this heading was low. The historic understanding has been affected both by legislation and through shifts in corporate governance. The Company Directors Disqualification Act 1986 aimed to improve standards through allowing the court to take misconduct of a director into account when determining whether a director should be disqualified.

With a similar intention to raise standards, the Insolvency Act 1986 introduced the requirement of assessing a director's own subjective skill and care. The Insolvency Act also introduced a dual objective obligation of making the director liable to contribute personally to the assets of the company when falling below an objective standard of skill and care.

The courts have made it clear that directors are to act in what the directors, not they, think are in the company's best interests, but nonetheless a contemporaneous growth of corporate governance guidance has made the position of the standard of duty and skill for directors a more objective and demanding one.

## 5. Companies Act 2006

Provisions concerning directors' duties are a significant part of the Companies Act 2006 and will be brought into force by October 2008. It aims to offer greater clarity on directors' duties by affirming that directors must act in the interests of shareholders, but it also introduces a need to pay regard to long-term issues, the interests of employees, suppliers, consumers and the environment. The seven duties are:

- a duty to act within powers;
- a new duty to promote the success of the company;
- a duty to exercise independent judgement;
- a duty to exercise reasonable care, skill and diligence;
- an expanded duty to avoid conflicts and possible conflicts;
- a duty not to accept benefits from third parties; and
- a new duty to declare an interest in a proposed transaction or arrangement.

Some aspects of this partial codification give cause for concern at the time of writing. The new duty to promote the success of the company, which replaces the well-established duty to act in the best interests of the company, has brought confusion to a previously clear concept. The 'enlightened shareholder value' introduces the need for a director to have regard to a list of non-exhaustive factors when discharging the new obligation which includes, for example, the interests of employees, the need to foster business relationships and the environmental impact of decisions.

The codification is attempting to establish the success of the company for the benefit of all members as the duty above all others. The government has said that 'success' will usually mean long-term increase in value, and that this is a matter of good-faith judgement for the director concerned. Nonetheless, it seems likely that the courts will be drawn into matters previously left to a director's judgement and it is unclear to what lengths the directors will need to go to show that they have properly considered all relevant issues. Where a director is also on a trustee board, he may have difficulty in carrying out his trustee functions if the actions are unlikely to promote the success of the sponsor company – many funding discussions would fit in this category. It may be possible to ease this difficulty by the sponsoring company providing an indemnity to the individual so that any attempt to sue him under this duty would lead circularly to him being indemnified by the company.

The duties will still be owed to the company (not other stakeholders). The breach of a duty may give rise to damages or compensation being payable. However, in practice, it is unlikely that there will be a surge of unwarranted claims because, unlike in US securities class actions, any damages recovered will be payable to the company, rather than the suing shareholder.

### 5.1 Duty to avoid conflicts of interest

Under the Companies Act 2006, a director must avoid a situation in which he has, or can have, a direct or indirect interest that conflicts, or may possibly conflict, with the interests of the company. However, the duty will not be infringed if it is authorised by the directors of the company. Where the duty to avoid conflicts of interest or the duty to declare interests in a proposed transaction or arrangement is complied with (via authorisation by or disclosure to the directors) by gaining the consent or approval of the members of the company, the transaction or arrangement is not liable to be set aside by virtue of any common law rule or equitable principle.

### 5.2 Indemnification

A company will be able to indemnify a director of a company who is a director of a corporate trustee of an occupational scheme for liability incurred in connection with the company's activities as trustee of that scheme. This will be via a qualifying pension scheme indemnity provision which cannot cover either payment of a criminal fine or regulatory penalty or any liability incurred in defending criminal proceedings in which the director is convicted.

## 6. Conflict of duties and occupational pension schemes

A fiduciary holding two roles is strictly prohibited. When a fiduciary acts for two principals, a strict interpretation of case law would suggest that there is an automatic breach of duty. Moreover, even when the trustee director has obtained informed consent, he is in 'double employment' and may not escape liability for a breach of this duty, if the strict interpretation is followed.

*Hillsdown Holdings Plc v The Pension Ombudsman* (1996) looked at the position where a trustee director is also a director of the employer. It was argued that the 'self-dealing' rule made the transaction voidable because of this conflict of interest. The High Court did not rule directly on this, but in passing, Justice Knox said:

> *I am not satisfied that the self-dealing rule is as hard and fast as to require a negotiation between pension fund trustees and the employer to be set aside automatically and without investigation if one or more of the trustees are directors of the employer. I accept that unless there is an express provision in the relevant trust deed permitting a trustee to act in negotiations with the employer under the scheme notwithstanding that the trustee is a director or employee of the company, the fact that negotiations have been conducted by persons one of whom had a conflict of duties puts upon those who say the transaction should be upheld the onus of proving that it was indeed reasonable and proper.*

The onus is on the trustees to demonstrate that conflicts have been recognised and dealt with appropriately. Trustees defending a claim that a decision is tainted by conflict have the onus of proving that it is valid. It is easier to do this if trustees are alive to the problem as they go along and have agreed (and complied with) protocols in place for dealing with conflicts.

Conflicts may be caused by an individual receiving information in his day job that would be relevant to his fellow trustees/trustee board directors. The individual is in a difficult position: does the duty to act in the best interests of the beneficiaries/in the interests of the trustee company mean he must pass the information on to the other trustees or does the original duty to keep it confidential override it? Case law (again, not in a pensions context) implies that the person with the fiduciary duty may be liable in damages for the failure to pass on the information, but is not required actually to hand the information over that he received subject to confidentiality requirements. Although untested in the courts, some trust deeds and rules/articles of association/service contracts are being amended to include wording protective to the individual absolving him of any obligation to pass on information. These amendments are being made in conjunction with confidentiality agreements obliging directors/employees to keep 'day job' information confidential and obliging trustees to keep information they are provided in connection with that function also confidential.

## 7. Resolving conflicts in occupational pension schemes

The Pensions Regulator requires trustees to manage conflicts and includes training in its trustee toolkit aimed at alerting trustees to the risk of ignoring conflicts. In practice, there are a number of ways of handling conflicts and, depending on the gravity of the conflict, reliance on one or a mix of the following may be necessary.

### 7.1 Section 39 of the Pensions Act 1995

Pensions legislation explicitly allows a scheme member with a personal interest to continue acting as trustee despite that conflict. However, it still does not allow an individual to wear two different hats during a conflict. Also, the section refers only to trustees and not to directors of corporate trustees. *Edge v Pension Ombudsman* (1997 and 1999) also addresses the position of a trustee who stood to gain from the decision in which he was involved – and held that equity should not intervene to preclude him from benefiting from the result of the decision.

### 7.2 Express authorisation in the trust deed and rules

Trust deed and rules regularly include wording which will permit actions to be valid notwithstanding that there may be a conflict – often subject to the conflict having been disclosed.

### 7.3 Implied authorisation in the trust instrument

Where the requirements of the pension scheme trust instrument require the appointment of a director as trustee when the fiduciary is subject to a conflicting interest or duty, the courts have determined that the strict interpretation may not apply by ruling that there will be no breach of fiduciary duty. On a case-by-case basis, fiduciary duties "may have to be moulded and informed by the terms of the contractual relationship".

### 7.4 Declaration of conflict

The Pensions Regulator and case law require a director/trustee to declare where he has a conflict. It may be possible for the board to conclude that the conflict is unimportant enough to be recognised and acknowledged, but for no other action to be taken.

## 7.5 Independent advice

The Pensions Regulator recommends taking independent advice to help manage conflicts. However, if a conflict exists, taking independent advice cannot absolve those who are conflicted. It can help conflicts be recognised and provide additional support to a board missing its usual source of expertise.

## 7.6 Consent to conflicting interest

A non-pensions case established that a director of the sponsoring employer may be released from a conflicting duty if fully informed consent of the person to whom the duty is owed is given. However, this is unlikely to be feasible because it is unlikely that the consent of all scheme members could be obtained.

## 7.7 Delegation/not taking part in the decision

This mechanism entails the director stepping out of a meeting where a conflicted issue is discussed or delegating to a sub-committee excluding the conflicted trustee. For this to work, the trust deed and rules/articles must not require all trustees to be present at a meeting to be quorate or that they vote unanimously for a proposal to be adopted.

## 7.8 Resignation

A trustee may consider that there is to be a period of time during which so many conflicts will arise that resignation may be appropriate. If the discussions relate to funding, then replacing a finance director with someone else from the finance department (who in turn reports to the finance director) may not address the conflict, but merely add in a level of personal conflict that did not previously exist.

## 7.9 Court approval

The courts also have the power to allow a transaction which would otherwise be a breach of fiduciary duty. Any court authorisation should be taken in advance of the conflicting action taking place, as the court may not be prepared to consider the issue after the event. However, the length of time necessary, the cost and the uncertainty make this an option worthwhile only where complete certainty is worthwhile.

# 8. Conclusion

Although the law surrounding how conflicts of interests operate in an occupational pension schemes context, and in particular how confidential information should be handled, has begun to develop, as yet there is no clear consensus on the practices that should apply. Although the issues have existed for many years, attention is currently focused on them due to the spotlight put on them by the Pensions Regulator and a renewed focus on corporate governance, all in the context, typically, of discussions between employers and trustee boards regarding deficit issues.

The issues are the subject of debate among pension lawyers and have been the subject of numerous papers, debates and workshops. Meanwhile, boards are handling matters on a day-to-day basis, making sense of the existing parameters as meaningfully as possible. As the case law develops, it must be hoped that boards will be able to continue to include members who will have potential conflicts of interest, recognising the expertise that they bring, and that boards will find a sensible framework to make decisions in a structured way that are appropriate for pension scheme members even where potential conflicts exist.

# The developing role of independent trustees

**David Archer**
Pitmans Trustees Limited

## 1. Introduction

The concept of a trust and the separation of legal and beneficial ownership of property has its modern origin in Republican Rome through the device of *Fideicommisa*, first decreed by Augustus, who ruled as emperor between 27 BC and 14 AD. After these early Roman developments, trust law then started to emerge in England as a creature of the English medieval legal landscape. In particular, trust law developed at the time of King Henry VIII to help avoid tax, and when the use of land trusts to hide ownership became a feature of protection from military service to the crown. To put an end to this, Henry VIII passed the 1535 Statute of Uses. This provided that a passive trust would be considered void and the beneficiary to it the real owner of the trust property. Also during the medieval period, guilds developed and started to provide financial help for the poor or elderly, alongside the church. The trust laws of 1597 and 1601 were the first tentative moves towards modern-day pension provisions. These developments took a leap forward under Victorian enterprise and philanthropy with the establishment of friendly societies. In the 19th century, as the Industrial Revolution gathered pace, occupational pension trusts were founded by some of the large emerging new industries. The Finance Acts of 1916 and 1921 then established modern-day tax relief and Inland Revenue approval for occupational pension schemes, giving birth to what are now about 90,000 occupational pension schemes registered with the Pension Schemes Registry today.

The essential legal role of the trustee has remained constant throughout this period of change. It is the same today as it always has been. Having said this, the role has developed rapidly in the last 20 years, for reasons that this chapter considers.

## 2. Trust and trustees

So what exactly is a trust? The word 'trust' is defined in the *Concise Oxford Dictionary* as being "a firm belief in reliability, honesty, veracity, justice, strength, etc, of person or thing… confidence reposed in person by making him nominal owner of property to be used for another's benefit; right of the latter to benefit by such property". The simple definition of a 'trustee' is "a person who holds property in trust for another". Several reported judgments from the 19th and first half of the 20th centuries sought to encapsulate the definition of a 'trust' in English or Commonwealth law. One leading example is that of Justice Mayo in the Australian decision *Re: Scott* [1948] SASR 193 at 196, which states as follows:

*No definition of a "Trust" seems to have been accepted as comprehensive and exact... Strictly it refers, I think, to the duty or aggregate accumulation of obligations that rest upon a person described as a trustee. The responsibilities are in relation to property held by him, or under his control. That property he will be compelled by a court in its equitable jurisdiction to administer in the manner lawfully prescribed by the trust instrument, or where there be no specific provision written or oral, or to the extent that such provision is invalid or lacking, in accordance with equitable principles. As a consequence the administration will be in such a manner that the consequential benefits and advantages accrue, not to the trustee, but to the persons called* cestuis que trust, *or beneficiaries, if there be any, if not, for some purpose which the law will recognise and enforce.*

There is, in effect, a bundle of legal obligations owed by trustees, all of which boil down to a strict legal obligation on trustees to act as wise and prudent stewards of the trust assets on behalf of the beneficiaries. In the case of pension schemes, the legal obligations of the trustees have been set out in Part V and so do not need to be set out again here. Why has the trustee role been changing recently? As much as the changes in pensions legislation have forced a change in the trustees' role, much of the demand for an independent trustee springs from a broader change in Western corporate culture over the last 20 years. This has been influenced by events such as the Cadbury Report concerning corporate governance, developments in the City of London since the 'Big Bang' in the late 1980s, the continuing move towards greater regulation with more emphasis on compliance management and, more recently, the post-Enron, Sarbanes Oxley Act in the United States. This has all contributed to the change in culture away from the *noblesse oblige* service provided by lay trustees. Coupled with an extensive range of complex changes to pensions law since the equalisation decisions arising out of the Treaty of Rome, the Pensions Act 1995 and the raft of new regulation and legislation since then, it is hardly surprising that many lay trustees feel bewildered and frustrated. Whether or not a change of corporate culture to try and control the unattractive side of capitalism is a good thing, the emphasis on caution seems likely only to develop further in the pensions arena as more and more trustees encounter scheme-specific funding issues for the first time following the first application of the new funding rules on January 1 2006. [1]

While it is clear that trustees have fiduciary duties to the members of a scheme, and indeed therefore to the spouses and dependants of members, do they also owe any duty to the employer company? The employer may be referred to in the trust deed and rules as an express beneficiary. As such, a duty would be owed. However, even if no mention is made of the employer's rights as beneficiary, it is still likely that the trustees do owe a duty of care to the sponsoring employer. This was stated in broad terms in *Edge v Pensions Ombudsman* [2000] CH 602; [1999] 4 ALLER 546. In that judgment, Lord Justice Chadwick stated that the trustees should:

*consider the effect that any course which they are minded to take will have on the financial ability of the employer to make the contributions to which that course will*

---

1 Part 3 of the Pensions Act 2004.

*entail. They must be careful not to impose burdens which imperil the continuity of the proper development of the employer's business or employment of the members who work in that business. The main purpose of the scheme is not served by putting an employer out of business ... the so called duty to act impartially ... is no more than the ordinary duty which the law imposes on a person who is entrusted with the exercise of a discretionary power ... if pension fund trustees [give proper consideration to the matters which are relevant and exclude from consideration matters which are irrelevant] they cannot be criticised if they reach a decision which appears to prefer the claims of one interest – whether that of employer, current employees or pensioners – over others. The preference will be the result of a proper exercise of the discretionary power.*

The decision in *Edge* concerned how surplus funds were to be distributed. It is thought likely that the judgment might instead have been more 'member friendly' if it had been ruling on circumstances in which the trustees were faced with a shortfall to pay. For example, in *Hagen Vici Chemicals* [2002] IR LR 31, Justice Elias stated, albeit at a risk of quoting him out of context, at paragraph [2], "the fiduciary obligations [of the trustees] are to the members of the scheme. It is only in the most exceptional cases that they would be justified in consenting [to any course of action inconsistent with their duty to the members]."

So now, the new scheme funding requirements lay firmly at the trustees' door the power and responsibility to decide how much money is required of an employer company. That is to say, while many employers continue to retain the right to fix contribution levels under their specific scheme deed and rules, the Pensions Act 2004 gives more power to the trustees to determine or accept contribution levels. Until the 2004 act, this duty sometimes sat lightly on the trustees' shoulders. The minimum funding requirement (MFR) used for calculating pension scheme liabilities until the end of 2005 was designed to operate as a science rather than an art. The MFR level has proved to be too modest. Trustees used to be much more sanguine about short-term problems with investment performance, not least because that relaxed attitude – otherwise known as a long-term view – was much more widely shared until the introduction of Financial Reporting Standard 17 reporting requirements a few years ago. However, it now seems that trustees were too lax about funding throughout the 1990s and into the first few years of this century. Even now, it is only as the new scheme-specific funding valuations are undertaken and reported on that the extent of the pension scheme deficits is becoming clear to trustees and employer companies for the first time. Trustees usually carry a legal responsibility for ensuring that scheme funding is, and remains, at proper levels. In the main, trustees have some justification for the decline in funding that they presided over and watched silently during the 1990s. Improving mortality, for example, is hardly the fault of a trustee body. On top of sharply improving mortality tables, unforeseen poor investment performance can seldom be blamed on the trustees.

Worries about current funding problems, coupled with the new scheme-specific funding requirements, have now compelled trustees, sometimes for the first time, to take a much closer and more educated interest in the scheme valuation process and the level of contribution payments to be required of the employer. Whereas before, trustees might simply accept a draft actuarial valuation, they must now pay careful attention to the report and agree the actuarial assumptions with the employer. In doing so, trustees now need to understand more fully the mortality assumptions applied and test their scheme actuary about the other assumptions adopted.

Trustees are expected to act much more like bankers than ever before. Often, the contingent pension scheme deficit – that is to say, the full value of the deficit on the buy-out basis – will be an employer's largest unsecured creditor. The trustees may decide to take security over employer assets and to monitor their exposure in the same way that a large creditor would behave.

## 3. Modern pressure on trustees?

With a list of regulatory and compliance requirements that could fill this chapter alone; with a requirement to demonstrate trustee knowledge and understanding; with the cost of professional indemnity cover and a much greater awareness of conflicts of interest, trustees are now more exposed than ever before to the risk of suit or penalty. Thus, the existence of an experienced and qualified independent trustee on trustee boards is a welcome way of helping to alleviate most of these concerns. A 2007 survey has stated that 50% of all trustee boards now include at least one independent trustee.[2] Ironically, perhaps, one disadvantage to scheme members is that having an independent trustee as part of the trustee body may help an employer adopt a much more rigorous approach to its dealings and negotiations with the trustees. However, in the round, any competent independent trustee will help to ensure that awkward finance issues are properly and carefully addressed, and that this is done in a cordial and collaborative way, but with independence and vigour when needed.

One further change introduced by the Pensions Act 2004 that is likely to lead to more independent trustees holding office arises out of the new mandatory requirement for member-nominated trustees. By October 2007 at the latest, schemes are required to ensure that at least one-third of the total number of trustees (or of directors of a corporate trustee company) are nominated by members, and employers will no longer be able to rely on an opt-out of this requirement. The Pensions Regulator has issued a code of practice to assist trustees with the new requirements. Moreover, there is a provision for the proportion of member-nominated trustees to be 50% of the total trustee body, possibly by 2009. However, a scheme with an independent trustee as its sole trustee is exempt from these new obligations.

Given also the requirement in the Pensions Act 2004 that trustees must acquire appropriate "knowledge and understanding" about pensions law, funding and investment, and comply with the codes of practice issued about these matters by the Pensions Regulator, increasing numbers of employers will decide that having an independent trustee offers the easiest way of coping with both the member-nominated trustee processes and the avoidance of time and expense of trustee training and education.

---

2 January 2007 PricewaterhouseCoopers survey on UK Pension Scheme Funding.

## 4. Engaging experts to help with funding

Lately, there has been a significant move, in part encouraged by the Pensions Regulator, towards commissioning independent reports from appropriate experts – often, but not necessarily, qualified accountants – about the strength of employer covenants. These reports are used to assist trustees to negotiate appropriate employer contribution levels, to assist with Pensions Regulator clearance applications or otherwise to safeguard trustees against criticism by justifying an inability of an employer to meet a higher level of contributions.

So, given the experience and knowledge that is to be expected of a good independent trustee, why should the employer also need to pay for a report on its own financial standing?

First, the Pensions Regulator has made it clear in the Code of Practice on Funding Defined Benefits[3] that it expects trustees to engage specialist advisers in appropriate circumstances so as to provide objective advice about the strength of employer covenants. Second, the process should not be nearly as painful as an employer might expect. If the employer's accounts and paperwork are in good order, and if the employer's financial officer and auditors are able to provide full support and up-to-date accounting figures, then the production of an independent report should be fairly quick and straightforward, even with sophisticated businesses. Third, the role of trustees includes a close overview of all aspects of scheme management, such as a good knowledge of legal, actuarial, administrative, investment and financial matters. Yet just as trustees are not qualified to give formal legal advice, no more are they expected to give formal objective financial advice about the strength of an employer's covenant. There will be times when trustees can properly decide to dispense with the cost of an independent review, but often it will be helpful to have one. Expert advice will be useful in measuring relevant criteria and what it means for the present and future ability of an employer to fund its scheme. Where an independent review is not commissioned, trustees will be expected to have a good reason for dispensing with a report, so much so that the trustees should minute that decision. Even with regard to fairly small pension schemes, where the cost of the report will be more of an anxiety, an independent financial review may still be necessary. All of the large firms of accountants and several specialist independent firms now have experienced teams ready to provide covenant review reports. Work in this area for trustees is likely to grow for the next few years.

## 5. Negotiation

Let us suppose that the trustees of the pension scheme are now armed with a new draft actuarial valuation report and an independent employer covenant review. Over the next decade, valuations are likely to include information about scheme funding deficits calculated on a buy-out basis. Indeed, in many cases the deficit may rank alongside the entire employer group net asset value in size. What do the trustees do? Do they press for contributions that then push the company into insolvency and in turn a winding-up of the scheme? Trustees might consider that this prevents the

3 Pensions Regulator Regulatory Code of Practice 03 paragraphs 58 to 60.

funding position becoming worse. Alternatively, do trustees nurture a plan with the directors to try and improve the overall scheme funding over the coming years? Ultimately it is for the trustees to strike the right balance in answering these questions. Naturally, any advisers who have reported on the employer covenant will give the trustees guidance on how far an employer company can be pushed. That is one of the purposes of such a report. However, there will usually need to be a negotiation process. This could test the skills and diplomacy of the trustees to the full. The trustees are in a unique position here, in that their duty is not just to the members of the pension scheme as a whole, but also to the different classes of membership which may sometimes compete. The active members will, for example, have a much keener interest in jobs being preserved than the deferred members. Is there any evidence of independent trustees colluding with employers to land schemes safely into the protection of the Pension Protection Fund (PPF) by allowing an employer company an easy ride in negotiation? None that has yet come to light. The Pensions Regulator can be expected to crack down heavily on any such behaviour. Moreover, trustees should assume that they owe a legal duty to the PPF, as contingent funder of last resort, to ensure that a scheme remains or becomes funded above PPF benefit levels where possible.

Where directors of an employer company are disheartened to find that all of their skill and energy in running a company may only be for the benefit of reducing its pension scheme deficit over the coming 10 years, many director bodies will look to other alternatives including, at one extreme, the administration or winding-up of the company under the Insolvency Act 1986. Increasingly, though, sophisticated reconstructing models are being used which may involve a more flexible approach by all of the interested parties, such as debt-for-equity swaps (subject to a complication provided by the statutory prohibition in Section 40 of the Pensions Act 1995 that not more than 5% in value of a scheme's assets can be held in the employer company equity). The more complex and creative such arrangements, the more likely that only an experienced independent trustee will be able to steer a scheme through the minefield of negotiation.

## 6. Resolving conflicts

If the trustees consider that they have pushed negotiations with their sponsoring employer as far as possible but are unable to reach an acceptable agreement, it by no means follows that their only option is to seek to trigger a winding-up of the scheme and sue for recovery of the scheme's funding deficit pursuant to Section 75 of the Pensions Act 1995, as amended by the Pensions Act 2004. While there may be occasions when it is essential to act quickly, litigation will normally be the last resort.

A handful of dispute resolution alternatives to court proceedings are available, such as arbitration, mediation or less formal dispute resolution processes. For example, the trustees and employer can agree jointly to appoint an independent professional, new to the parties and their advisers, with relevant industry knowledge to adjudicate on a dispute. The timetable and method of the dispute resolution process can be agreed between the parties. Sometimes this can take the form of what is called 'early neutral evaluation', in which an impartial adviser is asked to express a view, either binding or non-binding. If both sides approach the issue in dispute with a genuine desire, in good faith, to find a resolution, then such an informal process should and will usually be the quickest and least expensive way of reaching a resolution, particularly if the parties continue to keep without prejudice channels of communication open at the same time.

An independent trustee should be expected to take centre-stage in dispute resolution. Other trustees, if any, may be influenced by one or more biases – perhaps both as employees of the sponsoring employer and as members of the scheme. Awareness of the importance of actual or perceived conflicts of interest has been encouraged by the cultural shifts referred to at the start of this chapter. It was addressed by Professor Roy Goode in the 1993 Report of the Pensions law Review Committee:[4] "Trustees appointed by management frequently hold key positions within the company, whilst trustees appointed by members may feel obligations to those who appointed them ... . In the modern world, conflicts of interest cannot be avoided. They can, however, be managed."

In its Guidance for Trustees,[5] the Pensions Regulator underlines the importance to trustees of recognising the existence of a conflict of interest and taking steps to manage the conflict by taking independent advice.

Managing conflicts of interest will be particularly important when there is an open disagreement between employer and trustee. Depending on the importance of the conflict, options available to trustees in such circumstances include:

- the conflicted trustee stepping out of any discussion or vote on the contentious point at issue;
- application to court; or
- resignation of the conflicted trustee and/or appointment of an independent trustee.

Clearly all trustees are meant to be 'independent' – that is to say, to fulfil their functions as trustees independent of any bias towards the employer, union or member. However, it is now widely recognised that appointment of an outside, professional independent trustee is a quick and effective way of managing these differing interests.

## 7. Liability of independent trustees

Most trustees are provided in their scheme's deed and rules with an express exoneration from, or an indemnity against, liabilities for their acts or omissions, apart from claims arising from their fraud or dishonesty. In the absence of a clause to this effect, trustees would still expect to have recourse to scheme assets against their personal liability. For example, Section 31(1) of the Trustee Act 2000 provides that a trustee may have recourse to scheme assets to defend an action taken against him where it is found that he acted honestly and reasonably.[6] However, what of

4 Report of the Pensions Law Review Committee, chairman at Vol 1 (CM2342-I), para 4.5.54.

5 www.thepensionsregulator.gov.uk/pdf/webGuidanceForTrustees.pdf.

6 *Armitage v Nurse* [1998] Ch 241 [1997] 2 All ER 705.

independent trustees? There is ample moral and commercial justification for allowing unpaid lay trustees the comfort of having their personal assets not at risk, provided that they discharge their duties with honesty. However, the same justification does not sit so comfortably on paid, professional independent trustees, particularly when independent trustees would be expected to carry their own professional indemnity insurance. This is certainly the view of Pensions Ombudsman David Laverick. In a January 2007 decision, while he did allow an independent trustee to "shelter", as he put it, behind the exoneration clause, the ombudsman added his own disquiet at doing so: "It does not seem to me to be acceptable for a trustee who is being paid for his professional services to avoid the consequences of maladministration when carrying out such work."[7] These comments echoed the same view expressed in the ombudsman's 2005/2006 Annual Report.[8]

This view was shared in a family trust case in 2001 where the sole trustee was a solicitor.[9] It was claimed by the beneficiaries that the trustee had failed to take proper steps to realise an important trust asset with the result that the asset had become worthless. In the event, the claimants were largely unsuccessful. However, as to the question of whether the trustee was protected from liability by Section 61 of the Trustee Act 1925, being a similar provision to Section 31(1) of the Trustee Act 2000 referred to above, the court was much less sympathetic. Queen's Counsel Michael Briggs, sitting as a deputy judge of the High Court, opined that a lay trustee is required to act with the care of an ordinary prudent man of business in the handling of his own affairs, but that a solicitor trustee is required to bring to the administration of a trust that "degree of care and skill to be expected of an experienced solicitor, and there [is] no relevant distinction between his duties as an administrator and the solicitor's professional standard of skill and care".

With the developing involvement of professional independent trustees – who are usually, by nature of their role, either members of a profession or well-experienced advisers in the field – it seems likely that judicial opinion will shift towards independent trustees being liable to pay the price for their negligence despite the existence of any exhoneration clause in the scheme's governing documents

## 8. Conclusion

To summarise, the role of trustees has developed significantly since the early 1990s. Given the pressures on trustees described in this chapter, it would be surprising if an employer or the trustee body would not at the very least consider engaging an independent trustee in this climate. Employers might worry only about two negatives: control and cost. However, a competent independent trustee will not go into a new appointment 'boots first', upsetting good working relationships, unless – unusually – there is a need to do so. Parting with control of the trustee body is in fact exactly what an employer should be relieved to achieve. Doing so will help to protect

---

7 Pension ombudsman determinations for January 2007, Case N00827.
8 David Laverick 2005/2006 Annual Report (August 2006).
9 *Younger v Saner* [2001] All ER (D) 247 (Dec).

the company's directors personally from possible liability for breach of duty as directors and will also protect the company from accusations of failing to act in good faith towards its scheme. As to the question of costs, there is good scope for an independent trustee to add value to the way in which the scheme operates and in its decision making. As no one pension scheme is the same as any other, it is difficult to generalise, but when factoring in the cost of saved employer management time as well, a good independent trustee should be able to justify the cost of his service against the benefit to all concerned.

# Canada

**Mark Newton**
Heenan Blaikie LLP

---

Similar to trends observed in other industrialised nations, the pension sector in Canada has witnessed a dramatic change in the financial profile of pension plans in recent years. The average funded status of plans has sharply declined. In addition, unfunded pension liabilities have been a central focus of large corporate insolvencies. At the same time, perhaps due in part to the onerous funding requirements of defined benefit plans, employers have begun to shift towards providing defined contribution pension plans and other retirement savings vehicles rather than defined benefit plans.

## 1. Recent trends

All of the pension regulators across Canada maintain current statistics regarding the funded status of the pension plans within their respective jurisdictions. The information below is extracted from reports by the federal and Ontario regulators, which are the two jurisdictions that supervise the largest number of pension plans in Canada.

The federal government's pension regulator, the Office of the Superintendent of Financial Institutions (OSFI), published data on pension funding in its 2004-2005 annual report entitled "Building on Our Strengths". Surprisingly, the average solvency ratio for all defined benefit pension plans within OSFI's jurisdiction was 1.0, meaning that on average, defined benefit pension plans under federal jurisdiction are solvent. However, OSFI's report also indicated that 55% of federally regulated plans had a solvency deficit and of those plans in deficit, 57% had a solvency ratio of less than 90%.

In its June 2006 report entitled "Funding Defined Benefit Pension Plans: Risk-Based Supervision in Ontario", Ontario's pensions regulator, the Financial Services Commission of Ontario (FSCO), reported that as of 2005, only 40% of Ontario-registered defined benefit pension plans with a final average earnings benefit formula were fully funded on a solvency basis. Only 13% of plans with a career average benefit formula were fully funded on a solvency basis. Pension plans with flat benefit formulas, which is typically the design of collectively bargained pension plans, were the least well funded. Only 6% of these plans were fully funded on a solvency basis and 50% of them had a solvency ratio of less than 80%, meaning that if the plans were wound up, half of them would have less than C$0.80 for every C$1 of benefits required to be paid out.

Apart from government statistical reports, a number of studies conducted by industry organisations have pointed to a growing funding crisis in private pension plans in Canada. The Certified General Accountants Association of Canada published a study in 2005 entitled "The State of Defined Benefit Pension Plans in Canada: An Update" which outlines the continuing deterioration in the funded status of defined benefit pension plans in Canada. According to the report, the additional funding required to fund fully pension plan deficits grew from C$160 billion at the end of 2003 to C$190 billion at the end of 2004.

In August 2005 the Association of Canadian Pension Management published a report entitled "Back From the Brink: Securing the Future of Defined Benefit Pension Plans". In that report, the funding issues facing defined benefit pension plans are highlighted as part of the reason for the trend by employers towards offering defined contribution plans. The report points out the asymmetry between the risks and responsibilities a plan sponsor faces in funding a defined benefit pension plan and the restrictions the plan sponsor faces in being able to use or access surplus assets. The report also examines:

- the relative merits of requiring plans to be funded on a going-concern and solvency basis;
- the lack of flexibility in existing funding rules;
- the use of funding policies; and
- the application of letters of credit as a vehicle to cover solvency liabilities.

The legal and policy issues raised in the report echo some of the issues discussed as part of the Canadian Institute of Actuaries' November 2004 study entitled the "Report of the Task Force on Public Policy Principles of Pension Plan Funding". In addition to making eight specific recommendations regarding actuarial practices, this report called for clarification of the legal framework for surplus ownership and the 'pension deal' between employers and employees.

## 2. Regulatory regime

Pension plans in Canada are regulated by income tax legislation and pension standards legislation. Income tax legislation places limits on the contributions to pension plans and the amount and type of benefits that may be paid from pension plans. Pension standards legislation is more in the form of public policy legislation that sets standards for the proper administration of pension plans and ensures minimum benefits, such as vesting, survivor benefits and so on.

The Income Tax Act (Canada) is a federal statute that includes specific provisions and regulations pertaining to the registration of pension plans and the conditions for maintaining their qualified status. The act is administered by the federal Canada Revenue Agency. Within the Canada Revenue Agency there is a Registered Plans Directorate, which is responsible for overseeing all pension plans in Canada registered under the act. The sections of the act and the accompanying regulations prescribe in some detail the documents that must be filed to obtain and maintain registered status, contribution limits, the requirement to file actuarial reports (for defined benefit plans) and the specific conditions and limits in respect of retirement benefits, termination benefits, pre-retirement death benefits, post-retirement survivor benefits, bridge benefits, periods of absence and so on.

The federal government's pension standards legislation, the Pension Benefits Standards Act 1985, applies to pension plans sponsored by employers that, by the terms of the Canadian Constitution, are federally regulated entities. This includes employers in the banking sector, inter-provincial transportation, telecommunications and other federal undertakings. OSFI oversees pension plans registered under the act.

Most employers in Canada fall within the provincial jurisdiction. Each province (except Prince Edward Island) has enacted pension standards legislation, called either the Pension Benefits Act, the Pension Benefits Standards Act, the Employment Pension Plans Act or the Supplemental Pension Plans Act, depending upon the province at issue. For ease of reference, we refer to the provincial pension standards legislation as the Pension Benefits Act, to distinguish those regimes from the federal Pension Benefits Standards Act. Each province has a pensions regulator responsible for overseeing the pension plans registered in that jurisdiction.

A provincially related employer must register its pension plan with the province where the plurality of the pension plan members are located. Therefore, an employer with employees across Canada may have a pension plan registered under the Ontario Pension Benefits Act, despite the presence of employees working in a number of other provinces. In such a scenario, the employees outside of Ontario will still be subject to the pension legislation where they reside (or where they are paid from, if they do not report to work in the province of residence), despite the fact that the plan is only registered with FSCO, Ontario's pensions regulator. FSCO is responsible for administering the legislation of the other provinces for the plan members located outside of Ontario. The same logic applies to employers that sponsor pension plans covering employees governed by federal and provincial legislation. There is a reciprocal agreement between the regulators permitting the administration of the legislation in this manner (with some exceptions).

Typically, the rules respecting the funding and investment of pension plans are governed by the pension legislation under which a pension plan is registered. In the above example, the pension plan and fund registered under the Ontario Pension Benefits Act would be funded and invested in accordance with the Ontario Pension Benefits Act. This is important to keep in mind, given the different funding rules and legislative initiatives discussed below.

## 3. Funding rules

Both the Income Tax Act and pension standards legislation prescribe minimum funding standards. The general rule is that actuarial valuations must be performed no less frequently than every three years. The valuation reports must be filed with both the Canada Revenue Agency and the pension regulator. It is on the basis of the filed valuations that the plan sponsor contributes to the pension fund.

A valuation will set out the contributions on account of current service and the contributions for past service liabilities. The contributions for past service are expressed as a minimum and maximum. The minimum represents the amount required to amortise the past service liability over the longest permitted period of time. Regular unfunded liabilities may be amortised over no more than 15 years, while solvency liabilities may be amortised over no more than five years. Unfunded liabilities are past service liabilities calculated on a going-concern basis. Solvency liabilities are past service liabilities calculated on a wind-up basis.

Depending upon the specific rules of the jurisdiction in which a pension plan is registered, if a going-concern valuation indicates a solvency deficiency and the ratio of solvency assets to solvency liabilities is less than 0.8, then solvency valuations must be performed and filed annually until such time as the 'solvency ratio' improves to greater than 0.8. This is intended to reduce the likelihood of large deficiencies on the wind-up of a pension plan, at least as a proportion of the size of the pension plan liabilities.

## 4. Pension Benefits Guarantee Fund

The only jurisdiction in Canada with a government-sponsored guarantee fund is Ontario. The purpose of the Pension Benefits Guarantee Fund is to protect employee pension benefits in the event of the insolvency or bankruptcy of the plan sponsor. The fund was established in 1980 and is administered by the superintendent of FSCO. It is funded by premiums paid by those employers with pension plans covered by the fund regime. This is generally limited to defined benefit single-employer pension plans. Multi-employer pension plans and jointly sponsored pension plans are exempt from the fund regime.

In the event that an employer with an underfunded pension plan becomes insolvent, the superintendent must first declare that the Pension Benefits Guarantee Fund applies. If it does, the fund will top up pension plan members' pension benefits to prescribed limits based on the age and service of the members. The maximum benefit guaranteed by the fund is C$1,000 per month.

The Pension Benefits Guarantee Fund itself is significantly under-funded. As of the end of 2005, it had a deficit of C$250 million, negative cash flow and a loan of C$330 million from the Ontario government. A large proportion of the under-funding had been built up prior to the much-publicised insolvencies of Algoma Steel and Stelco, discussed below. This placed the government in a difficult situation when it came to dealing with these two insolvencies in which the pension funding shortfalls were potentially very large.

## 5. Risk-based monitoring

In view of the funding issues with defined benefit pension plans, some jurisdictions in Canada have adopted a more proactive model of risk-based monitoring of pension plans. The main objectives of risk-based monitoring are to:

- establish criteria to identify plans with a higher risk profile;
- allocate more regulatory resources to these pension plans; and
- take corrective action.

For example, as a general rule, if the solvency ratio of a defined benefit pension plan with a final earnings formula is less than 0.8, further screening by the regulator may be warranted. The regulator will also review the actuarial methods and assumptions with greater scrutiny. If there are irregularities, the regulator will initiate discussions with the plan sponsor and, depending upon the authority given the regulator in the legislation, it may impose conditions on the plan sponsor in relation to the funding of its pension plans.

OSFI, the federal regulator, probably has the strictest and most interventionist risk-based programme of plan supervision. OSFI has automated early warning tests that are based on filed information. In 2004-2005, 25% of pension plans that filed information were subject to more detailed review. OSFI also tests for plan solvency on a semi-annual basis, for all defined benefit pension plans. If a pension plan's solvency ratio is close to or less than 1.0, the plan's risk profile is moved to the high range, upon which OSFI will consider various interventions, as occurred in relation to Air Canada's pension plan (see below in the discussion of pension insolvencies). One powerful type of intervention at OSFI's disposal is to request early filing of actuarial reports, which will update the financial position of a pension plan and, in many cases, will identify further deficits that require expedited funding. OSFI also identifies pension plans in which contribution holidays were taken by the plan sponsor, and of those contribution holidays which, in its view, were imprudent. In those cases, OSFI strongly encourages the plan sponsor to recommence contributions.

OSFI also conducts on-site examinations of pension plans. It maintains a watch list of pension plans based on the size of a pension plan's deficit and the plan sponsor's capacity to fund it. To compile its watch list, OSFI accesses public information regarding an employer's financial position, together with the information it has on the employer's pension plans, to determine whether intervention is required.

OSFI's risk-based supervision efforts have yielded obvious results. As discussed above, OSFI's 2004-2005 annual report indicated that an average solvency ratio of 1.0 existed for the defined benefit pension plans under OSFI's supervision.

## 6. Response to pension insolvencies

There have been several high-profile insolvencies in Canada in the past few years in which pension liabilities and the associated solvency funding requirements have played a key role. Two very prominent steel producers with pension plans registered in Ontario, Algoma Steel and Stelco Inc, filed for restructuring under the Companies Creditors Arrangement Act in 2001 and 2004, respectively. The Companies Creditors Arrangement Act is the equivalent of Chapter 11 under US law. Air Canada, the largest airline in Canada, filed for Companies Creditors Arrangement Act protection in 2003. Air Canada is a federally regulated business and, as such, its pension plans are governed by the federal Pension Benefits Standards Act, under the supervision of OSFI. Due to the different regulatory jurisdictions responsible for the pension aspects of these restructurings, it is instructive to examine both the steel and airline situations in closer detail. With respect to the steel industry, the commentary below focuses on Stelco's restructuring because it is more recent than the Algoma situation.

### 6.1 Steel restructurings

In the case of both Algoma and Stelco, the pension liabilities and funding obligations precipitated insolvency proceedings. This created a very serious situation for the creditors, shareholders, employees and pensioners of those companies. In addition, and perhaps more crucially, the bankruptcy of either company would have pushed the Ontario Pension Benefits Guarantee Fund into insolvency unless the Ontario government provided hundreds of millions of dollars to pay the benefits guaranteed under the Pension Benefits Act.

Notably, Ontario's legislation contains a unique feature applicable to pension plan wind-ups. In the event of a partial or full wind-up of a pension plan, members are entitled to 'grow in' to any special early retirement or other subsidised benefits under the pension plan, which may otherwise be forfeited on wind-up. Members 'grow in' to these benefits as if their service had continued to retirement age. This feature would have added significantly to the value of pension benefits payable to the Algoma and Stelco pension plan members, and would have put a further strain on the Pension Benefits Guarantee Fund.

As a result, the Ontario government was motivated to do what it could to prevent these companies from going into bankruptcy proceedings. The end result in both cases was that the Ontario government relaxed the Pension Benefits Act's funding rules by enacting special regulations that applied specifically to these companies.

The following are comments specific to Stelco. Stelco had previously made an election under the Pension Benefits Act to exempt itself from the solvency funding provisions in the regulations to the Pension Benefits Act. This election was available up to June 28 2002 for pension plans with assets of at least C$500 million. This exemption was a special provision in the Pension Benefits Act directed at the largest pension plans, which exist primarily in the automotive and steel industries. As a result of exercising this exemption, the solvency position of Stelco's pension plans was not what it would otherwise have been had the plans been funded in the same manner as pension plans subject to the solvency funding requirements. Stelco's solvency deficiency in its pension plans amounted to approximately C$1.25 billion.

The agreement Stelco reached with the Ontario government required Stelco to make an initial contribution of C$400 million to its pension plans, and for the remaining solvency deficiency to be paid according to a schedule of payments over 10 years (instead of the Pension Benefits Act's regular five-year period for funding solvency deficiencies). The Ontario government also advanced Stelco C$100 million in the form of a loan, three-quarters of which will be forgiven if Stelco eliminates the pension plan deficiency by the end of the 10-year period. In the years since this crisis, steel prices have rebounded and both Algoma and Stelco's balance sheets are much stronger.

### 6.2 Airline restructuring

Air Canada's solvency deficiencies in its pension plans were of the same magnitude as Stelco's, in the order of C$1.3 billion. In March 2003, OSFI ordered Air Canada to perform a valuation of its pension plans and immediately to make catch-up payments that amounted to approximately C$500 million. The contributions due and payable into the pension plans constituted a deemed trust under the Pension Benefits Standards Act. OSFI threatened to enforce the deemed trust if Air Canada did not make the required payments. This directive pushed Air Canada into Companies Creditors Arrangement Act proceedings.

Under the federal Pension Benefits Standards Act, unlike the Ontario Pension Benefits Act, there are no special 'grow-in' provisions and there is no guarantee fund. Therefore, there was perhaps less pressure on OSFI than there was on the Ontario government to arrive at a successful resolution of Air Canada's funding crisis. In the event that Air Canada went bankrupt and the pension plans were wound up, the pension plan members would receive benefits only up to the degree of solvency. In Air Canada's case, the pension plans were over 90% solvent, notwithstanding the enormous deficiencies.

OSFI finally reached an agreement with Air Canada and entered into a funding relief protocol in May 2004. Under the terms of the protocol, the deemed trust would be waived in favour of promissory notes issued by Air Canada. In addition, the solvency deficiencies would be funded in accordance with a 10-year schedule instead of the regular five-year funding under the Pension Benefits Standards Act. In order to protect against further deterioration of the pension plans' solvency ratio, any future plan amendments would be subject to the prior approval of the superintendent of OSFI. In September 2004, the terms of the protocol were implemented in the form of special regulations to the Pension Benefits Standards Act. These regulations apply only to Air Canada's pension plans.

## 7. Regulatory reform

As can be seen from the above, the approach of the regulators to corporate restructurings has been largely reactive in nature and specific to the circumstances that may arise. While the regulators across Canada have witnessed the declining solvency of pension plans and an increased number of insolvencies, they have been slow to enact any broad-based or sweeping reforms to help alleviate the situation. Partly as a result of the key role played by pension deficits in the high-profile insolvencies discussed above along with the lobbying efforts of many organisations that are calling for reform, some pension regulators have begun to act, albeit slowly. Specifically, the federal government, as well as the Quebec and Alberta provincial governments, have either enacted legislation or made reform proposals with the intent of enacting measures in the near future. These initiatives are summarised below.

### 7.1 Proposed federal regulations

The federal government introduced draft changes to the Pension Benefits Standards Act regulations in June 2006. The proposed changes would permit employers to choose between a few different funding relief mechanisms:

- to consolidate all existing solvency deficiencies and amortise over a new five-year period;
- to extend the five-year solvency payments to 10 years with a requirement for member consent, such that no more than one-third of plan members object, and

- to extend the five-year solvency payments to 10 years, in combination with a letter of credit to guarantee the difference.

Member consent would not be required if a letter of credit is used.

The changes proposed by the federal government, if enacted, would apply only to federally regulated employers. The measures are temporary in nature as well, applying to solvency deficiencies identified in an actuarial report prior to January 2 2008.

Clearly, the federal government has attempted to balance the competing interests of plan sponsors and plan members. Generally speaking, the federal government appears to be maintaining its belief that the five-year funding timeline for solvency deficiencies represents an appropriate balancing between member security and sponsor funding, so no permanent changes to this aspect of the funding rules have been proposed.

### 7.2 Regulatory measures in Quebec

The Quebec government amended its pension legislation in 2005 by introducing a temporary measure (Bill 102) in anticipation of more substantial and permanent reforms in respect of pension funding. The temporary measures permit the extension of funding of solvency deficiencies from five years to 10 years and also permit previously identified solvency deficiencies that remain outstanding to be combined under an amortisation schedule. The rules also permit the use of a letter of credit to secure the amount of the difference in funding between the five and 10-year amortisation amounts. If a letter of credit is not used, member consent must be obtained, unless the plan sponsor is a municipality or university. Consent is deemed to be given unless 30% or more of the members object. These measures apply to the first valuation conducted after December 30 2004.

Quebec was the first jurisdiction in Canada to permit the funding of pension plans, even partially, through letters of credit. There have been many proposals by industry organisations, such as the Association of Canadian Pension Management, advocating in favour of recognising letters of credit as a valid funding mechanism. Use of letters of credit remains somewhat controversial and has been the subject of litigation in the courts. The British Columbia Court of Appeal released a decision in 2005 in which it decided that a letter of credit was not a valid investment under existing pension regulations.

Quebec's Bill 102 above was passed into law in anticipation of Bill 30, which was introduced in June 2006. Bill 30 is more robust legislation that proposes sweeping reforms in a number of areas, including plan funding, governance and plan administrator responsibilities. If passed, Bill 30 is scheduled to come into force on January 1 2010. Between now and then, the Quebec government is engaged in the consultation process. The permanent measures included in Bill 30 provide for:

- a provision for adverse deviations that affect solvency;
- an increase in the amortisation period for solvency deficiencies from five years to 10 years;
- the consolidation of solvency deficiencies in the first valuation after December 30 2009;

- the use of letters of credit to guarantee up to 15% of solvency deficiencies;
- the determination and funding of the cost of plan amendments on the basis of solvency; and
- a provision for the plan administrator and the members to agree in advance regarding the allocation of surplus assets.

Another measure relating to ongoing funding limits contribution holidays to the year immediately following an actuarial valuation.

The changes introduced in Bill 102 and Bill 30 were the result of a comprehensive study by the Quebec government that was published in 2005 as a Working Paper entitled "Toward Better Funding of Defined Benefit Pension Plans". The changes proposed by Quebec are the most comprehensive, proactive and forward-looking measures of any jurisdiction in Canada.

### 7.3 Alberta proposals

In December 2005, the Alberta government tabled draft legislation that would permit plan sponsors to cover an entire solvency deficiency with a letter of credit. Under the proposals, the government would approve a list of financial institutions to issue letters of credit. The regulations would set out the detailed provisions as to how the system would function. The letter of credit would cover the principal sum of the solvency deficiency, but not the interest accruing on the deficiency. The letter could not be cancelled until the solvency deficiency was reduced to zero. The letter would therefore be called if not replaced or if the plan sponsor were unable to make payment by reason of insolvency or otherwise. The Alberta government enacted other changes to its pension legislation in August 2006, but those amendments did not include the letter of credit proposals, which are still under consideration.

## 8. Conclusion

The pension regulatory regime in Canada is in need of a concerted and unified effort to resolve the funding and other issues pertaining to defined benefit plans. The pension plan deficits and the associated consequences faced by plan sponsors, plan administrators, regulators, advisers, plan members and other stakeholders in Canada are not unique. However, they are serious, and without some resolution the attraction of defined benefit pension plans may continue to erode. The predictable result is that defined benefit plans will predominate only in the public sector and with unionised workforces.

# Germany

**Christoph Crisolli**
Kliemt & Vollstädt

The German pension system has been receiving increasing attention in recent years, and not just in connection with the structural impact of demographic developments. German employers also face the impact of significantly unfunded pension obligations in the light of the strict banking requirements under the new Basel II regime. According to a recent report by Mercer Human Resource Consulting, German employers have the worst pension deficits in Europe.[1] The highest deficits are among companies listed on Germany's DAX-30 index: in 2005, the aggregate liabilities of these companies amounted to almost €250 billion.[2]

Germany is one of the few countries where the internal funding of pension obligations via book reserves is an accepted standard. Since the adoption of US generally accepted accounting principles (GAAP)/International Financial Reporting Standards, pension liabilities have become transparent and international investors are increasingly aware of the risks arising from unfunded or under-funded pension obligations.[3] As a reaction to these deficits, rating agencies have reduced the short-term and long-term bond ratings of employers as substantial as Deutsche Post AG and ThyssenKrupp AG.[4]

This chapter explains the background to the pension liability exposure of German employers and the steps that have been taken to find a solution to reduce the deficits through the outsourcing of pension liabilities, in particular through contractual trust arrangements (CTAs).

## 1. Unfunded pension schemes

In addition to the statutory public pension scheme, employees in Germany are often covered by supplementary occupational schemes such as direct pension commitment plans, support funds, pension funds, direct insurance or deferred compensation arrangements. Well over half of all pension obligations of German employers are in the form of direct pension commitments based on unfunded or funded pension schemes. By engaging in such commitments, employers withhold a portion of employees' salaries in order to pay them directly a pension in retirement.

1 "Germany hardest hit by pension fund deficits", *The Guardian*, August 8 2006.
2 *"Demographischer Wandel und Pensionen"*, *Frankfurt Allgemeine Zeitung*, September 4 2006.
3 Heubeck/Seeger, *"'Ungedeckte' Pensionsverpflichtungen im Rating von Unternehmen"*, *Der Betrieb* 2004, pp 993 *et seq*.
4 "Standard & Poor's downgrades ThyssenKrupp two notches to BB+: Loss of investment grade status", ThyssenKrupp press release, February 21 2003.

In return, employees obtain a claim against the company, which must make accounting provisions for such deferred payments.[5]

In contrast to the separate funding found in most other countries, German tax legislation has historically favoured a 'direct pension commitment' approach. For unfunded pension plans, the employer pays pensions from cash flow; consequently, pension payments do not affect cash flow before they are due. When pensions are internally financed in this manner, employers accrue book reserves corresponding to the existing value of pension commitments as liabilities on their balance sheets, and write off the accruals from their taxable income. For the recipient, income tax does not fall due until the pension is actually paid and the book reserves are drawn down. Currently, the accrual of book reserves is still the most widespread method of financing occupational pension plans in Germany, accounting for almost 60% of total pension liabilities in 2004.[6]

In recent years, however, employers have increasingly moved to match direct commitments with external funding and investment. In such funded pension plans, the employer transfers money to an external fund, which invests it and pays the pension at retirement. The employer guarantees the amount of the future pension (defined benefit plan) in the event that the value of the fund's assets becomes insufficient to cover such obligations and the pension plan becomes underfunded.[7]

## 2. Outsourcing of pension liabilities

To reduce the risks inherent to unfunded or under-funded pension schemes, the outsourcing of pension obligations makes commercial sense. However, in order for employers to improve key balance-sheet numbers and increase their credit rating, the transfer must be carefully structured and the disadvantages weighed against the advantages.

The following strategies may be considered.

### 2.1 Outsourcing of liabilities to a pension fund

The 2002 German Retirement Savings Act introduced the concept of the pension fund and made it possible to make tax-favourable asset transfers to pension funds in order to fund unfunded pension commitments without creating a tax liability for the employees concerned. Employers can thus extinguish their past-service pension liabilities by undertaking a transfer to a pension fund. Employers also use the pension fund approach in M&A situations for relatively moderate obligations where the purchaser is reluctant to assume responsibility for pension liabilities.

A pension fund offers almost unrestricted capital investment possibilities and is therefore attractive in terms of returns. However, several issues regarding transfer possibilities are still unresolved from a legal standpoint. Although the legislature has

5 "By accepting a portion of their compensation on a deferred basis, the employees essentially become creditors of the company" – Standard & Poor's Criteria for Assessing Post-retirement Obligations March 20, 2003, p 1.

6 Gerke/Mager/Reinschmidt/Schmeider, *Empirical risk analysis of pension insurance*, 2006, p 3.

7 Reichel/Schmandt, *Betriebliche Altersversorgung bei Unternehmenskauf und Umstrukturierung*, 2006, pp 280 *et seq*.

established a framework for the tax-free transfer of assets to a pension fund in return for the assumption of pension obligations, corresponding regulations have not yet been introduced under German labour law. It is therefore unclear whether the individual consent of the beneficiaries must be obtained.[8] In addition, pension funds must calculate their liabilities conservatively, in a manner similar to that adopted by insurance companies when pricing annuity business. Thus, the amount that would need to be transferred to 'buy out' plan liabilities can substantially exceed the value that employers would typically hold on their accounting books for such liabilities. Finally, a pension fund is not specified as a suitable transferee of pension obligations in the Company Pension Act, the law which regulates company pension schemes. As a result, most providers of pension funds are currently unable to 'mirror' the defined benefits under existing payment plans in their pension plans.

It is hoped that legislation will reduce the need for such a large contribution in order to finance past-service liabilities, which would make such transfers more attractive. However, any advantage of this approach must be weighed against the fact that if transferred assets plus future returns prove insufficient to pay promised benefits, the employer will be obliged to make up any deficit.

### 2.2 Transfer to a contractual trust arrangement

CTAs are gaining increasing acceptance as a method of outsourcing pension obligations in Germany. A CTA is a reliable way to convert existing company assets into pension plan assets that are recognised under Financial Accounting Standard 87 and International Accounting Standard (IAS) 19. The legal framework may be structured without changing the investment structure or tax treatment of the assets. Nearly half of all companies listed on the DAX-30, and many German subsidiaries of foreign corporations, have a CTA in place.[9] Contributions to CTAs are considered company assets and do not represent taxable income of employees.

A CTA is usually implemented by 'two-way trust' models instead of 'pledge' models. If implemented via a trust, the pension reserves and the relevant assets are transferred from the sponsoring employer and are cancelled from the balance sheet. This is possible not only for accounts in accordance with IAS or US GAAP, but also pursuant to Section 292 of the Commercial Code for group financial statements and, since 2005, also for the individual statements of German companies.[10] Since no change of pension debtor occurs in this scenario, the beneficiaries' consent is not required.

While it is not required that employee representative bodies be consulted prior to the implementation of a CTA, it is advisable that employers involve works councils to achieve higher acceptance among employees.

Trust models are generally characterised by the fact that assets of the employer

---

8 The Federal Labour Court recently ruled that the transfer of pension liabilities from a former employer to a new legal entity in a transfer of undertakings scenario does not require the consent of either the employees concerned or the pension security association – see Federal Labour Court decision of February 22 2005, 3 AZR 499/03.

9 Passarge, "*Aktuelle Fragen zur Auslagerung von Pensionsverpflichtungen mittels* Contractual Trust Agreements", *Der Betrieb* 1995, p 2746.

10 Höfer, BetrAVG-Arbeitsrecht, 2004, p 1408.

are provided exclusively for the purpose of fulfilling its pension obligations and are separated from its other assets. Assets in respect of pension obligations are usually outsourced to a legal entity with the legal form of a registered association – that is, to an independent legal entity charged with the administration and investment of the assets transferred, and bound by provisions set out in the trust agreement. The key feature of these 'two-way trusts' is that the trustee assumes the function of an administrative trustee with respect to the employer (the settlor), while at the same time assuming a security trusteeship with respect to the employee entitled to pension benefits (the beneficiary). This security trust is arranged in such a way that the beneficiary acquires proprietary rights to payment against the trustee on the occurrence of a security event (ie, the entitlement to payment of a benefit). In this regard, the trust agreement to be concluded between settlor and trustee constitutes what is known as a third-party beneficiary contract.

As a CTA is not a pension vehicle, it is not subject to the EU Occupational Pensions Directive (2003/41/EC). There are no restrictions on capital investment with the CTA model. The system also has the advantage of fully flexible allocation as regards the expense for the beneficiary's pension. This means that there is no limitation on the amount which may be contributed for the beneficiary and there is no obligation to pay the same or increasing rates of contribution, so it is possible to link contributions to employer success.

From a legal standpoint, the CTA model first requires the establishment of a trust as an independent legal entity – usually a registered association or a limited liability company – to which the means for the fulfilment of pension commitments can be outsourced. Articles of association and internal procedural rules for the management board must be drawn up for the trust. A trust agreement is then concluded between the employer and the trust which, in addition to administration of the trust for the employer, must assume the obligations of a genuine security trusteeship in relation to the employee as beneficiary. Such a third-party beneficiary contract is crucial to ensure that the employee is sufficiently protected from insolvency under private law.

From a tax standpoint, companies usually wish to transfer the means without reversal of hidden reserves, to avoid the value of the reserves becoming subject to taxation on earnings. It is crucial to obtain the view of the tax authorities on this issue prior to implementation. Depending on the companies involved, issues under banking supervision regulations may also require clarification prior to implementation. The recent code of practice published by BaFin, the German financial services regulator, confirms that fiduciary companies operating within CTAs are conducting regular banking business – that is, financial commission business, depositary business and, in certain circumstances, guarantee business.[11] As a result, CTAs are in principle subject to approval, with the exception of so-called 'company CTAs', which are subject to the law governing banking business. Banking law stipulates that a CTA fiduciary which exclusively undertakes 'internal' business with a parent, sister or subsidiary company does not require BaFin permission. Thus, fiduciary constructs which are not part of an external company, independent of

11 See www.bafin.de/merkblaetter/0511.htm.

intention, investments and scope, but are rather administered exclusively internally, are not subject to approval. All other CTA constructs are, under certain circumstances, subject to an exception under German banking law.

A CTA structure may be illustrated as follows.[12]

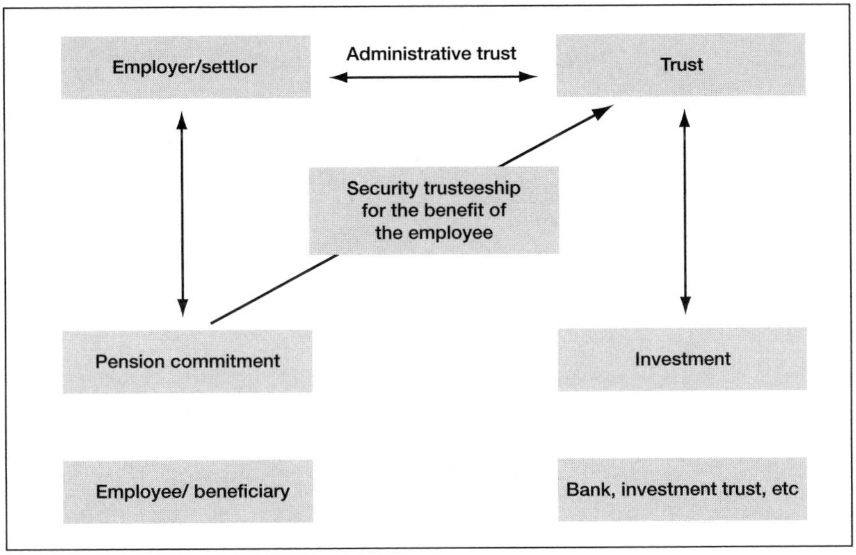


The advantages of clearer accounting and additional benefit security are countered by the main disadvantage of CTAs: namely, that the transferred assets may no longer be used for other purposes, such as capital expenditures or acquisitions.

A number of transfer methods should not be considered. The first is where a third party assumes the responsibility to fulfil future pension obligations within an internal relationship with the employer only. In such case the employer remains directly liable for fulfilment of the pension obligations in relation to the beneficiary, even if the third party takes over the entire administration of the pension scheme.

The second arises where future pension obligations are transferred to a pension fund society or direct insurance policy. In such case the transfer of assets to an external pension debtor in return for assumption of pension obligations will render the transferred assets subject to wage tax, except in the event of liquidation. In addition, the strict investment regulations of the Insurance Supervision Act apply to such external pension schemes, with the effect that the expected return on capital invested is lower than it would be with an optimised free investment strategy.

## 3. Conclusion

German employers with unfunded pensions are increasingly aware of the attendant

12 Reichel/Schmandt, *Betriebliche Altersversorgung bei Unternehmenskauf und Umstrukturierung*, 2006, pp 280 *et seq*.

financial risks, particularly where they have invested company assets to pay future pensions. In this context, sensible financial structuring can improve both accounting treatment and insolvency protection without changing employee benefits. There are indications that the trend towards CTAs is likely to continue among larger companies and spread to small and medium-sized organisations.

# Ireland

**Fiona Thornton**
LK Shields Solicitors

## 1. Overview

The Pensions Act 1990 requires defined benefit pension schemes to be funded at a basic level known as the 'minimum funding standard'. Schemes are required to be valued by an actuary every three years, following which the actuary must certify whether the scheme meets the standard. The actuary must also opine on an annual basis as to whether he considers the scheme would meet the standard. Where the standard is not met, the trustees must file a funding proposal (as agreed with the sponsoring employer) with the Pensions Board (the equivalent of the UK Pensions Regulator) demonstrating how the scheme shall meet the standard by a date agreed with the Pensions Board. If the proposal is not filed, the board has power to reduce benefits. Where a scheme fails the standard, its trustees are given a statutory power to refuse any early retirements, notwithstanding that they may have no such power under the scheme's governing rules. While the Pensions Board has power to prosecute breaches of the Pensions Act, there is no debt on the employer legislation in Ireland, nor any pension protection fund. When a scheme is established, it is feasible to enable the employer to wind it up at any time without the employer being required to make good any funding deficit arising at the time of wind-up.

Employers do not set up pension schemes with a view to winding them up. However, external influences such as accounting standard Financial Reporting Standard 17 and increased regulation, coupled with the recent bear markets, have had the effect of prompting several employers to wind up their defined benefit pension schemes, especially where the scheme has a deficit on the funding standard basis and the employer is faced with the prospect of paying in significant extra contributions in line with a prospective funding proposal. Some employers are reorganising their pension arrangements either to close their defined benefit scheme to new members or to reduce the future accrual rate. Others have wound up their defined benefit schemes which are running a deficit. In some cases the employer will effectively make good the deficit for active members by making extra payments to newly established alternative pensions vehicles. When an insolvent defined benefit scheme is wound up, the first priority of entitlements requires benefits to be secured for additional voluntary contributions paid by members and for pensions in payment. Other beneficiaries rank second. Consequently, where an insolvent pension scheme is wound up, the deferred members are most likely to suffer the greatest reduction in benefit as the employer may take steps to ameliorate the position of its current workforce, and pensioners are a first call on the assets of the scheme.

## 2. The minimum funding standard

This applies to any occupational pension scheme other than a defined contribution scheme or a small scheme which became frozen before January 1 1993. A 'small scheme' is one with fewer than 100 members entitled to, but not receiving, pension benefits. It also applies to any cross-border defined benefit scheme which is authorised to accept contributions from an undertaking in another EU member state. Occupational pension schemes which are not cross-border and which fail the funding standard may have a relatively long period within which to fund up to the required level. Cross-border schemes do not enjoy this leeway and are required to be fully funded at all times. Many public sector schemes are exempted by regulations from compliance with the funding standard on the basis that their benefits are paid in whole or in part out of monies provided by the state's Central Fund or by the Irish Parliament. Such schemes are funded on a pay-as-you-go basis.

The funding standard is calculated on a discontinuance basis. The actuary is required to assume that on the effective date the scheme is discontinued and wound up and the certification must show whether the assets at that date are sufficient to meet the liabilities, assuming the scheme was wound up on that date. The standard is met if, in the opinion of the actuary, the resources of the scheme would be sufficient had the scheme been wound up on that date to provide for:

- benefits in respect of additional voluntary contributions and the transfer of accrued rights from other schemes to the extent that the rights to which the transfer relates were originally secured or granted by way of additional voluntary contributions;
- pensions in the course of payment;
- a transfer of accrued rights from another scheme;
- benefits for current active members and deferred pensioners; and
- the estimated expenses of winding-up.

The actuary may assume that the liabilities of the scheme on that date can be provided by transferring benefits to another pension scheme or to a buy-out bond. Pensioner liabilities must be valued on the basis of open market annuities.

## 3. Triennial certificates and inter-valuation statements

Under the Pensions Act 1990 the trustees of a defined benefit pension scheme are required to ensure that its assets and liabilities are valued at intervals of no longer than three years. Such valuations will usually precede a triennial certification. During the two inter-valuation years the actuary must make an annual certification. Without this, members would be unaware of a funding problem until the next actuarial valuation. Instead, the scheme's annual report must contain a statement which incorporates the scheme actuary's opinion as to whether he is reasonably satisfied as at the last day of the reporting period of the annual report that if he were to prepare an actuarial funding certificate period, he would certify that the scheme satisfies the funding standard.

## 4. Trustee obligations where scheme fails the standard

Where the scheme fails the standard the trustees must notify the Pensions Board. They also must prepare and submit a funding proposal which must be agreed with the sponsoring employer. There are various filing deadlines and procedural steps which must be met in this process, and these can be difficult to meet in practice.

For example, the funding proposal is expected to be delivered at the same time as the certificate which indicates that the scheme does not meet the standard. This may be problematic to accomplish due to the fact that the employer is required to agree the funding proposal. If the employer is a subsidiary, it may need to get sign-off from its parent. Also, since there is no legal requirement on the part of the employer to meet the cost of any funding deficit, the employer is likely to want time to evaluate whether it wishes to continue the scheme.

The proposal must be accompanied by a certificate from the scheme actuary indicating that the proposal can be reasonably expected to satisfy the funding standard.

The Pensions Board has power to modify some of these procedural steps, but has no role in approving or otherwise commenting on the contents of a funding proposal.

It usually adopts a very sympathetic attitude to a scheme in distress once it is aware that a problem has arisen. Its aim is to facilitate the continued existence of defined benefit schemes, while also carrying out its statutory functions as a regulator. A funding proposal usually demonstrates that with additional funding made by the sponsoring employer over a specified period, the standard will be met during or by the end of that period. The usual period covered by a funding proposal is three years.

Following the significant fall in stock markets in 2001 to 2003, the Pensions Act was amended to give the Pensions Board discretion to extend the period within which trustees of an insolvent defined benefit schemes are required to bring the scheme back into equilibrium.

Where the trustees seek a longer funding period, the Pensions Board will facilitate funding over a longer period of up to 10 years, provided it considers that appropriate circumstances have arisen and the failure to meet the standard relates wholly or mainly to either or both of two sets of circumstances. (Exceptionally, the Pensions Board will allow a longer period, but no longer than the average working life of the active members.)

The circumstances are that:

- both:
  - the assets are less than expected due to market performance of scheme assets where that performance is consistent with the general performance of those markets; and
  - having regard to the general performance of investment markets, the Pensions Board considers that specifying a later date is necessary or appropriate and not contrary to the scheme members' interests; and
- the liabilities of the scheme are greater than expected where this is due to prescribed factors (being adverse experience relating to price inflation or rates of interest underlying the actuarial values over the relevant period; relating

to increases in pensionable earnings; and relating to the payment of benefits other than pensions).

Where an extension to the usual funding period is sought, the Pensions Board will expect the funding to be spread evenly over the period and the new contribution rate to be at least equal to the aggregate of the normal contribution rate (as if the scheme had neither a surplus nor deficit) and the contribution rate necessary to fund the deficit over the working lifetime of active members.

## 5. Employer's position

Larger schemes are more sophisticated than smaller ones. As at December 31 2005, 35 defined benefit schemes had over 1,000 members and were subject to the funding standard. It is not known how many of these had funding difficulties at that time. In order to ward off a deficit, three routes are contemplated:

- tinkering with the liabilities (eg, changing the future accrual rate, increasing retirement age, restricting future pensionable salary increases and changing salary policy by the introduction of non-pensionable bonuses);
- altering the investment policy by persuading the trustees to take a more aggressive attitude to risk; or
- using other means such as the deployment of contingent assets.

It is unclear how many sponsoring employers engage in deficit reduction strategies such as the employment of letters of credit and the use of parental guarantees, although some may be considering the use of such strategies. There is no information in the public arena regarding such practices, but practitioners are considering their application. There are technical legal issues that are relevant to such strategies: parental guarantees may be helpful to give trustees comfort where they are asked to adopt more aggressive investment strategies than they might otherwise contemplate, but, if called upon, the guarantee may give rise to breach of self-investment rules. Letters of credit may need to be spread over more than one financial institution if the value exceeds 10% of the scheme's assets; otherwise a breach of concentration rules would arise. The practical effect of such a breach is that the investment may not be taken into account by the actuary when certifying the scheme's solvency. Given the relative size of Irish defined benefit schemes, relative to the UK market, and that provided the scheme rules so permit, the employer is free to wind up a plan at any time (subject to employment law and human resource considerations), there is probably less pressure to be creative as the values are significantly less and there is no debt on employer legislation or pension protection fund levy. Straight funding is still the most common solution when a deficit actually arises, along with seeking a time extension over which the deficit is eliminated, provided the relevant conditions are met.

## 6. Trustees' position

Trustees usually exercise expected caution and will take all relevant factors into account when a deficit arises. Their main aim is to continue the scheme (on a solvent basis) and they will have checked the extent of their powers and what controls they may have over the employer. As a matter of course, the employer's funding covenant will be examined along with its rights to vary or discontinue the scheme. Few schemes in Ireland have an employer funding covenant which cannot be discontinued. One of the chief difficulties facing trustees is compliance with the legislation's timetable as regards the submission of the required actuarial certifications and funding proposal (where a deficit arises). Given that the employer must be a party to the proposal, the trustees will usually inform the Pensions Board if late filings are likely.

## 7. Pensions Board's role to prosecute and direct a reduction in benefits

The Pensions Board can prosecute the trustees for failure to submit a funding certificate or, where appropriate, a funding proposal and it is its policy to do so. In both circumstances the board may issue a written notice to the trustees requiring them to reduce the benefits of active members. Members must be notified of the reduction. The reduction must be of such magnitude that the funding standard will be satisfied directly after the reduction has taken place. It may be difficult for the trustees to comply with such a dictat, as they may not have adequate up-to-date information on members to enable a proper evaluation of how benefits ought to be appropriately reduced. Once the board issues the notice there is no facility for it to be withdrawn. Neither is there any statutory right for members to have their reduced benefits enlarged were the scheme to move into surplus. At the end of 2005, one-third of all defined benefit schemes in Ireland were in deficit and had submitted a funding proposal or were in negotiations with the Pensions Board. Most funding periods are in the usual three-year range. To date, the Pensions Board has never used its powers to require the trustees to reduce benefits and it is thought that the existence of this power is enough for some employers to dig deep and make good the deficit. Few employers elect to wind up their scheme and fewer still organise their affairs to the detriment of deferred members.

# United States

**Robert P Flanagan**
**Mary K Samsa**
Seyfarth Shaw LLP

---

In the past several years, financial trouble has compelled many major US companies to freeze or terminate their defined benefit pension plans. In many cases the underlying reason these plans were terminated was tied to outdated federal pension laws that mandated certain assumptions that may not have been realistic given current market conditions. The flood of pension plan defaults forced the US Congress to address the outdated pension laws, strengthen the US worker's retirement security and reduce the prospect of a future multi-billion dollar taxpayer bailout.

## 1. How does the US Pension Benefit Guaranty Corporation support the US pension system?

In the United States, when a company defaults on its pension obligations, a US governmental organisation, called the Pension Benefit Guaranty Corporation (PBGC), assumes responsibility for paying all or a portion of the company's pension obligations. The PBGC insures US employees against the loss of pension benefits due to a company's bankruptcy. It insures most private sector pensions offered in defined benefit plans, which are those in which pension benefits are defined based on years of service and salary levels, without regard to investment performance (eg, 401(k) plans which are not insured).

Pension plans pay insurance premiums directly to the PBGC. The PBGC receives no supplemental revenue from the US government. As such, the PBGC is financed by insurance premiums, the assets assumed along with liabilities from pension funds taken over due to insolvency and bankruptcy recoveries.

Notwithstanding the above, PBGC insurance is intended to be the third layer of pension benefit protection for US employees. The primary responsibility resides with the companies offering the pension plan to provide the pension benefits they promise. The secondary responsibility falls on the qualified trust which is funded with collateral to satisfy the pension responsibilities. The PBGC steps in only when both plan sponsor and trust seem unlikely to cover the financial obligations promised. In that event, it assumes the qualified trust's liabilities, assets and activities or, for multi-employer plans, lends the necessary funds to the trust.

## 2. Why was US pension reform necessary?

Through the PBGC, the US government has stood behind retirement benefits promised to US employees since 1974. This financial burden eventually filters down to US taxpayers. As the assets available to the PBGC become insufficient to support the growing pension liabilities it has assumed over the past several years, the pension amounts necessary to keep the PBGC going must come from somewhere and hence are borrowed from the US government. To cover this additional expense of the US government (which adds to the US deficit), these amounts are recouped in the form of taxes from US taxpayers.

In today's economy, the PBGC currently has an operating deficit of roughly $20 billion to $25 billion. Because of the significant increase in pension plan terminations by US companies, the US Congress decided that comprehensive reform of the US pension system was essential to ensure that millions of hard-working Americans who rely on these pension benefits can continue to count on them for the future. Their solution was the Pension Protection Act of 2006.

## 3. The six principal reforms of the Pension Protection Act

The US Congress focused on six key reforms when drafting the Pension Protection Act, as follows:

- Certainty – the act establishes a permanent interest rate to calculate more accurately US employers' pension liabilities to ensure they fund their worker pension promises.
- Common sense – the act gives US employers incentives through higher deduction limits on contributions to help build up a cushion in their worker pension plans during good economic times.
- Stability – the act closes funding loopholes and reduces volatility in worker pension plans by ensuring US employers make adequate and consistent cash payments to their plans.
- Transparency – the act ensures US employees and retirees are given timely, accurate and straightforward information about the health of their plans, and thus their own financial future.
- Honesty – with hundreds if not thousands of significantly underfunded pension plans across the United States, the act includes reasonable restrictions to ensure US employers and union leaders cannot dig the pension hole even deeper by promising extra benefits if a plan is insufficiently funded.
- Portability – the act helps resolve legal uncertainty to ensure hybrid plans, such as cash balance pensions, can be designed to provide portable benefits that are designed to grow evenly throughout a worker's career.

This chapter describes the above reforms and how they impact on the current pension protection system.

## 4. Use of permanent interest rate for actuarial assumptions

Employers must be able to predict, and budget for, annual pension contributions. If companies are unable to do this because pension costs fluctuate too much from year to year, the sponsor may choose to freeze and/or terminate its pension plan. The US Congress recognised this economic reality and decided it must act to stabilise annual contribution requirements.

Prior to the passage of the Pension Protection Act, pension plan sponsors were allowed to calculate pension benefit liabilities using a 'reasonable' interest (discount) rate selected by the plan's actuary, in its sole discretion. The mortality table was prescribed by the Department of Treasury. In the past, the effective discount rate was typically based on either the US corporate bond interest rate or the US 30-year Treasury bond rate. These are market-based rates that fluctuate with the US economy. Consequently, plan sponsors' pension contributions have traditionally been subject to significant swings from year to year.

The Pension Protection Act will generally require US employers to use an interest rate based on a modified yield curve approach. Under the modified yield curve approach, the rate of contributions will depend largely on the plan's demographics. Employers operating plans with more retirees and older participants, and that offer lump-sum pension payments, would generally be required to contribute at a more accelerated rate. On the other hand, employers operating plans with younger participants and fewer retirees, and that do not offer lump-sum distributions, would be allowed to make contributions at a less aggressive pace. This approach is designed to match the pace of funding with the maturity of the obligations. It provides US employers with greater certainty and predictability in their pension funding obligations.

Under the modified yield curve approach, the Pension Protection Act specifies interest rates in three maturity 'segments':

- liabilities due in five or fewer years;
- liabilities due between five and 20 years; and
- liabilities due after more than 20 years.

The new interest rates are derived from a yield curve comprised of corporate bonds of appropriate maturities. A pension plan sponsor may disregard the three segments and instead use a 'true' yield curve tied directly to the plan's liabilities. However, if an employer elects to take this approach, it may revoke the election only with the permission of the Department of Treasury. Additionally, the interest rates used to measure both liabilities and assets for funding purposes may be averaged – or smoothed – over 24 months. Under the current rules, asset values could be smoothed over a five-year period.

Given the new interest rate mandate, US employers must now reassess the funding status of their US pension plans. With the new interest rate approach for actuarial assumptions, the Pension Protection Act could adversely affect a plan's funded status, especially if the existing assumptions were unrealistic. The modified yield curve approach is phased in over a two-year period beginning in 2008.

## 5. Increase in the maximum deductible contribution

According to the report made to the US Congress by the US House Committee on Education and the Workforce, the prior funding rules often prevented US employers from making additional contributions to their pension plans during good economic times. Many employers then had to endure accelerated contribution requirements during economic downturns. The Pension Protection Act now permits US employers to make additional deductible contributions up to 150% of the pension plan's funding target. This means that the Pension Protection Act allows employers to fund over and above the target funding liability. For this purpose, the employer may take into account the impact of future pay increases. This gives US employers more flexibility to make generous contributions during good economic times to provide a cushion for plan participants.

## 5. Funding through required contributions

The most significant funding change in the Pension Protection Act is a rule that requires sponsors to accelerate pension funding obligations. Currently, plan sponsors may contribute an amount necessary to fund current-year pension liabilities and certain past-service liabilities amortised over a 30-year period. Pension plans are generally required to be only 90% funded. The long amortisation period was identified as one of the primary reasons for the massive underfunding that currently exists with US pension plans.

In addition, US employers are currently permitted to use credit balances as an offset to their annual funding requirement. Under US law, a 'credit balance' occurs if a pension plan sponsor makes a contribution to the pension plan in excess of the minimum required contribution. The excess, plus interest, is treated as a credit balance that can be drawn upon for future required contributions. Congress determined that credit balances were often fictitious assets for pension plan purposes. This is because the credit balance typically grows at a rate of return which does not necessarily correspond with actual investment experience under the pension plan. Some US employers with severely underfunded pension plans were continually using credit balances to avoiding having to make annual contributions. This loophole often caused underfunded pension plans to become even more poorly funded.

Beginning in 2008, the Pension Protection Act replaces the current funding system with a much-simplified single funding regime designed to fund fully most pension plans over a number of years. Under this new regime, the minimum required contribution for any plan year equals:

- the present value of all benefits that are expected to accrue under the pension plan during the current plan year; and
- the 'shortfall contribution' necessary to amortise over seven years the difference between the pension plan's current assets and 100% of liabilities on the first day of the plan year.

In determining the above liability, credit balances are generally required to be subtracted from pension plan assets, unless the plan is 100% funded.

The Pension Protection Act also provides an 'all or nothing' transition rule. Plans that meet a graded minimum funding requirement (set forth below) are exempt from making the full shortfall contribution for that year. This means sponsors that have funded their pension plans well under current law will have the benefit of a five-year transition period. However, sponsors of plans funded less than 90% must meet the new 100% requirement when the law becomes effective. The graded funding requirement is 92% for 2008, 94% in 2009 and 96% in 2010. Beginning in 2011, all plans must fully fund their shortfall contribution. If an employer misses the target funding percentage at any of the above levels, it will be subject to full funding the following year. Accordingly, some employers may wish to increase the funding of their plans to ensure they will meet the transition minimum funding requirement beginning in 2008, and for each year thereafter.

The new law creates a special category for plans deemed to be 'at risk'. If a pension plan is at risk, it may not use the above-referenced graded funding schedule. Under the Pension Protection Act, a pension plan is 'at risk' if the pension plan's funding target attainment percentage is both less than 80% without regard to the at-risk liabilities and less than 70% counting at-risk liabilities. The 80% test will be phased in from 2008 through 2011. Plans with 500 or fewer participants are not subject to these new rules. However, if a pension plan is considered to be at risk, its liabilities are calculated by assuming that employees eligible to retire in the next 10 years will retire as early as possible. The at-risk exception was designed to address the pension plans that present the greatest financial exposure to the PBGC and to the retirement security of the participants.

## 6. Meaningful disclosure of pension plan health to participants

Besides addressing the pension funding problem facing US employers, one of the primary objectives of the Pension Protection Act is to provide employees and investors more timely and useful information regarding the financial status of the pension plan, and to ensure greater transparency and accountability. Currently, US employers are required only to provide participants with a summary annual report that provides limited information regarding the pension plan.

Beginning in 2008, the summary annual report requirement is repealed and replaced with a new pension plan funding notice for single-employer pension plans with more than 100 participants. This notice must be provided within 120 days of the close of the plan year to participants, beneficiaries, unions and the PBGC. The funding notice must contain the following information:

- the total assets and liabilities of the pension plan for the current and two preceding years;
- the number of participants in the pension plan, broken down by active participants, retired or separated participants receiving benefits, and retired or separated participants eligible for future benefits;
- the pension plan's funding policy and the asset allocation of the pension plan's investments as of the end of the year;
- a summary of any material pension plan amendments or events taking place in the current year, and a projection of the event's affect on pension plan liabilities;
- a summary of the pension plan's Employee Retirement Income Security Act plan termination rules;
- a general description of the pension plan benefits eligible for PBGC insurance, with an explanation of any limitations;
- a statement that the person may obtain a copy of the annual report upon request; and

- a statement if the pension plan was required to file a PBGC 4010 notice (ie, that the pension plan is underfunded by more than $50 million).

## 7. Restrictions on increasing benefits (US employers keeping their promises)

The US Congress determined that, in some instances, financially troubled companies were amending their pension plans to offer greater benefits to retain and motivate their US workforce, even when the company was in financial difficulty. The US Congress determined that these practices must cease to avoid worsening the pension funding crisis.

The Pension Protection Act now limits the benefits a pension plan may pay if its adjusted funding target attainment percentage falls below certain levels. A pension plan's 'adjusted funding target attainment percentage' is the ratio of pension plan assets (minus carryover and pre-funding balances) to the target pension plan liability (without regard to at-risk status). This percentage is then adjusted by adding the amount of annuity purchases for non-highly compensated employees in the last two years to both the assets and the liabilities. The restrictions are as follows:

- If the adjusted funding target attainment percentage is below 80% for the plan year, the pension plan is prohibited from increasing benefits.
- If the adjusted funding target attainment percentage is between 60% and 80%, lump-sum pension benefit payments are limited to the lesser of:
  - the present value of the participant's PBGC guaranteed pension benefit; or
  - 50% of the lump sum the participant would otherwise receive.

  The participant's remaining pension benefit is payable in the form of an annuity.
- If the adjusted funding target attainment percentage is below 60% for a plan year, the Pension Protection Act prohibits the pension plan from triggering shutdown benefits or accelerated payments, including lump sums, and would freeze benefit accruals.

These restrictions do not apply to plans that are 100% funded (determined without reducing assets for credit balances). In addition, special rules apply to new plans and plans of employers in bankruptcy.

To curtail this problem, the Pension Protection Act also prohibits a public company from funding any non-qualified deferred compensation arrangement for certain key executives while its pension plan is considered to be at risk. This prohibition includes deposits into any trust or other arrangement that is subject to the claims of creditors. Any funding (ie, the actual setting aside of money) that violates the restriction will be immediately taxed to the executive, with the executive subject to an additional 20% penalty tax. Moreover, any tax 'gross-up' payments made to the executive to cover the tax penalties will also be subject to the same penalties, with no tax deduction for the employer.

The new law also prohibits employers from funding deferred compensation for the chief executive officer of a public company, the other four officers whose compensation must be disclosed in the company's proxy, or any officer or director subject to Section 16 of the Securities Exchange Act of 1934, during any of the following periods:

- any period during which the employer or any member of its controlled group is undergoing bankruptcy proceedings;
- six months before or after the employer, or a member of its controlled group, terminates an underfunded pension plan in a distress termination; or
- any plan year during which any pension plan maintained by a controlled group member is in at-risk status for funding purposes.

This rule is imposed to prevent the key executives from enjoying retirement security while the rest of the employee population (which needs greater protection) is left with an underfunded pension plan. In other words, if the retirement benefits for the general employee population are not secure, the key executives cannot receive special treatment for their non-qualified benefit – at least until the pension plan funding problem is resolved.

## 8. Legal certainty in cash balance plan to secure greater portability

Over the last decade, a large number of US pension plan sponsors converted their traditional defined benefit pension plans to hybrid plans, such as cash balance plans. Many other employers have established new cash balance plans. Cash balance pension plans have become a significant component of many US employees' retirement security. In recent years the legal status of cash balance plans and cash balance plan conversions has been called into question. One of the biggest questions has been whether such plans are inherently age discriminatory. Litigation over this and other issues has created a lot of uncertainty regarding the viability of these arrangements. These issues also threatened to expose sponsoring employers to significant legal risk. The Pension Protection Act directly addresses the legal questions surrounding cash balance plans.

The Pension Protection Act includes a number of provisions intended to clarify the legal status and requirements for hybrid plans, such as cash balance plans. It is important to note that the Pension Protection Act is generally effective prospectively. The statute states that the new law is not intended to contain any inference regarding the status of cash balance plans before the law was enacted. This means that current sponsors of cash balance plans may remain exposed to some historical liability. The following are some of the key provisions of the law with respect to cash balance plans:

- Age discrimination – effective retrospectively to June 30 2005, the Pension Protection Act provides that a hybrid plan does not violate the age discrimination rules if a participant's accrued benefit would be equal to or greater than that of any similarly situated, younger individual who is or could be a participant. In determining a participant's accrued pension plan benefit for this purpose, the accrued benefit may be expressed as the balance of a hypothetical account. 'Similarly situated' means that the participants are identical in every respect (ie, period of service, compensation, position, date of hire, work history), except age. This provision is intended to address the age discrimination risk that was originally articulated by the Federal District Court for the Southern District of Illinois in *Cooper v IBM*. That court found that the cash balance pension plan at issue violated age discrimination rules. Since the legislation was passed, however, *Cooper v IBM* was reversed on appeal by the Seventh Circuit.

- Conversions – the Pension Protection Act imposes restrictions on converting a traditional defined benefit plan into a hybrid plan. Specifically, the Pension Protection Act would prohibit the wear-away of pre-conversion accrued benefits if the conversion occurs after June 29 2005. ('Wear-away' is when a participant does not earn new benefits for a period until his or her total benefit, taking into account the change, exceeds the benefit accrued up to the time of the change.) In addition, the Pension Protection Act requires the employer to preserve early retirement subsidies associated with benefits accrued under the pre-conversion plan.
- Interest rate requirement – effective as of January 1 2008, any interest credited by a hybrid plan must be at a rate that is not less than zero and is not greater than a market rate of return. The Internal Revenue Service is to issue rules governing the calculation of a market rate of return.
- Whipsaw – The Pension Protection Act eliminates the 'whipsaw' calculation for distributions made on or after the date of enactment by allowing a hybrid plan to pay a lump-sum distribution equal to the hypothetical account balance. 'Whipsaw' occurs when the interest rate used to project a participant's account balance out to an age 65 benefit – which is generally required under current US law – is greater than the rate used to discount the benefit back to present value. The resulting lump sum in this scenario would be greater than the participant's hypothetical account balance – hence the term 'whipsaw'.
- Vesting – effective January 1 2008, hybrid plans must provide that a participant is 100% vested after three years of service.

By clarifying the rules around cash balance plans, US employers can move forward in structuring retirement benefits through the cash balance model without fear of litigation. The portable nature of the cash balance benefit (most plans permit lump-sum distributions) makes these plans very attractive to US employees.

Cash balance plans are particularly attractive to employers because the annual contributions for funding purposes are much more predictable than with traditional defined benefit plans. Now that the legal status of cash balance plans appears to be settled going forward, more US employers will likely offer these plans, especially as an alternative to traditional defined benefit plans.

## 9. Conclusion

Each of the above Pension Protection Act changes is aimed at increasing pension protection for US employees. However, some of the requirements (eg, the new funding rules) may ultimately prove to be too financially burdensome for many US companies that sponsor traditional defined benefit plans. We expect that the current trend of plan freezes will continue for employers sponsoring traditional defined benefit plans. The rules clarifying the legal status of cash balance plans may cause some of those employers to convert to the cash balance model. We may see some other employers establish cash balance plans.

# Future developments

**Kevin Wesbroom**
Hewitt Associates

The experience of dealing with pension scheme deficits during the early 2000s was a bruising and painful one for many companies, often forcing them to take actions they would have dearly wished to avoid. At the time of writing – the second quarter of 2007 – we have witnessed a period during which two of the key factors that contributed to deficits have gone into reverse:

- Investment returns on equities have been favourable – the recovery from the depths of 2003 is the second biggest bull market in UK history (even if it did not feel that way); and
- Long-term interest rates have increased, leading to a reduced value of liabilities, calculated on a mark-to-market basis.

Of course, other factors have not reversed – longevity improvements seem to be a one-way street; there is no sign of reversing Advance Corporation Tax changes; administration costs continue to rise; the costs of governance and operating a scheme and complying with the never-ending raft of legislation continue to rise inexorably; and so on. But we are in a position where we are close, on average, to deficits being reduced or even eliminated - and all of this well within 10 years of the scheme-specific funding regime coming into effect. This begs a fundamental question – how will companies react if and when deficits start to disappear?

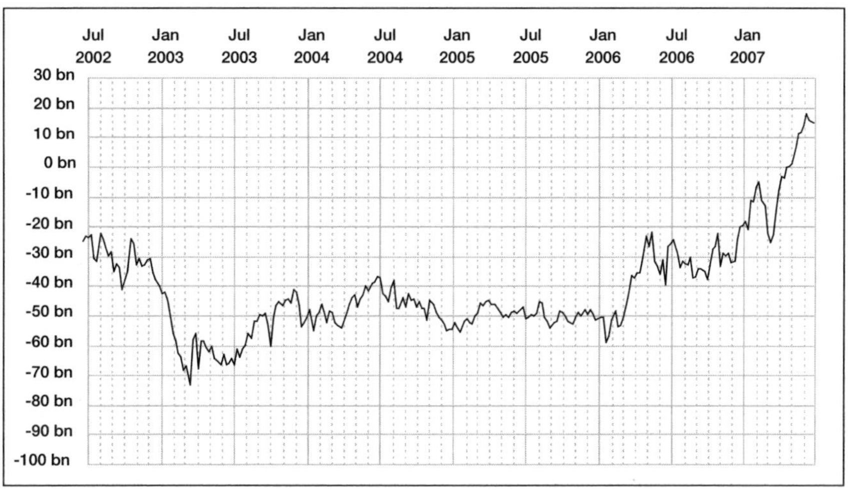

Of course, some of their decisions may be taken away from them. Hard-pressed trustees might take the opportunity to strengthen their 'technical provisions' or valuation reserves in old currency. For example, who could argue against trustees adding in further allowance for future improvements in post-retirement longevity, given the overall uncertainty about the outcomes for future life expectancy? Surely a first charge on any emerging surplus will be to adjust the mortality allowance from short cohort to medium cohort, to medium cohort plus a minimum underpin, to long cohort plus an underpin and so forth. Who really knows what constitutes a prudent allowance for future improvements?

The Pensions Regulator might also decide to look for some convergence with insurance regulatory standards on the back of a more favourable climate. Can schemes be sure the goalposts of 'full funding' are well and truly fixed in the ground and will not be subject to movement? Will funding or accounting standards move – justifiably, perhaps, if the inverted yield curve remains a feature of the UK bond markets? The United States has already moved to a three-point yield curve approach for funding – this may sound a technical move, but it leads to higher reserves for funding.

Meanwhile, members and their trade union representatives might look to have any emerging surplus applied to counteract some of the painful changes in dealing with deficits. Perhaps member contributions could return to previous levels, early retirement incentives be re-introduced or other benefit cuts be reversed? Companies will need to think long and hard about 'sharing' the good news of surplus. The asymmetry of benefit improvements (on the back on the huge surpluses in the 1980s and 1990s) should be a salutary lesson to companies in thinking about how to 'spend' any new surpluses that might arise.

The more thoughtful companies will reflect long and hard on their experience of deficits and work out – perhaps for the first time – just exactly what their ultimate objectives might be in operating a defined benefit (DB) pension plan. The following table summarises two polarised points of view that they might reach.

| | **Minimise cost** | **Managed exit** |
|---|---|---|
| Overall philosophy | This is a strong employer, well able to withstand the volatility of global equity markets, which believes that defined benefit pensions can offer a source of competitive advantage in tight labour markets | This is an employer that believes it is not rewarded by its shareholders for operating DB pension liabilities. The strategy should be to remove all DB liabilities, at an acceptable price, and focus on running the core business |
| Attitude to funding and employer contributions | On the assumption that cash invested in the business will generate higher returns than portfolio investments (eg, pension fund assets), the amounts paid by the employerto fund pension liabilities will be minimised | The correct comparison is not between return on equity in the business and return on pension fund assets, but is rather to treat the pension fund deficit as debt alongside other corporate borrowings. If the company does not wish to 'borrow' money from its pension funds, it should repay this debt as soon as possible. Higher contributions will be acceptable, since the eventual goal is buy-out |
| Attitude to investment | Accepting that equities are likely to generate longer-terms returns, the investment policy will be equity orientated to maximise the long-term returns and so reduce the cost to the employer | The consequences of risk aversion and viewing pension fund obligations as debt would be to have a more cautious investment policy, with a higher proportion of bonds, more similar to an insurance company |

| | Minimise cost | Managed exit |
|---|---|---|
| Accounting implications | There will be lower disclosed pension costs, but balance-sheet deficits will be highly volatile; this is acceptable since pension liabilities are not material in the corporate context | There will be less volatility in pension deficits, since there will be higher funding and a more conservative investment policy. However, disclosed pension costs will be higher |
| Member security | Members are looking to the ultimate strength of the sponsoring company, or the parent in the group, to deliver the pension promise | The ultimate goal is to buy out all pension liabilities from an insurance company and all other steps will be consistent with this objective. Member security will be high since it will become insurance backed (a more secure regime than pension regulation) |

These two routes could be seen as the extreme ends of a spectrum and many companies will doubtless try to position themselves somewhere in the middle ground – but this could simply be a failure to work really hard to answer the question, "Why do we have a DB pension plan?" This fundamental question is seldom asked – but, faced with life-threatening deficits over the past few years, several companies have tried to address it. While it is true that some strong, well-diversified (and typically multinational) companies may continue to make use of the 'minimise cost' route, an increasing number of companies in the private sector may well decide to go down the 'managed exit' route. They may decide that they have had enough management distraction with pension scheme deficits and want to refocus on their core business activities. They are more likely to do so if they have already taken the (big) step of closing their final salary plan to future accruals, leaving only a set of deferred and immediate pensions to be paid.

Companies in this camp may welcome the arrival of new entrants such as Paternoster, Synesis Life and PIC set up specifically to take away their DB liabilities. They might be less delighted when they learn about the cost of making their exit from DB provision. Buy-out costs will be significantly higher than accounting or funding targets – and in many cases, will look impossible to reach. But then we will have good runs, as in 2006 and early 2007, when markets are favourable and yields increase, so that perhaps a target of 125% of International Accounting Standard 19 liabilities does not look impossible. This raises interesting questions of corporate psychology and attitudes to DB pension provision:

- 'Never again' – the company does not want to experience again the pain of deficits, the changing (reduction) of benefits for members, the polarisation of the workforce into the 'haves' and 'have-nots', and so on. Any improved conditions will simply hasten the time when this company can exit from pensions or equivalently good news reduces the cost of the eventual buy-out.

- 'Here we go again' - deficits were a bad experience, but now things are back to 'normal'. Pension fund surpluses have returned and are making a helpful contribution to improve the company's accounting bottom line. Painful memories are soon forgotten – or perhaps a new management team is now in place – and the company may as well continue with some sort of DB provision. After all, members prefer it – don't they?

For those that continue with DB provision, it seems unlikely that this will involve the 'traditional' 1/60th of final salary scheme with all of its 'bells and whistles'. Even large employers that stick with DB seem likely to adopt some form of career average revalued earnings scheme, or hybrid defined benefit/defined contribution scheme or other risk-sharing mechanism. What we can expect is a change in mindset towards consideration of the risk aspects of DB provision and new scheme designs that target these risks explicitly.

And what of those companies that adopt the managed exit route? The new entrants to the annuity buy-out market are bringing not just extra capacity, but plenty of innovation in the ways in which they will work with sponsors to manage – and eventually eliminate – their DB risks. The capital markets seem poised to offer new commercial solutions for eventual exit strategies. And we seem on the verge of new, active markets in financial instruments that will allow companies to hedge and manage their longevity exposure, in the same way as they can hedge interest rate and inflation risks at present, should they choose.

In this environment, it is looking increasingly feasible to map out a managed exit strategy over, say, a 10-year timeframe. For many schemes this will involve a partial buy-out strategy: securing current pensioners' benefits with an insurer, but then tackling deferred members through a transfer incentive exercise (with eventual buy-out of those deferred members who choose not to accept the incentive). The 10-year exit plan might involve some purchase of insurance policies, but keeping other assets in the much freer pension regulatory regime. This has the advantage that the sponsor can use the greater investment freedom to gain benefit from equity exposure and to use this to meet the ultimate target of 100% buy-out. Within a finite investment timescale to meet buy-out costs, it is fair to assume that the capital market players will look to sell increasingly specific and targeted products that deliver the desired end result. These products or processes might involve mechanisms to capture and lock in upward 'spikes' in markets (such as that witnessed in 2007) to ensure they are not lost if markets subsequently turn down. Products might offer to do this mechanically inside a 'black box', with some sacrifice of upside returns being applied to provide downside protection. It might seem unrealistic as yet, but there could be potential upside over even the cost of buying out benefits if one looks over 10-year timeframes and starts from progressively improved funding levels. Some insurers have indicated that they are prepared (at a price, of course) to guarantee future buy-out terms, making targets over a 10-year timeframe that much more concrete. If sponsors are lucky – and well prepared – they might be able to take advantage of any hoped-for pricing war between the new entrants, capturing opportunities to purchase annuity 'slices' at favourable rates. Once the strategic direction is confirmed, there are many tactical opportunities and issues that can be addressed.

Sorting out deficits once and for all could well become the main preoccupation for the majority of DB plan sponsors for the next five to 10 years. In the ultimate of ironies (or is it just the circularity of events?), we could see DB pensions provided predominantly by the insurance industry. The DB pensions industry developed back in the 1970s and 1980s on a self-administered basis, as a response to what were perceived as the unattractive terms of insured pension contracts, which had been the norm until then. The wheel may turn full circle.

# About the authors

**Mark Alexander**
Partner, Lane Clark & Peacock LLP
mark.alexander@lcp.uk.com

Mark Alexander is a qualified actuary who works as a pensions and employee benefit consultant for Lane Clark & Peacock LLP. He advises a wide variety of pension scheme and corporate clients, and works on all aspects of pension provision, from benefit design to scheme wind-ups.

**David Archer**
Founding director, Pitmans Trustees Limited
DArcher@pitmans.com

David Archer is the founding director of Pitmans Trustees Limited, incorporated in 1994. Pitmans Trustees Limited is a wholly owned subsidiary of Pitmans Solicitors. Pitmans Trustees Limited is on the Pensions Regulator's register of independent trustees.

Mr Archer qualified as a litigation solicitor with Norton Rose in 1985 before working with Baker & McKenzie in Australia and with Clifford Chance. He joined Pitmans as a partner in 1992 and specialises in corporate reconstruction, pensions dispute resolution and independent trusteeship.

**Camilla Barry**
Barrister, Macfarlanes
Camilla.Barry@macfarlanes.com

Camilla Barry graduated in philosophy and modern languages from Wadham College, Oxford before completing a diploma in law. She has specialised in pensions law since 1997. She joined Macfarlanes in 2007.

Ms Barry advises trustees and employers on all aspects of pensions law, including day-to-day advice to trustees, benefit and scheme changes, winding-up, transfers to the PPF, pensions-related litigation and complaints to the pensions ombudsman. She has extensive experience of advising on the pensions aspects of corporate transactions, including advising on the powers of the Pensions Regulator and transfers from the public sector.

Ms Barry is a member of the Association of Pension Lawyers and a former contributor to Sweet & Maxwell's *The Law of Pensions*.

**Däna Burstow**
Partner, Allen & Overy LLP
dana.burstow@allenovery.com

Däna Burstow is a partner at Allen & Overy, an international legal practice specialising in banking and finance, capital markets, corporate, employment, pensions and incentives, litigation, private client, real estate and tax law. Ms Burstow is part of the pensions practice, advising both trustees and employers on all aspects of pensions law.

Ms Burstow has recently advised on scheme mergers, liability reduction exercises, contingent funding arrangements, disputes, scheme deeds and rules and their interpretation, and pensions issues arising on sales and outsourcings. She sits on the education and training committee of the Association of Pension Lawyers.

Ms Burstow is a regular speaker on pensions matters and delivers trustee training.

**Mark Catchpole**
Partner, Stephenson Harwood
Mark.catchpole@shlegal.com

Mark Catchpole is a partner at Stephenson Harwood, where he heads the employment and pensions department. He has specialised in pensions law since qualification in 1989. He is treasurer of the Association of Pension Lawyers and a member of the Statement of Recommended Practice (SORP) No 1 working party of the Pensions Research Accountants Group, which has statutory authority for the SORP.

**Penny Cogher**
Partner, Speechly Bircham LLP
Penny Cogher is a recognised authority in the pensions field. She advises companies, trustees, fund managers, high-net-worth individuals, employees, senior executives and insurers. Her clients range from leading multinational companies with UK subsidiaries to charities. Ms Cogher has established two sectionalised schemes and lectured on these at the Association of Pension Lawyers' autumn conference in 2006. She was also a contributor to *Guide to the Pensions Act 1995* (FT Law and Tax), and sits on the pensions committee of the Charity Finance Directors' Group. Ms Cogher is a regular contributor on pensions articles for various publications, including the *Financial Times* and the charity press.

**Christoph Crisolli**
Partner, Kliemt & Vollstädt
Christoph.Crisolli@kliemt.de

Christoph Crisolli heads the Frankfurt office of Kliemt & Vollstädt, one of Germany's leading employment law boutiques. He advises clients on all matters of individual and collective employment law. Central interests of his practice are consultancy on company transactions and restructuring, including pensions. He also specialises in occupational pension plans, with a particular emphasis on the harmonisation of pension schemes, test cases and the spin-off of pension liabilities for corporate accounting purposes. He has particular expertise in implementing cross-border outsourcing projects. Mr Crisolli is an author and a frequent speaker at employment law seminars.

**Kenneth Donaldson**
Head of actuarial services,
Higham Dunnett Shaw plc
kenneth.donaldson@hdsplc.com

Kenneth Donaldson joined Higham Dunnett Shaw in 2005 to shape the development of the company's pension strategy. He has been involved with a number of projects spanning traditional pension schemes and the new approaches being taken to liabilities in the insurance buy-out market.

Mr Donaldson was formerly a director of Hazell Carr, where he helped to establish and develop its pension consulting business into a successful and profitable organisation.

Between 1999 and 2003 he was the expert, actuarial speaker and subsequently chairman of the Institute of Actuaries' seminars on how to manage successfully the focused winding-up of a pension scheme.

Mr Donaldson began his career at Clay and Partners (now part of Aon). His responsibilities included acting as an expert witness, independent trustee and consulting actuary, and he also led major due diligence exercises.

**Robert P Flanagan**
Partner, Seyfarth Shaw LLP
rflanagan@seyfarth.com

Robert P Flanagan is a partner practising in the area of employee benefits for the Chicago office of Seyfarth Shaw LLP. Mr Flanagan serves as lead employee benefits counsel to many companies, both public and closely held. He counsels companies with regard to qualified and non-qualified retirement plans, health and welfare plans, and cash and equity-based incentive compensation programmes. He also advises trustees, boards of directors, investment committees and other plan fiduciaries regarding their powers and responsibilities under the Employee Retirement Income Security Act. He also assists companies on employee benefits issues in the context of mergers and acquisitions.

**Ian Gault**
Partner, Herbert Smith LLP
ian.gault@herbertsmith.com

Ian Gault has been a partner in the pensions group of Herbert Smith since 1988. He has extensive experience as a pensions lawyer, advising on all aspects of pensions law and practice. He is a member of the legislative and parliamentary committee of the Association of Pension Lawyers, the Council of the Society of Pensions Consultants and the executive committee of the Pensions Research Accountants Group. Mr Gault also participated in the consultation panel that assisted the Department for Work and Pensions in developing its proposals on scheme-specific funding.

**Steven Hull**
Partner, Ashurst
Steven.Hull@ashurst.com

Steven Hull is a partner at the international law firm Ashurst and leads the London pensions team. He has over 18 years' legal experience of a wide range of pension-related matters in acting for employers and trustees. He has particular expertise in pension scheme reorganisations and mergers, deficit reduction and surplus resolution strategies, changing benefit structures, the pension aspects of corporate transactions and dealing with the new legislative regime following the Pensions Act 2004 and Finance Act 2004.

Prior to joining Ashurst in 2005, Mr Hull established and led the pensions team for over five years in the London office of a large US law firm. Prior to that, he spent over 12 years training, qualifying (in 1989) and working in the pensions team at a well-known London law firm that for many years was widely acknowledged as having the most highly regarded pensions team of any law firm in the United Kingdom. His time there included a two-year secondment to the employee benefits department of a well-known New York law firm.

**Paul Jagger**
Corporate Pensions Consultant, Hewitt Associates
paul.jagger@hewitt.com

Paul Jagger is a qualified actuary at Hewitt Associates who specialises in advising clients on pension and employee benefit strategy. He is currently head of the UK merger, acquisition and divestitures team based in London, and focuses on global M&A situations and full-scale benefit reviews. He helps companies to understand the pensions risks and liabilities they may be taking on during a transaction, and guides them through implementation post-completion. He has over 15 years of employee benefits consulting experience and enjoys making a difference to the bottom line.

With more than 65 years of experience, Hewitt Associates is the world's foremost provider of human resources consulting and outsourcing services. The company consults with more than 2,300 organisations and is located in 39 countries, employing approximately 24,000 associates.

**Julian Jones**
Consultant, Lane Clark & Peacock LLP
julian.jones@lcp.uk.com

Julian Jones is a qualified actuary who works for Lane Clark & Peacock LLP. He spends a significant part of his time advising on the pensions aspects of mergers and acquisitions. Other areas of involvement include providing trustee advice, accounting for pensions costs in company accounts and assisting with a wide range of one-off corporate projects.

**Sally Ling**
Consultant, GR Communications
sally@grcomms.co.uk

Sally Ling joined GR Communications in 1998, where she leads communications and research projects. Before this, she spent five years as a journalist for *Occupational Pensions* magazine. She also has hands-on experience of pensions management and administration, having worked in-house and in both the insurance and consultancy sectors.

**Mark Newton**
Associate, Heenan Blaikie LLP
MNewton@heenan.ca

Mark Newton, BA (hons), LLB, is a lawyer in Toronto with Heenan Blaikie LLP, a large multi-service national law firm. He specialises in pensions and benefits law and has almost 25 years of experience in this field, having been called to the Ontario Bar in 1983. He is founding chair of the National Pensions and Benefits Law Section of the Canadian Bar Association and past chair of the Pensions and Benefits Section of the Ontario Bar Association. He is a frequent speaker and writer on pension and benefit issues, and serves on the editorial advisory board of the *Benefits & Pensions Monitor*, the leading pensions and benefits publication in Canada. Heenan Blaikie LLP is Canada's pre-eminent management-side labour law firm and has over 20 lawyers across Canada practising pensions and benefits law.

**Kulin Patel**
Actuary, Higham Dunnett Shaw
kulin.patel@hdsplc.com

Kulin Patel is a senior actuary at Higham Dunnett Shaw, a leading provider of specialist consultancy and outsourcing services to the life and pensions industry. Higham Dunnett Shaw's discontinuance team delivers actuarial and administration services to more than 80 discontinued schemes, either in wind-up or in a PPF assessment period, representing over 25,000 members. Mr Patel has been instrumental to the design and delivery of Higham Dunnett Shaw's services for discontinued schemes, including PPF preparation services. He has over 10 years' combined experience in the occupational pensions industries of both the United Kingdom and Canada.

**Daniel Peters**
Investment consultant & actuary,
Aon Consulting
daniel.peters@aonconsulting.co.uk

Daniel Peters has been with Aon since 2000 and currently works in the investment consulting practice. He advises both trustees and employers on a wide range of investment matters, with particular focus on liability-driven investment and advising on alternative asset classes. Having spent time working within the actuarial practice, he utilises his knowledge and understanding of pension scheme liabilities to bring optimal solutions to issues currently facing trustees and employers. His overriding philosophy is that "the solution has to be right for the client".

**Andrew Powell**
Consultant, Hammonds
Andrew.Powell@Hammonds.com

Formerly head of the pensions team at Hammonds, Andrew Powell is now a consultant with the firm. He is the editor of *IDS Pension Law Reports* and a member of the Association of Pensions Lawyers' Legislative and Parliamentary Committee. He is a regular contributor to *British Pensions Lawyer* and other trade magazines.

**Diane Preston**
Partner, Trowers & Hamlins
DPreston@trowers.com

Diane Preston LLB is a partner at Trowers & Hamlins, which she joined in 2006 from Ashurst, and heads the firm's pensions team. Ms Preston became interested in pensions law during her articles and joined the pensions department at Lovells (then Lovells White & King) after qualifying as a solicitor in 1988. She specialises in all aspects of the law relating to occupational pension schemes, particularly issues relating to legislative compliance, documentation, scheme amendment, scheme mergers and wind-up. Recent work experience includes negotiating with the Pensions Regulator and advising on new compliance issues. She has a particular interest in the legal aspects of managing scheme deficits.

Ms Preston is a former member of the public relations committee of the Society of Pension Consultants and of the divorce sub-committee of the Association of Pension Lawyers (APL), and is a full member of the APL.

**Mary K Samsa**
Partner, Seyfarth Shaw LLP
msamsa@seyfarth.com

Mary K Samsa is a partner in the employee benefits practice group in the Chicago office of Seyfarth Shaw LLP. Her primary practice is in the area of executive compensation (both domestically and internationally, and with respect to for-profit as well as not-for-profit entities). She also focuses her practice in the areas of qualified retirement plans (eg, 401(k) and pension plans) and employee stock ownership plans.

Ms Samsa has also developed significant expertise in international employee benefits issues. She is a certified public accountant with a master's in taxation.

**Jonathan Seres**
Partner, Sacker & Partners LLP
Jonathan.Seres@sackers.com

Jonathan Seres is a former chairman of the Association of Pension Lawyers and has served on its international committee. He led the trustees' legal team in last year's Marconi clearance, which netted £675 million for the £2.4 billion pension fund on the sale of a majority of the telecommunications businesses to Ericsson. This included an escrow arrangement for £490 million of the nett sum.

Mr Seres is a practising lawyer and a partner at Sacker & Partners LLP, and in 2005 co-authored *Pensions Risk and Strategy* (City & Financial), focusing on finance directors' needs, including an outline commentary on the United Kingdom's new legislation and practical advice on defined contribution benefit structures. Mr Seres has acted in high-profile scheme mergers and obtained court approval to one of these. He has also advised on major clearance applications to the Pensions Regulator.

**Gary Smith**
Senior Consultant, Watson Wyatt
gary.smith@watsonwyatt.com

Gary Smith is a senior member of Watson Wyatt's defined contribution (DC) pension consulting team and a member of the firm's European DC management group. His particular responsibilities include devising the strategy for, developing and marketing the firm's DC services across Europe, as well as advising a portfolio of DC clients.

He started out as a trainee actuarial consultant after leaving university in 1990 and worked for Bacon & Woodrow from 1994 to 1999, where he helped develop the firm's DC capabilities, led on many major DC client projects and set up the firm's specialist DC consulting team. In 1999 he joined Schroders, with managerial responsibility to build and develop its DC business. He joined Watson Wyatt at the beginning of 2004.

Mr Smith is chairman of the Watson Wyatt Pension Research Forum and a frequent conference speaker and press commentator.

**Frances Phillips Taft**
frances.phillipstaft@btopenworld.com

Frances Phillips Taft is a dual-qualified attorney (US/UK) and has a fellowship in international practice. Ms Taft has experience working with multinational companies on a broad spectrum of domestic UK and cross-jurisdictional matters, including international benefits and pan-European pension arrangements. She is a member of the American Bar Association, International Section and the International Pensions and Benefits Lawyers Association.

**Fiona Thornton**
Partner, LK Shields Solicitors
fthornton@lkshields.ie

Fiona Thornton LLB, solicitor is a partner with LK Shields Solicitors and heads up its pensions and employee benefits practice. She has more than 25 years' experience and has practised as a tax consultant. She is a member of the Law Society of Ireland, the Association of Pensions Lawyers in Ireland and the International Pensions and Employee Benefits Lawyers Association. She is a member of the benefits and international committees of the Irish Association of Pensions Funds.

**Danny Tsang**
Partner, K&L Gates
danny.tsang@klgates.com

Danny Tsang is a partner and head of pensions in the London office of K&L Gates. He has specialised in pensions law since he qualified as a solicitor in 1994 and has extensive experience in pension plan restructuring. He has advised on numerous pension plan mergers, changes to benefit structures and other projects relating to pension fund deficits. Mr Tsang is a member of the Association of Pension Lawyers and of the International Pension and Employee Benefits Lawyers Association. He joined K&L Gates in February 2007. Previously, he was head of pensions and incentives in the London office of another international law firm.

**Kevin Wesbroom**
Principal Consultant, Hewitt Associates
kevin.wesbroom@hewitt.com

Kevin Wesbroom is an experienced pension consultant who has been advising high-profile clients for over 30 years. He is a qualified actuary who has been involved with many different aspects of pension, investment and broader employee benefits: he was responsible for establishing Hewitt's UK defined contribution team, and is currently leading work on the close-out market and risk-driven solutions.

**Susanne Wilkins**
Professional Support Lawyer, Herbert Smith LLP
susanne.wilkins@herbertsmith.com

Susanne Wilkins has been the professional support lawyer to the pensions group of Herbert Smith since March 2005. Before that, she practised pensions law in the City for seven years, advising corporates and trustees on all aspects of pensions law.

**Stephen Yeo**
Senior Consultant, Watson Wyatt
stephen.yeo@watsonwyatt.com

Stephen Yeo is a senior consultant in Watson Wyatt's benefits practice, based in London. As well as acting as an account manager, Mr Yeo communicates the views of the firm and its clients to the press, opinion-formers in politics and the benefits community, and contributes to Watson Wyatt's research initiatives. He is therefore a regular commentator on pensions issues on television and radio, and in the national and trade press.

Mr Yeo qualified as an actuary with Clay & Partners, where he spent nearly 20 years, including six as a partner.

Prior to joining Watson Wyatt in 2004, Mr Yeo spent two years employed as pensions policy adviser to the Conservative Party. Jointly with Shadow Secretary of State David Willetts, he wrote the pamphlet *A fair deal for everyone on pensions,* in which the Conservative Party pledged to reverse the spread of means testing by restoring the earnings link on the basic state pension.